goodbye Iran

BASED ON A TRUE STORY

BY

M. HOSSEIN TIRGAN

Goodbye Iran

First Edition: 2012

Printed in the United States of America

ISBN-10: 0985655305
EAN-13: 9780985655303
Library of Congress Control Number: 2012911474

I dedicate this book to all the Iranians

- *who suffered the death of a loved one because of the revolution of 1979,*
- *who suffered the death of a loved one in the war of 1980-1988,*
- *who since 1979 have fled their homeland and sought refuge elsewhere,*
- *who continue to live under the repressive regime.*

M. Hossein Tirgan

Life is an opportunity, benefit from it.
Life is beauty, admire it.
Life is a dream, realize it.
Life is a challenge, meet it.
Life is a duty, complete it.
Life is a game, play it.
Life is a promise, fulfill it.
Life is sorrow, overcome it.
Life is a song, sing it.
Life is a struggle, accept it.
Life is a tragedy, confront it.
Life is an adventure, dare it.
Life is luck, make it.
Life is too precious, do not destroy it.
Life is life, fight for it.

— *Mother Teresa*

TABLE OF CONTENTS

INTRODUCTION

Among all the subjects we studied in high school, *history* was the one that I always struggled with, because history is for most part the study of events that occurred in the remote past, whereas I was more concerned with the present, and even more so with the future, *my* future. So it was ironic that as the years passed, I wound up personally observing some extraordinary historical events, life-altering, world-changing events that evolved before my very own eyes. When you are a teenager, busy daydreaming about all the exciting things that will happen to you in your life and all the successes you will achieve as an adult, you never stop to consider for one moment that someday you may become an eyewitness to events that will undoubtedly change the course of history, not to mention your own life.

For most of us, the United States' invasion of Iraq, the war in Afghanistan, and the overthrow of Gaddafy in Libya are so recent, so contemporarily topical, that we may not even consider them history, yet these are exactly the kind of events that become history. Momentous events such as these have already affected the lives of millions of people, and will continue to do so for generations to come.

For Americans, September 11 stands out as an earth-shattering black mark on the calendar of this great nation's past. It left a grave and profound impression on almost every aspect of the country and its people. We see its ongoing effects more than a decade later. An event of such great magnitude has an almost incomprehensible impact upon the lives of so many people, especially those at its epicenter. Just as in an earthquake—the more powerful it is, the more damage it causes –those living near its center suffer the most. In addition, all human beings, wherever they reside, will at some point encounter an event that will change the course of history.

As a high school student in Iran, I had to learn the ancient history of my country. We studied our past kings, and all the significant happenings that occurred during their reigns. We learned about King Darius, what he did for Iran, and how he conducted his famous attack on Greece. Those people whose lives we analyzed had been dead for hundreds of years—whatever their contribution to our present-day lives, surely it was long-since eroded away.

All my life, I believed that to study history was to study the past fruitlessly. Then, after high school, history came crashing unbidden into my world. I saw with my own eyes the fall of the Shah of Iran and the change of the governing regime of my country that occurred in 1978 and 1979. I then realized that history was not only a thing of the past, it was something constantly developing, unfolding right in front of us all. Suddenly, I understood that we are all part of it, every one of us, whether we give our consent to be involved or not.

History put its mark on every Iranian as the new government rolled out its agenda in an attempt to enforce its rule over the masses. The Islamic regime killed thousands of Iranians, men and women, young and old, in the name of God. Anyone who opposed the new way of life in Iran, or voiced his opinion criticizing the regime, was killed. Those of us living in Iran at the time remember a cleric by the name of *Khalkhali*. The Grand Ayatollah Ruhollah Khomeini appointed him to cleanse the society of those who either sided with the Shah or opposed the new regime. Nicknamed, "*Executioner Khalkhali*" this cleric became the most powerful revolutionary judge in Iran. Twentieth century Iran, a country with thousands of years of illustrious history, was now entering its dark ages. The county fell under the forces of fear. A new rule of law decreed a new dress code for the country, and almost overnight, put women under veil and banned music, chess, and backgammon. Decades later, I can now see how this one particular historical event impacted my own life, the lives of more than seventy five million Iranians who live in today's Iran, and the lives of more than five million Iranians who live outside Iran.

Soon after the fall of the Shah of Iran in 1979, the aggressor country of Iraq chose to take advantage of the weakened central government of Iran, and invaded my country. All of the sudden, on top of dealing with fear of the new government, we were also at war, a full-fledged war that had its own unique impact on every single Iranian. Saddam Hussein, ruler of Iraq at that time, with whom most of the world is now familiar thanks to the recent war and invasion by U.S. forces, would never have dared to consider a war with Iran, but the fall of the Shah's monarchy, the takeover of the government by the Islamic clerics, and the introduction of Islamic ideology to the military had seriously weakened the country's defense infrastructure. Saddam Hussein saw his chance. Without hesitation, he made his opportunistic advance on Iran.

The war between Iran and Iraq lasted from 1980 to 1988 and claimed more than one million Iranian lives. To defend the country against the invasion, the government relied heavily on its manpower, and for the most part, on the youth of the country. It drafted hundreds of thousands of young Iranians and sent them to the front with inadequate equipment and minimal training. Those inexperienced combat soldiers, instead of bearing the advanced weaponry necessary for them to protect their precious lives, received a promise for a place in heaven and a good afterlife as a reward for fighting and dying in a war over which they had no control.

During the war, every draftee assumed that he was facing a death sentence, although one delivered in the name of Allah. They were supposed to find solace in the belief that their death carried special blessings from the Ayatollah Khomeini, and that they would enjoy an eternal afterlife in a much more beautiful world, in paradise.

The human survival instinct, however, can be unwaveringly strong and this primal impulse forced thousands of Iranian families to find ways to avoid the war by moving to Northern or Eastern parts of Iran. Some chose to leave Iran altogether, and immigrated to other countries. Those who did not want to die during the war, or did not want to play a part in the merciless killing of others (that is to say, the Iraqi soldiers), did everything they could to leave Iran and find a safer place to live.

The Iranian government counteracted this efflux of people by banning overseas travel for most Iranians, especially young men and those who could potentially serve in the army. Leaving the country against those rules was simply illegal. Borders were impenetrable to young Iranians. The passport office would not issue travel documents to youths, and all of the sudden some new words were added to the Persian vocabulary: *mamnuol khorouj*—a complex word, made from two distinct Arabic words. *Mamnu,* meaning 'not allowed, banned or illegal,' and *khorouj* meaning, 'to exit,' and in this case, it was applied to traveling outside the country. With the establishment of the clerics' government, many people became *mamnuol khorouj.* Courts had the power to take away one's right to travel from Iran. All those old enough to serve in the army, without exception, soon found themselves in this category.

The fight for freedom, on the other hand, did not recognize any of these newly imposed rules on young and energetic Iranians who did not want to live in a dark age or die in the war. In their minds, the borders between Iran and its neighboring countries remained open. Although they could not get a travel document, and could not cross through official border checkpoints, they knew that this did not mean that the borders were absolutely closed to them.

Thousands of Iranians, citizens of all kinds who refused to live under the new regime, chose to leave their homeland, legally if they could, or illegally by crossing the borders of Turkey or Pakistan, seeking refuge in other countries. Such travel was not without severe and unforeseen risks. As with Mexicans who illegally cross the U.S. border to come and live in America, many Iranians risked their lives in their journey to escape from the oppressive regime and find freedom elsewhere.

The ban on international traveling, and the war, spawned a new and dangerous, yet lucrative trade in Iran: "people smuggling." For a substantial fee, one could hire a team of professional smugglers to take him or her to either Turkey or Pakistan. For many, the potential for greater freedom and a life without daily fear of the regime was more than worth the hefty sum they handed over. Despite all the risks, thousands of young and old Iranians—men, women, children, and entire families—risked their lives on journeys so perilous that each is worth its own authored novel.

This book is based on the true story of two young Iranian men, Hamid and Hossein, who lived in Tehran but desperately craved to escape from the regime and the war. Their sole focus was to find a better place to live outside Iran.

At the time, Hamid was only eighteen. He graduated from high school in the summer of 1982, and within a few months, in the fall of that year, he entered into the military as a draftee, scheduled for deployment to the war front that winter. Hamid felt he had received a death sentence and was simply waiting for his turn to face the firing squad.

During the war years, high school students had very few options following their graduation. Acceptance by a university in Iran was the best way to avoid the military draft, yet getting into a university at that time was possible only for the top five to ten percent of high school graduates. Despite working hard, Hamid's grades were not high enough to gain him acceptance. The path for male high school graduates such as Hamid was perfectly clear: they would serve in the military, go to the front lines and give their lives for a cause they did not even understand, much less believe in.

Hossein, on the other hand, was studying to become a doctor. He was less than a year away from graduation, also destined to serve in the war. All male medical school graduates had to serve in the army immediately after graduation, and work in forward military medical bases. Iraqi bombs had annihilated many of those medical camps, a fact of which Hossein and his classmates were lucidly aware.

CHAPTER ONE
THE TRUTH

Jamshidieh, like many other military bases in Tehran, was a training ground where new draftees lived round the clock during the workweek, receiving passes to go home only on weekends. In Iran, the work week began on Saturday. The weekend consisted of just Thursday evening and Friday. Draftees left the training bases on Thursday afternoon to go home and spend time with their families. They were, without fail, to report to the base promptly, early Saturday morning.

Hamid lived with his parents in Narmak, a suburb of Tehran. Obedient and punctual, Hamid reported to the base each Saturday morning and attended all the courses and training sessions required of him. However, beneath his apparent conscientiousness, he could think of nothing other than finding a way to escape from the military.

The military machinery of Iran at the time would not allow anyone to leave. Those attempting to escape were tried in military courts and received various uncompromising punishments, inclusive of execution. Leaving the military and abandoning your duties was not only illegal, but also a crime against the Islamic laws of the country, a new set of rules that were enacted after the fall of Shah. The country needed every soldier they could get, and simply would not tolerate any attempt at escape.

New soldiers received only the briefest of formal training, limited to just several weeks of learning how to handle weapons such as machine guns, how to set bombs, and how to neutralize explosives. Training also involved strenuous physical and endurance exercises. Men were taught to be machines, stripped of whom they were to their families and friends—personality and emotions replaced by a weaponized human. The war zone was on the Iran-Iraq border, and all soldiers, including Hamid, eventually went there.

One Saturday, Hamid woke at four in the morning to his alarm clock. Another restless night had passed, another fleeting weekend with his family over, and it was time for him to get ready to go back to his military base. The thought painfully tugged at his insides. Reluctantly, he got himself up and sat on the edge of his bed for a while, thinking about the past, his family, his friends, and even daring to consider what may lie ahead for him in the next few months.

I am not ready to go to war. I am not made to kill anyone. I am not willing to die. Hamid repeated the mantra in his head over and over.

He knew thoughts of this nature would not help his situation, but he could not stop himself from thinking such things. Nevertheless, after a few minutes, he released a heavy sigh and forced his legs to transport him to the full-length mirror attached to his closet door. For a long while, he just stared at the man who stood before him. Who was he now? Who is Hamid? A soldier? No. No, of course not. The Iranian war machine was doing its best to mold him into a cold and detached warrior, but it could not take away the fact that he was peaceful, compassionate, and empathetic. He was not an animal whose sole purpose was to survive as the strongest member of the pack, no matter what the cost. He could not justify killing another innocent human being. Yet Hamid had no choice. He opened the closet door, took out his military outfit, and dressed himself in the uniform that signified something he just did not believe in.

Almost robotically, Hamid walked to the bathroom, washed his face, brushed his teeth, and shaved. He dried his hands and face, took a deep breath, and went downstairs to join his parents for breakfast. He had until he reached the kitchen to compose himself, to appear strong and fearless in front of his parents.

Mom and dad were already up. They had prepared breakfast for their brave young soldier. Hamid's older brother, Mahmood, joined them too. The family greeted each other and sat on the floor, the traditional way of enjoying mealtime in Iran. Hamid, however, was not hungry.

Nasrin, Hamid's mother, chose to quietly read the Quran, as she did every morning, praying in her heart for her son's well-being and for the war to end. Her thought was simple—the end of the war meant her son would live.

Mom, I love you. Thank you for all you have done for me, repeated Hamid in his heart before succumbing to another uninvited thought: *I cannot leave you Mom. I am not ready to die Mom.*

Hamid tried very hard to resist such thoughts, the worst ones, the idea of how his mother would suffer and how hard she would cry for him if he were to die at war, but they refused to go away, rising from his subconscious with growing intensity until he caved in and acknowledged them. He shook his head in a vain effort to eliminate the troubling thoughts once more. Instead, he assumed a false smile of courage and told his mother how much he loved to share the mealtime with her. With his eyes, Hamid was following her every move, as she arose to get him tea, as she gently walked to and from the kitchen, as she bowed her head praying and reading from the Quran. He glanced at the clock; time was flying by.

As Hamid was leaving, at the door Nasrin held his face with both hands, kissed him on his cheeks, hugged him, said her farewells and prayers, and wished him a wonderful week. She would never know how hard it was for Hamid to get through those moments without releasing the hot tears that threatened to cascade down his cheeks.

"Before you know, Hamid, it will be Thursday again, and you will be home," said his mother. "Would you like me to invite Hossein and your aunt Parvin for dinner?"

Hamid nodded his head in agreement. The lump in his throat was still wedged firmly in place and prevented him from speaking. He tried to force himself to cheer up—the dinner plans would give him something positive to focus on over the coming week. Mahmood and then Haj Agha, their father, took their turns to hug and kiss him, and all of them waved as he walked away from the comfort and familiarity of his home. The streets were still quiet, and the sky broodingly dark.

"Goodbye, Hamid. We will see you soon, my love," said his father.

Haj Agha was an honorary title that Hamid's dad had acquired several years ago after his religious pilgrimages to Mecca. Despite what he said, however, deep down Hamid's father was very upset. He had always wanted his son to study at the university, but those dreams evaporated the instant he discovered Hamid had not passed *Konkoor*, Iran's national university-entrance examination. He had tried very hard not to reveal his bitter disappointment in front of his son, but whether he had succeeded, he was unsure. The three watched Hamid walking away from home, and when he was out of sight, they closed the door and went back inside the house.

In the quiet of early-morning Tehran, Hamid ambled lethargically to the bus station. His bus arrived soon after he did. The driver waived the fare for him, one of the few advantages that came with wearing a military uniform, and welcomed him warmly onto the bus.

"We are proud of you, son," said the driver. "The country is proud of you. Without you, we could not fight against that bastard, Saddam Hussein." The driver pulled his window down and started spitting out of the window with great anger, as if he were actually spitting on Saddam Hussein's face. "The bastard, Saddam Hussein!" Hamid was transfixed. The bus driver was almost beside himself with fury. After several more expletives, the driver calmed himself and said, "Take a seat, my son."

Hamid walked back to take a seat as far away from the driver as he could. He was in no mood to have a conversation with him. The early-morning bus was almost empty, and Hamid wrapped himself in isolation and gazed out the window.

Eventually, the bus moved away from the station and set off along its scheduled route. As it chugged dutifully down the road, Hamid silently immersed himself in the past. He recalled his first day on the military base, the location of the *Konkoor*, his last day at high school, his classmates, his cousin Hossein who had passed the *Konkoor* and was studying medicine, the good old times, the times when they would travel with Hossein and his family to the Caspian Sea, memories of swimming in the Caspian Sea as a child, the 1979 regime change in Iran, the demonstrations that preceded the fall of the Shah, simple uprisings in the streets to million-man marches in Tehran's main roads. All these thoughts and memories passed tumultuously through his mind, hastening the journey to the base.

Hamid had lately found that remembering the good old days was an effective defense mechanism. The colorful world of carefree smiles and joyous experiences, from which he could exclude the outside world, had become a comforting refuge each day. Acquiescing to this fantasy world allowed him to avoid thinking about his terrible reality and what may lie ahead. The war had dictated his destiny, and he knew it full well. What good would come of constantly reciting the awful and inevitable truth in his head?

Hamid missed playing soccer with his friends. He had a genuine interest in the game and even had a table-soccer in his room. Hamid and his brother Mahmood used to play against each other all the time back in the good old days, exhibiting friendly and good-natured rivalry. Then, as he rode along in the bus, floating in those pleasant thoughts, another, more unsettling thought started to rise, fighting its way into his consciousness.

Is there any way that I can get out of this whole mess? thought Hamid. *I am not made for this. I was not born to be a soldier. I hate war. I cannot bear arms. I do not want to go and fight. Even if I am not killed, I do not want to kill anyone.*

More, and more troubling, thoughts came unbidden from his subconscious, gushing and surging to the surface of his mind. *What for? What does it all mean? Why should I kill another human being, an Iraqi soldier, who is probably someone like me, someone who did not choose to go to war? I am sure that he also, like me, has a family, a loving mother, a father, and a brother. He may even be married with kids. How can I kill him and have his death on my conscience? Why are our countries even at war? Why cannot we make peace? How long will this go on? What do I do now? How can I get out of this?*

They were thoughts he had many times on the long bus rides between his home and the military base, but this morning they felt different, this torrent of familiar thoughts, spilling out with a sense of urgency that he could not ignore. Typically, he used the ride back to the base as a time to brainstorm, and as the weeks rolled by, he began increasingly to think about, and consider a way out or an escape from the military. This unspooling of his imagination started as whimsical notions, and over time developed into plausible ideas, and this morning rapidly evolved into a convincing plan.

Maybe I can act as if I am sick, thought Hamid. *I could pretend to be deaf, or blind in one eye. Can they figure that out? Can they detect that I am lying? Maybe I should act as if one of my legs is paralyzed? Is this legal? What if they discover that I am lying? What are the penalties? Maybe I should ask Hossein. He is a doctor! Yes, that is a good idea. I am sure he will tell me what to do. He is smart.*

Hamid embraced this plan, and finally felt as if he may have found a way out, and to an extent, this was already true, for the idea brought him some peace. Deep in his heart he was relieved, at least temporarily.

Mom said that Hossein will be coming over next weekend, Hamid said to himself. *I will ask him. I can trust him. I am sure that he will give me some answers and perhaps some inventive ideas.*

The bus stopped across from the main entrance to Hamid's military base.

"Jamshidieh Military Base - Death to Saddam Hussein," announced the bus driver in an authoritative voice that tore through Hamid's reverie and snapped him back to reality. Hamid got up, walked down the aisle, and exited through the rear door of the bus, purposefully avoiding the face of the driver. Almost involuntarily, he crossed the street, paused at the gate to show his ID card, and entered the base. He was in autopilot mode. The air was fresh, and the street noise was vanishing behind him as he approached his dormitory to meet with other soldiers.

Days were long at the base. He was there with hundreds of other new soldiers who, mostly like Hamid, did not pass the *Konkoor* and so had to do their mandatory two years of military service. He looked at his young comrades and knew that in eight weeks they would all be at the front, with rifles in their hands and high expectations of being able to fight Iraqis. He also was acutely aware of the statistics that hung faintly but constantly in the air that enveloped him and his fellow draftees, like a smell that would not go away: within a year, 80 to 90 percent of them would be either dead or severely disabled by war injuries. Hamid blinked. Why was his mind torturing him? He did not want to think about death, and he did not want to think that most of these kids would not return to their homes and families. No, he could not prevent himself from contemplating who among them would survive and who would die. His eyes trailed from one face to the next, and fleetingly past a small mirror hanging on the back wall. His heart sank.

The official training day at the base ended at five in the afternoon, when soldiers were free to go to their dormitory or simply hang out on the premises until dinnertime.

At night, long after the sun had set; groups of soldiers would gather around someone's bed and engage in friendly chitchat. This was a time for them to get to know each other, learn where each of them was from, what their parents did, or even what plans they had for their lives. It was a time to make new friends, and during one such occasion Hamid found that he had a friend in Ali, another draftee who was also eighteen. Ali was a recent graduate of a high school in a wealthy neighborhood of Tehran. The two young men had clicked instantly, quickly becoming very good friends, but each had his own unique set of beliefs.

Ali had decided to go to war and fight for his country; even if he not been forced to the frontlines, this would have been his choice. He hated Saddam Hussein almost as much as he hated the idea of Iraqis invading his country. Ali was not afraid of war. He did not think about dying at all. He was determined to fight the enemy.

"Hamid, are you afraid of dying?" asked Ali.

"Do you want to hear the truth, or a formal answer we all give to the sergeant?" asked Hamid.

"Of course the truth, Hamid," said Ali.

"I am very scared," replied Hamid gravely. "I know that you are brave, and determined to go to war. You are fearless, but I am not. I just cannot do it. Why should I go and kill another human being? What for?"

And so began another of the nightly conversations that would continue among the newly drafted soldiers until those hushed post-dusk discussions were no longer an option, and their tired bodies eventually fell asleep.

CHAPTER TWO
THE QUEST

It seemed to take forever, but Thursday afternoon, the official end of the work week, had finally arrived. Hamid could not wait to get home. He had spent all day rehearsing the questions he had for Hossein. He was now obsessed with the thought of getting out of the military. It had started as a small spark of an idea in one corner of his brain and had grown in size and vigor, multiplying rapidly and infecting every cell of his body. By the time he arrived home, his cousin had already arrived, accompanied by his mother, *khale* Parvin. Hamid's mother, Nasrin, kissed and greeted him. As sisters, Parvin and Nasrin, were very close to each other, and had raised their children together, virtually in one large and extended family.

Dinnertimes such as this were happy occasions for the two families to share. They were wonderful opportunities to catch up with one another and discuss everything new in their lives. Hamid's mom had again made her signature dish, a meal everyone rapidly devoured amid approving sounds. Her *Ghormeh Sabzi* was everyone's favorite. The room was full of voices and laughter. Hamid's dad told a story with great animation to keep his two youngest boys entertained. The delicious smell of food had filled the air. These certainly were happy times.

The joyous scene prompted Hamid's brother to nostalgically recall a scene from former times. He spoke directly to Hossein, but his conversation commanded the attention of everyone in the whole room. "Do you remember, Hossein, when all of us used to go to the Caspian seashores every summer?" asked Mahmood. "Remember the narrow stream of water in front of the rental home, where we used to search for frogs?" He paused briefly and smiled, "Locals used to sit beside the same stream, washing their clothes and dishes. Remember that, Hossein?"

Mahmood's smile faded as reality tore through his recollections.

"Now it is all about war. The shadow of this war is all over us. Look at Hamid. In just eight weeks, they will force him to go to the front. Then what?"

It was a rhetorical question; an answer was neither expected nor appropriate, but everyone near Mahmood had heard.

The mood in the room then swiftly changed. Silence ensued and for a while, the loving family members looked across at Hamid's young face. No one communicated their feelings, but at that moment, everyone was acutely conscious that this dinner could be one of the last ones they might have with Hamid. An uneasy, sorrowful air engulfed the room.

"Come on, Mahmood, don't ruin the dinner." interjected Hamid with a lightheartedness he did not feel. "Let's enjoy the food and the company of *khale* Parvin and our cousins. I am here only for the weekend, and I would like to relax and have a good time with all of you. I hear enough about war at the base all day—six days a week—that is more than enough for me. So, please no more talk of war. I want to enjoy this dinner and have fun with you."

Hamid's dad nodded in agreement, but kept his gaze firmly down.

"How about some music, Hamid? What would you like to listen to?" asked Haj Agha. It was the ideal diversion.

Mahmood stood and walked to turn on the music. Without hesitating, he chose Hamid's favorite song, *Booye Gandom,* "The Scent of the Wheat Farms," a song by Iran's legendary singer, Dariush. Gentle music filled the room and the smell of delicious food filled everyone's nostrils, yet the mood remained low.

Hamid's dad attempted to break through the somber atmosphere.

"Hossein, Jaan, how are your studies coming along?" he asked. "When will you be finishing medical school?"

"I am in the last stretch of my studies," replied Hossein, "I have another seven to eight months to graduate."

"You must love medicine," said Haj Agha.

"I just started my internship in surgery," said Hossein. "I do love medicine, and will work very hard to become a good doctor. You know, although I am doing a rotation in surgery this month, I don't think that I will ever want to become a surgeon."

At the same time, at the other end of the room, Hamid's two younger brothers were getting into a verbal fight.

"Hey you two, keep it quiet. It's dinner time," said Haj Agha to the younger boys. "There is enough soda for everyone to drink."

With that, the mood gradually reverted to what it was before; smiles and laughter returned.

Trying to retain the buoyancy of the conversation, Mahmood asked, "Hamid, have you learned any new jokes at the base?"

The corners of Hamid's mouth twitched upward slightly as he recalled a joke he had overheard the other day. It was a type of Iranian joke that makes fun of an ethnic minority in the country.

"Have you heard this one? Two friends were out on the street, walking and chatting. They had just finished lunch at a local restaurant. As they were walking away from the restaurant, one of the two, who happened to be a Tork, without notice or warning to his friend, started climbing up a tall tree. His friend, shocked by this unusual behavior, stood speechless under the tree and watched him for a minute. 'Hey, Abbas Agha, why did you climb the tree? What are you doing up there?' asked the friend. Abbas Agha yelled back down, 'I am up here to eat some cherries. It feels so good to be eating cherries on top of a tree.' But this only confused his friend further, 'this is not a cherry tree, Abbas Agha. This is an apple tree.' His friend, undeterred, replied 'I know that. The cherries came from my pocket—I brought them with me to eat here and enjoy the view.'"

Hamid burst into laughter himself as he said the punch line. Everyone else laughed with him.

"He was a Tork," said Hamid.

"Good joke, Hamid," said Hossein. "Thanks for making us laugh."

After dinner, the three cousins went out for a walk on the street. The air was still warm. Although fall had already descended on the town, the chill of winter was still far away.

Away from the rest of the family, Mahmood spoke openly about his concerns. "You know, Hossein, we are all worried about Hamid. His life is in danger now. He is scheduled to go to the front in about eight weeks." He looked at Hamid and hesitated. He knew he should not be saying these things in front of him, but he also knew that Hamid was already acutely aware of the danger of his predicament—no point hiding it or pretending everything was fine. Anyway, this was a good opportunity to discuss things with Hossein.

"I don't know what our mother will do when Hamid goes to the front. She is already crying every day. Her daily prayers have lengthened considerably. She is constantly praying for the war to end, so Hamid won't have to leave."

Then Hamid spoke up. He was keen to hear Hossein's thoughts. "What do you think, Hossein? When do you think this war will end?"

"I think, to our government, we are dispensable, much like the leaves are to a tree in the fall," was Hossein's philosophical response. "Do you think anyone cares if *we* fall? No. Do you think they are concerned about all the young people killed in this war? No, of course not. To them, war is a good excuse to solidify the government's position, to justify the shortages, and to unite the masses of people for their own gain. This war, in my opinion, is not going to end anytime soon. It is much like the Palestinian and Israeli conflict. When do you think that conflict will end? The war is good also for Iraq and for the Western world. Think about it—the West is ridding itself of stockpiles of their antiquated war machines. Because of this war, and the threat it brings to the supply of oil from the Persian Gulf, international oil prices have climbed to all-time highs. And who benefits from that? Exxon. BP. Not you, and not me for sure. Superpowers prosper during wartime. Did you know that the United States was in its worst economic depression during World War II and that the war helped them get out of it? American industry was revitalized by the war. What else do we know about the economy of World War II? How was the economy of Hitler's Germany before that war?"

"Let's not become too involved in the recession and economy, Hossein," said Mahmood.

"I am sorry, Mahmood. I am just so upset at the entire thing," said Hossein. "We are the casualties of this war, yet we have nothing to do with it. Thousands of us have died already. Day and night, Saddam Hussein is dropping bombs on us. We hide in our basements almost every night, as the air-defense sirens go on. No one in the government cares about our well-being. They could not care less whether Hamid returns alive from the war or in a body bag. They do not care whether any of us will survive the air attacks. They won't look after us, so we need to care for ourselves."

"What is the mood among the doctors at the hospital? Do all of them feel the same as you?" asked Mahmood.

"I have already lost one year of my life to the so called revolution, so have all my classmates," replied Hossein. "With the establishment of the clerics, the universities were closed. The medical school closed for one year, other schools for even longer. Why? To instigate the 'cultural revolution.' It took them a year to do what they wanted to do. They expelled a dozen students and several university professors just because they were of the Baha'i faith. They also expelled some students who were agents of SAVAK" the Shah's Secret Service.

"Oh, and not forgetting the 'Islamic philosophy' class added to the medical school's curriculum," continued Hossein. "We had to spend a whole semester studying the faith of various Emams of early Islam. Why? Is that going to help us treat our patients any better?"

"So what are your plans for the next year or two?" asked Mahmood, unfazed by the passion with which Hossein spoke.

"I am planning to leave Iran as soon as I am finished with school," said Hossein. "I know of someone who can take me out of Iran. For ten thousand dollars, he promises to get me to Istanbul. The rest will be up to me. I would like to do my postgraduate training in the United States." Hossein broke off, suddenly conscious of the time he had been talking. "I am sorry, guys, if I am talking too much."

The three strolled down the street. Hamid, absentmindedly, found a small stone on the sidewalk and threw it on a vacant piece of land. Mahmood was lost in his own thoughts. Hamid then broke the silence.

"Guys, do you think there may be a way for me to get out of the military, somehow escape it? At my military base, so many of the soldiers go to the nurse's office, throwing up, looking or acting sick, complaining of back pain, headaches, so that they can get an exemption from serving in the army. Last month, they let one person out because he had some kind of problem with his feet. The military clinic and the doctors there are strict on letting people out. You have to be sick as a dog to get a day off, let alone exemption from duty altogether."

Hamid turned to Hossein and asked, "Do you know under what medical circumstances one could get out of serving in the military?"

"I don't think that is a matter of public information Hamid," replied Hossein. "I would have to research that for you. My gut feeling is that a person would have to have a chronic condition, with a poor outlook, and no chance of recovery with treatment, or you would have to be physically unfit to perform the duties of a soldier. For example, someone suffering from kidney failure or liver failure, or major orthopedic problems, or chronic asthma, or something of the similar nature should get a medical exemption. Those conditions would make it impossible to serve in the military and fight in the war."

"Have you ever been to the base's clinic?" Hossein continued, "Do you know how they assess soldiers who go in and complain of being sick?"

"I don't know," said Hamid. "I have never been inside, but every day I think about faking an illness so that they will let me out. A medical condition may be an ideal excuse to get out of the military."

Hossein knew that this would be no easy feat. "Just let me think for a minute, Hamid." Hossein looked down contemplatively at his feet as the three walked on. Hamid and Mahmood knew this side of Hossein well. Whenever they asked a serious question of him, he would take his time and think deeply before he responded. Hossein was a thinker—part of what would make a good doctor. After what seemed a lifetime, Hossein spoke up.

"Guys, I have an idea," said Hossein. "Something just sparked in my head. We need to somehow make Hamid sick, extremely sick—not life-threateningly ill, but sick enough to leave the military. He will need to suffer from a disease, a chronic disease with a poor outlook. At least that is how it should seem. With that in place, we should be able to convince the doctors that he has a serious illness that prevents him from serving in the military. Now this would be no quick fix, guys. It may take several months, but I think it is possible. It may be his only chance to get out of the military."

"So how do we do that, Hossein?" asked Hamid. He trusted Hossein's judgment implicitly, and although he tried to keep his emotions in check, he could not help feeling his hopes lift.

"I have some ideas," replied Hossein. "You have to remember that his is not a simple task, but I think it can be done. Almost daily, we have patients who come to our neurology clinic with all kinds of paralysis, blindness, or deafness, yet they are not truly ill. They simply fake it. We diagnose these easily. For most people, this is a way out of something. Last month, we had a fourteen-year-old girl presumably paralyzed on the right half of her body, but she could talk, laugh, and play with her left arm. She had us all confused, but you know what? She was faking it. Acting out paralysis is easy to do, yet it is also easy to diagnose. For you, Hamid, we need something better. This may be your only chance out of the military, so we need to be clever about it. The only way to stop people from doubting your diagnosis is to actually make you sick, so you won't have to act."

"Really, Hossein?" asked Hamid. Despite the notion of him actually being ill, not merely faking an illness, he felt no apprehension, only hope for a future away from the military. "Do you think that we have a chance?"

"I need time to think this through better, but I think we can definitely do something," he replied. "And once we make you appear sick, all you need to do is to go to the clinic and tell them you don't feel well. Let them figure out what is wrong with you. Whatever we do, needs to result in plenty of physical findings and concrete evidence with which they cannot argue. I have some ideas now, but let me research this some more and talk to you about this next weekend. How is that?"

Hamid was more than happy. Like an excited child, he kept asking his cousin for more information. But Hossein gave nothing more away. He did, however, promise him a plan by next weekend.

By the time the three returned home, everyone was having dessert.

"Where have you all been?" asked Hamid's dad. "Sit down. Have some dessert." They took their places with the others, enjoying tea and the best of Persian desserts.

"Mahmood, we need to inform your dad too," said Hossein in a hushed voice. "Do you think he will be okay with it?"

Mahmood already knew what his father's response would be, but he said, "Let's ask him."

"Haj Agha, can we go upstairs to talk privately for a minute?"

Mahmood's father was taken aback. His son spoke in such a serious tone. "Of course, my son, what is wrong?"

"Dad, let's go upstairs," said Hamid.

Without protest, Haj Agha followed his boys upstairs to the library.

Haj Agha was concerned about what he was going to hear next, but the familiar surroundings of the old library put him at ease. He loved this room. It was so peaceful—his own little sanctuary.

Mahmood spoke first. "Dad, you know that Hamid has another seven to eight weeks before he is deployed to the front. We are of course very concerned about that, and I know you are too."

Haj Agha said nothing. He just waited patiently for his son to reveal the news he was evidently so eager to share.

"We have discussed this with Hossein, and he has some ideas that we wanted to run by you. We want your input too," continued Mahmood.

Haj Agha was intrigued, but wary. "Hossein Jaan, what is on your mind?"

Hossein took the lead. "I think there may be a way to get Hamid a medical exemption from the military; we would do this by making him sick. I have some ideas, but before we go further, I wanted to be sure you are okay with the concept."

This was not what Haj Agha was expecting. "Tell me more. I am somewhat confused. Hamid is very healthy. What do you mean by making him sick? You mean have him fake an illness? Because I don't think..."

"No, Haj Agha," Hossein interjected. "I am thinking of actually making him sick, real sick, temporarily though, so that he can get a medical leave from serving in the army. I have a few ideas, but need more time to refine them and come up with a solid plan."

Like most people, Haj Agha trusted both Hossein's medical prowess and his honest nature. "In general, I support whatever you can do to get him out of the military," he said. "Of course I would rather Hamid be sick and at home than be fighting Iraqis at the front." You have my support, but I want to know more details."

"Of course, Haj Agha. Thank you for trusting me," said Hossein. "How about we meet next weekend to discuss this further?"

"To me, you are like Hamid and Mahmood," said Haj Agha. "I treat you like my own children."

Haj Agha stood, hugged, kissed Hossein, and told him, "I trust you. I will let you do whatever you think we should do. You can count on my support because I know you have Hamid's best interests at heart."

It was a memorable moment for all the men in that room. Hamid was witnessing how concerned everyone was about him. Haj Agha was impressed with Hossein and how his nephew was stepping in to help his son and potentially save his life. Mahmood saw how his family's unity was encircling Hamid. He loved his younger brother, and the idea of losing him was something to be fought against by any means they had.

Despite his outward confidence, Hossein was now feeling the heavy load of responsibility on his shoulders.

What if something goes wrong? He asked himself, as Haj Agha was talking to him. *What if we are caught? What if Hamid is caught? Will they torture him and interrogate him on who planned this and carried it out? Will Hamid be able to keep this entire thing a secret?* Hossein knew very well that both their lives and their futures would be in jeopardy if something were to go wrong with whatever plan he was going to implement to get Hamid out.

"One more thing," Hossein said, interrupting Haj Agha's speech. "It is essential that we keep this a complete secret. This conversation stays here, in this room among the four of us only. No one else should know—not my mother, not even your mother. "

Haj Agha nodded his head in agreement.

"Absolutely, Hossein," said Haj Agha. "You are completely right. Never should anyone know what we are doing—not now, not next year, not even in the next thirty years. The consequences of this thing leaking out are tremendous. It doesn't bear thinking about."

The four men left the room, walked down the stairs, and joined the rest of the family. For the first time in a long time, Hamid was feeling good and was seeing a sliver of hope before his eyes.

Before the night was over, Mahmood pulled Hossein into a quiet corner.

"Can you tell me what our chances of success are?" whispered Mahmood.

"Mahmood Jaan, the plan I have should succeed," said Hossein with conviction. "I am not going to risk Hamid's life and devise a plan that might fail. Give me a few days. I need to work out a few wrinkles that I can already foresee, but don't worry."

"Okay," said Mahmood, satisfied with the response he received.

"To succeed, all of us need to remain focused, have positive attitudes, and maintain a steady course," said Hossein. None of the men realized what would be in store for them soon.

CHAPTER THREE
THE CHALLENGE

Over the next few days, Hossein spent every hour of his spare time in the hospital library. He spent hour after hour brainstorming various scenarios and reviewing the relevant medical literature, solely focused on Hamid's situation. Every time he felt tired, all he had to do was close his eyes and picture the hope that had flickered across his cousin's young face on the night he conceived the plan; immediately he would return to his work with a newfound determination to succeed.

Hossein thought aloud, muttering under his breath, as if verbalizing his ideas would make them more effective. *Whatever illness it is, it must reveal legitimate physical or biological findings so the military doctors have no choice but to believe him.*

Hossein had compiled a mental list of the characteristics that Hamid's illness should have to gain him exemption from duty. *The illness has to be objective and convincing, be reversible so when the entire thing is over, Hamid would fully recover. It should not result in any form of long-term injury and it should not raise any suspicion of malingering or foul play as a potential cause. It also has to be chronic in nature and seemingly incurable, or debilitating.*

Hossein was good at detecting malingering and foul play in the patients he saw, so he was well aware of the things to avoid.

Who could ever imagine that to save a life, I would have to make someone sick? thought Hossein. The irony of his profession and the task at hand was not lost on him.

One afternoon as he paced the library, deep in thought, a voice called out to him. It was Afsaneh.

"Hello, Hossein, what is it that you are so deeply indulged in?"

"Afsaneh, how are you?" replied Hossein. He raised his voice slightly, and it displayed a warmth that reflected his feelings towards the woman who had stood by his side. The pair had been best friends for many years. They had known each other for more than six years and had many mutual interests, most importantly, both wanted to leave Iran and continue their postgraduate studies in the United States.

"Busy as always, and you?" replied Afsaneh, temporarily distracted from her initial question. "Studying hard? Preparing for ECFMG?"

ECFMG was the name of an examination, given by the Educational Commission for Foreign Medical Graduates that foreign-trained physicians had to pass to continue their education in the United States.

"Yes, dear," replied Hossein.

"Want to come to our house tonight?" said Afsaneh. "My mother is making your favorite dish. You are more than welcome to join us."

Hossein loved spending time with Afsaneh's family. They were truly hospitable, good-natured and, above all, caring people. "Afsaneh. I would love to join you for dinner. I will be there at seven," said Hossein.

Hossein had a wonderful time with Afsaneh's family that night and, as always, the food was divine, yet he remained preoccupied by the illness he was going to create in Hamid.

What if something goes wrong and this plot is discovered? he thought as he was riding in the taxicab on the way home. *Will I be able to get out of Iran by July next year, in time to take my examination? My own future is in jeopardy too.*

For as long as he could remember, Hossein had wanted to go to the United States. Continuing his medical education there would be a dream come true. He felt the familiar surge of adrenaline-fuelled anticipation as he pictured himself and Afsaneh studying there. The fall of the Shah's regime and the war between Iran and Iraq, however, had created several obstacles that Hossein would have to overcome to be able to go to the United States and continue his education there.

Over the next several days, and since his promise to Hamid and Haj Agha, Hossein had taken a new approach to assessing his own patients. Not only did he treat their ailments, but now he also constantly asked himself whether he might be able to safely induce any of their illnesses in Hamid, and whether the induced ailment would meet all the criteria Hossein had established.

One day as he was working in the emergency room, he considered two of the patients in his care: one had a fractured hip, and the other had sustained a fracture in his pelvis. Hossein dismissed both options. *Although they would most definitely result in exemption from military service, such serious fractures are hard to induce and can cause all kinds of complications. This cannot be a choice for Hamid.*

In the emergency room, Hossein encountered heart attacks and strokes regularly. Hamid, however, was too young to develop either; nor was Hossein able to reproduce them in his cousin. Even if he could, the damage to Hamid's body would be tremendous. Hossein was looking for a condition from which Hamid could fully recover without long-term ill effects.

Hossein's primary field of interest was hematology, the study of blood disorders. For the past several years, he had debated whether to become a surgeon or a hematologist. Hossein knew that most of his friends, interns, and residents shied away from hematology because they found it hard and complex. Then an idea arose in Hossein's mind.

There are all kinds of blood disorders that we can mimic, and I bet if my friends and other interns and residents don't like hematology, and don't understand this field of medicine, the military doctors won't get it either. In addition, with the short supply of hematologists in Iran, I bet they do not even have one on their own staff. They will most likely have to refer their patients to an outside hematologist.

One afternoon, when he was done with his routine work, he made a short walk to the hematology ward. The staff there liked and respected Hossein for his genuine interest and depth of knowledge in this field of medicine.

Most of the patients in the ward had bad hematological conditions, such as leukemia and life-threatening lymphomas. Hossein knew that Ardeshir, one of his classmates, would be on duty that night. Sure enough, there he was loitering at reception, talking casually to a smiling nurse. He caught sight of Hossein and turned to greet his friend.

"Hey, Hossein, how are you? What are you doing here?"

"I am fine Ardeshir, thank you. I have a few free hours and just thought I would stop by to check on the patients whom I took care of during my rotation here," said Hossein, reciting his rehearsed line perfectly.

"So are you enjoying your time here Ardeshir?"

"Not really, this is a mandatory rotation." Ardeshir shrugged his narrow shoulders. "It is a difficult rotation. I have to study so much, and it is difficult to understand what is behind these complex illnesses. Honestly, it's all rather confusing with so many forms of leukemia."

"Well, I won't stay and bother you," said Hossein to Ardeshir glancing around the ward. "I can see you have plenty to do. By the way, how are things going between you and the tall, skinny unit receptionist? What is her name?"

"You mean Ms. Tehrani," replied Ardeshir with a smile on his face. "She is friendly, and a good flirt," Ardeshir paused for a second, looked around, and then whispered. "I will tell you about it next time we meet. Let me get back to this other friendly nurse. She is just out of nursing school and has some medical questions for me."

"Of course Ardeshir, and what kind of questions do you have for her?" replied Hossein as he smiled back at Ardeshir. "Go and educate her, I am just going to look through the charts to see if I recognize any patients."

Hossein reviewed several patient charts and paid visits to handful of them. By the time he left the ward, he was convinced that the way out for Hamid was to have a hematological disorder, one that would confuse everyone who would see him.

By the time he reached home, Hossein was closer to a solution.

Anemia can be induced, he thought. *If I draw enough blood from Hamid regularly, he will undoubtedly become anemic. This will show on his lab tests. Severe anemia will be convincing enough to prevent him from performing his daily duties, and most importantly, I will have full control over the degree of his illness. If need be, I can make him more anemic. On the other hand, I can make him less anemic. I can fine-tune it as time passes.* The plan solidified in Hossein's mind. It seemed the ideal solution, and so simple to implement.

Again, on the following Thursday night, everyone gathered at Hamid's house for dinner. Just as the week before, Mahmood, Hossein, and Hamid left the house to go for a walk in the neighborhood.

"So how was your week, Hamid?" asked Hossein.

"It was okay," replied Hamid. "A new group of draftees came to the base. They replaced another group that had gone to the front. Have you had a good week?"

"Busy. I spent a great deal of time in the library," said Hossein calmly. "Researching what we can do for you mostly. I still need to iron out some wrinkles, but I have devised a plan," He paused. He could not help building the tension slightly. He had spent plenty of time contemplating this solution and he was rather excited about revealing his thoughts to the other men.

"What I am proposing is to make Hamid anemic. Most of those who develop anemia have it because of excessive bleeding or occasionally their bodies don't make enough blood cells." He waited for their reaction.

"And how are you going to make me anemic, Hossein?" asked Hamid. He did not seem apprehensive or worried in the slightest.

"You will have to lose blood, lots of blood," replied Hossein. There was no point sugarcoating the pill—Hamid needed to realize what he would be imposing on his body. "We will do it is by drawing a lot of blood from you, much like those who go and donate blood to the Red Cross. The difference is that we will have to take your blood regularly, once a week at the beginning, then as often as we need to keep your blood counts within a range that will safely make you appear ill."

"How will that affect me? How will I be feeling throughout this?" asked Hamid.

"By making you anemic, you will feel weak and fatigued," replied Hossein. "You will also look pale." He started to recognize unease settling on Hamid's face and tried to put his mind at rest. "That is what we want, though. We want you to appear really ill so no one would even think that there is any wrongdoing or foul play."

Mahmood interjected. "So when he is pale and ill, all he needs to do is to show up in the medical clinic at the base and say he is sick?"

"Correct, Mahmood," replied Hossein. "Hamid, I think we can make you anemic in about two to three weeks. At that point, all you will need to do is to show up in the medical clinic and tell them you are not feeling well. The rest will be up the doctor there. He will have to figure out what is going on with you."

"I am really excited and want to get started as soon as we can, Hossein," said Hamid. "Time is running out on me."

"Just remember that drawing blood is only one aspect of this," said Hossein. "We will need to do other interventions, but right now drawing your blood is the most important part of this plan."

Mahmood was confused. "What else do we need to do?"

"Well, if we just draw Hamid's blood, it will result in a particular type of anemia," said Hossein. "It causes what we call iron-deficiency anemia. I am thinking about complicating his clinical picture, to confuse the doctors who will be taking care of him. Iron-deficiency anemia is too simple, too easily treated. A more sophisticated type of anemia would not be so easy to diagnose, it could raise the suspicion of leukemia, something that will really scare them."

"Hossein, do you really think you can do that?" asked Hamid.

"I think I can. It will be a stepwise process."

"I actually had to visit the nurse's office this week," said Hamid. "During one of our exercises, I fell and wounded my knee. The group sergeant noticed me falling. I did not think the wound was particularly serious, and honestly, I dreaded going into the clinic, but my sergeant insisted that I go in and at the least get a tetanus shot."

"And?" asked Hossein, curiosity presenting itself as an evident inflection in his voice.

"It was a frightening scene in the clinic," said Hamid. "Like something out of a movie. Just as I got there, they brought in a soldier who had sustained a major injury to his face. There was blood all over his uniform. The poor guy was screaming."

"Did you meet the doctor there?" asked Hossein unaffected by Hamid's description of the base clinic. After all, this was what he saw every day.

"Yes, I did," replied Hamid. "The doctor there was not a pleasant guy. He wore a military uniform, and he looked at you as if you had already done something wrong. After the nurse triaged me, he came in and asked me why I was there. 'What is wrong with you, soldier?'" said Hamid mimicking the stern tone of the military-base doctor. He talked to me as if I owed him something. "I said, 'Nothing, sir,'" Hamid tried to recite the conversation he had with the doctor. "I said, 'I did not want to come in to bother you. I know you are busy, but my sergeant insisted that I come in and get a tetanus shot.' He asked me, 'Did you cut yourself?' and I rolled up my pants to show him my right knee that was badly scratched and bleeding. It actually looked worse than it felt. Well anyway, he took a quick look and started yelling. 'This is nothing, why are all of them wasting my time here? NURSE!' he yelled. 'Clean his knee with Betadine, some Bacitracin ointment and cover it with gauze. Also, give the sergeant a tetanus shot. I mean the soldier, not the sergeant.'" Hamid was laughing as he recited the conversation. "And the doctor walked out," said Hamid.

"Did you get the impression that he is an intelligent man?" asked Hossein, deliberately ignoring the comedic aspect of Hamid's anecdotal account.

"I don't know. I cannot judge him," replied Hamid. "He was too abrupt, obviously overworked, and was mad about something. At first, I assumed he was angry with me, but thinking back, he just seemed angry in general."

"He took care of you, though?" asked Hossein. "He looked at your wound, right?"

"Yes, right," said Hamid.

"I can imagine that he was stressed, but at least he was attentive enough to look at your knee and give proper instructions to his nurse," said Hossein.

"So, Hossein, what are the next steps? When can we start with the blood drawing from Hamid?" asked Mahmood.

"When can we start? Hmm," replied Hossein. "How about we get started tonight? We also need to talk to your dad to make sure he is okay with this. You are his son—he needs to be fully informed."

Hamid was thrilled with the idea and the plan that Hossein had proposed. He now knew that something would happen. It finally felt real. He could not envision anything beyond that. Having hope, even a sliver of hope, can make a significant difference in one's life.

After a hurried walk home, Mahmood with the other two men in tow went immediately to find his father. "Dad, we need to talk to you."

"What is up?" replied Haj Agha. Although he had already guessed what this was about.

The four men walked upstairs to Haj Agha's study room. Haj Agha sat behind his large, imposing desk. Hamid and Mahmood sat on the sofa, and Hossein sat on the armchair closest to Haj Agha.

"Haj Agha, I wanted to go over the plan that I have devised for Hamid," said Hossein. "We wanted to get your input, and hopefully your approval, to go ahead with the plan."

"Sure. Tell me, Hossein Jaan," said Haj Agha. "Tell me. What did you have decided to do?"

"I have thought this through extensively, and I think I can make Hamid anemic," said Hossein. "Once he is anemic, he will naturally appear sick to the doctors at the military base. They will need to do lots of blood work and other medical studies to figure out the cause of his anemia."

Hossein paused for a second, and then continued. "With the kind of anemia that I have in mind for Hamid, they will soon be at a loss. They will not have a clue about what is wrong with him. After a while, they will devise some diagnosis. We will work with whatever diagnosis that may be, and take it from there."

Hossein went on to explain how he would implement his plan. He reassured Hamid's father that he would carefully monitor his blood count to make sure Hamid did not become *too* anemic.

"Hamid also has to take supplemental iron," said Hossein. "If we just draw his blood, he will be developing iron-deficiency anemia, which is a simple, treatable condition. He should also take multivitamins. They will possibly check his vitamin B12 and folic-acid levels, as part of routine anemia workup. We want all those measurements to be completely normal. I will also need to put him on some antibiotics."

"Why antibiotics?" asked Haj Agha with a smile on his face. He could not help it. It sounded such an absurd idea. His smile broke the tension in the room and, for no obvious reason, all of them burst into laughter, including Hossein.

"Haj Agha, this is complicated," said Hossein. "I will try to simplify this. Hamid is fully healthy. As he becomes anemic, his body will react to compensate for the lost blood. Bone marrow is the organ in the body that produces blood. His bone marrow will respond, trying to activate the normal compensatory mechanisms to produce more blood. We can measure this response of the bone marrow by doing a simple test. We call it a reticulocyte count or *retic count* for short. Reticulocytes are the youngest and freshest red-blood cells. Doing a retic count is a routine workup for anemic patients."

"So Hamid's retic count is normal now?" asked Haj Agha.

"Correct, Haj Agha. Right now about one percent of the red cells in Hamid's blood are reticulocytes," replied Hossein. "Once he becomes anemic, that number will climb. An elevated retic count means that the bone marrow is healthy, and it is properly responding to blood loss. As a side effect, some drugs and antibiotics can suppress production of blood cells from the bone marrow and potentially lower the retic count. And when the retic count is low..."

Haj Agha suddenly interrupted Hossein and said, "The bone marrow is unhealthy and cannot make enough blood."

"Very good, Haj Agha, you got it," said Hossein.

"Well done, Hossein," said Haj Agha. "I enjoyed your 'Anemia 101' lecture tonight. I fully support this plan. In some ways this is like a game of chess, and I know that you play good chess, Hossein Agha."

"Yes, I do," said Hossein, smiling at the analogy.

"You are playing white, and you are going to make the first move of the game, making Hamid anemic. The opponent, black, will respond to your move by evaluating Hamid's anemia. You will fine-tune his anemia according to what they will do, and so this game will go on."

"Until we checkmate the black," laughed Hossein conspiratorially. "And I would like to start playing this game tonight."

"Hamid, are you okay with this plan?" asked Haj Agha, noting his son's silence.

"Yes, Dad, I am all for it," replied Hamid. "I fully trust Hossein."

"And Mahmood, what do you think?"

"Dad, I trust Hossein," replied Mahmood. "He is smart, and I am sure he can do this."

Hossein reviewed his plan, going over more details with the three men, and he expressed his concerns about the risks of disclosure of information or any form of leakage.

"Everything we do in life has a risk," said Hossein. "Haj Agha, the risks of what we are going to do for Hamid are several. Medically, however, Hamid will be okay. If worse comes to worst, we stop, and the anemia will resolve on its own. The greater risk lies in the highly unlikely event that our cover is blown. But remember, whatever happens, even if, say, they take Hamid away or jail him, or jail me, whatever the situation, all of us must deny everything. Deny, deny, deny, okay?"

All of them nodded in agreement.

"Okay, Hamid?" asked Hossein. "If someone under pressure asks you something, your answer will be always, 'I don't know what you are talking about.' Are you okay with that?"

Hamid agreed. Haj Agha walked over, kissed, and hugged Hossein and his two sons.

"Did you say we were starting this tonight, Hossein Agha?" asked Haj Agha.

"Yes, Haj Agha, right now," replied Hossein. With that, Hossein started instructing Hamid and Mahmood about what he needed to start the blood drawing process.

"Hamid, why don't you go and get changed in something more comfortable. I will need to work on your right foot,"

"Mahmood, can you please get me a few bottles of Pepsi while I go downstairs to get my briefcase?"

"We only drink Coke in this house, Hossein, how could you forget?" Mahmood joked.

The two went downstairs. Hamid wend to his room and changed his clothes. Mahmood returned with four bottles of Coke and four glasses, all on a neatly organized tray, and a bucket of ice and some cookies. Hamid returned to the room, now wearing more comfortable clothes.

Mahmood made the drinks as Hossein was giving instructions to Hamid to lie on the sofa. Hamid felt unexpectedly nervous, but he did not let it show. Instead, he thought about how good it would feel to walk out of the military base a free man.

Hossein sat on a chair next to Hamid. Haj Agha and Mahmood were both standing, ready to observe what he was about to do.

Hossein pulled out his blood-pressure machine and stethoscope, and checked Hamid's pressure.

"Your blood pressure is 120/80, Hamid," said Hossein. "Great. So are you ready?"

Hamid swallowed hard. This was it. This was the start. "Let's do it," he replied.

Hossein took a needle out of his briefcase.

"What is this?" Hamid asked. Nerves made him curious.

"This is a butterfly needle," replied Hossein. "On one end, as you can see, is a needle central to this yellow plastic wing. I can maneuver the needle by holding this wing between my thumb and index finger. As you can see, the needle is connected to this long plastic tube."

Hossein reached into his briefcase and took out a large syringe, deftly unwrapping it, and connecting its tip to the plastic end of the butterfly needle.

"Hossein Agha, why don't you use a simple blood-donation bag? Isn't that easier?" asked Haj Agha. "You can also donate his blood to someone who needs it. That will serve a good cause."

"We cannot do that, Haj Agha," replied Hossein. "Although theoretically we could utilize his blood by donating it to the Red Cross, we cannot do so without divulging identification and records. What we are doing must be untraceable. Another problem with using the blood-donation bags is that the needles in that system are part of the bag, permanently connected to the tubing of that system. They are also thick. They will leave a noticeable mark on Hamid's skin. Last, obtaining the blood-donation bags, and disposing them once they are filled, may raise some suspicion."

"So what will you do with his blood?" asked Haj Agha.

"I will show you in a few minutes," said Hossein. "Hamid, please take off your socks."

"Take off my socks?" asked Hamid.

"Yes, Hamid," said Hossein. "I will take your blood from the back of your right foot. We cannot put a mark on your arm. You cannot have a bruise on your arm. Every doctor knows what a needle-stick site looks like. If they examine you, they may look at your arms, but they most likely will not pay attention to your feet. I do not want you to have any questionable marks on your arms right now. We will wait until the military docs start doing blood tests on you before we start drawing from your arm."

"So many precautions," said Hamid, half-worried by the situation and half-impressed by his cousin's cautious approach and attention to so many details.

"Yes, Hamid," said Hossein. "We just need to be as careful as we can."

Hossein pulled a yellow rubber band out of his briefcase and wrapped it just above Hamid's right ankle. He then cleaned the skin on the back of Hamid's foot and carefully inserted the butterfly needle into a large vein there.

"Aoucchhhhhhhhhh," said Hamid.

Haj Agha turned his face the other way. It did not matter how old his children got, they would always be his children, and he fought the instinct to protect his son from the pain Hossein could not avoid inflicting.

"Guys, I am going to step out for a minute," said Mahmood to excuse himself to leave the room "I am not good with looking at blood."

Using a tape, Hossein secured the butterfly needle to Hamid's foot and then started pulling back on the plunger of the syringe, and by doing so Hamid's blood started flowing into the syringe.

"So what are you going to do with the blood, Hossein Agha?" asked Haj Agha.

"Haj Agha, would you please pass your empty bottle of Coke?" asked Hossein.

The syringe was almost full of Hamid's blood. Hossein bent the plastic tubing to stop the flow of blood from the butterfly needle, and then separated the syringe from the tubing and emptied the contents, Hamid's blood, into the Coke bottle.

Haj Agha's eyebrows rose quite high at the sight of Hossein virtually dumping his son's blood into a Coke bottle.

"Never seen blood in Coke bottle!" said Haj Agha, disconcerted.

"Haj Agha, there is always a first time for everything," said Hossein. "I have not seen it either."

"Hamid, are you okay?" asked Haj Agha.

"Yes, Dad, I am perfectly fine," replied Hamid.

"Haj Agha, Hamid is young and healthy. He will be fine," said Hossein.

"Do you have any pain, Hamid?" asked Haj Agha.

"No, I don't, Dad. I don't even feel the needle anymore," said Hamid.

Hossein connected the syringe to the tubing again and repeated the process several times, each time taking more blood from Hamid.

"Haj Agha, may I have another empty Coke bottle?" said Hossein after he had filled the first bottle with Hamid's blood.

"That is it; we are done. I took nine syringes, for about 450 cubic centimeters of blood. We are going to stop here."

Hossein took out the needle from Hamid's foot and placed a Band-Aid on the site of the needle stick.

"Hamid, please keep your foot elevated and apply pressure here for the next five to ten minutes," said Hossein.

"Are you dizzy at all?" asked Haj Agha of Hamid.

"No, Dad, I am just fine. This was nothing," replied Hamid honestly.

"Okay, Hamid. Please rest here until I come back. Don't move, and keep your foot elevated," said Hossein. "Haj Agha, I am going to dispose of the blood now. Can you please check to make sure the upstairs bathroom is vacant? It is imperative that no one sees this."

Haj Agha stepped out of the room. "Come, Hossein, come."

Hossein took the two blood-filled Coke bottles with him to the bathroom where he tried to empty them in the sink, but the blood had clotted inside the bottles and was not coming out easily.

"Damn, I did not think about this," said Hossein. Normal blood containers contained anticoagulant to prevent the natural clotting process, which normally begins on contact with glass. He mentally chastised himself for overlooking such an obvious detail.

Hossein then tried to empty a half-full bottle; that seemed easier.

"I have to think of something else for the next time," said Hossein.

With great difficulty, Hossein emptied the bottles in the sink. He then rinsed the bottles and cleaned both the inside and outside of them with lots of soap. He washed his hands and the sink thoroughly. Once everything was clean, he washed his hands again, and he carefully and quietly started opening the bathroom door. As the door opened, there was a loud and menacing, booming noise from outside. Hossein's blood ran cold.

Mahmood was supposed to be standing guard at the bathroom door. It only took Hossein a second to realize what was going on. In a moment of boyish mischief, he had decided to try to frighten his cousin. Hossein laughed, relieved that the noise was little more than Mahmood's ridiculous ghoulish moan. He should have expected this. Mahmood had been playing tricks on him ever since they were small boys.

"You scared me, Mahmood," said Hossein playfully. "Now do the honors. Here are your Coke bottles. Make sure you recycle them."

Mahmood took the bottles from Hossein, eyeing them with revulsion. They walked to Haj Agha's study room where Hamid was still lying on the sofa with his foot elevated. Hossein sat on the chair next to Hamid.

"Let me check your blood pressure again and look at your foot."

Hossein checked Hamid with the same care and attention he gave his patients.

"Everything looks fine. There is no bruise or bleeding. This was the first of a series of blood draws that we need to do. We have just started. Are you up for this?"

"Yes, I am," replied Hamid.

"The next blood draw should be done tomorrow," said Hossein.

"I will take your *khale* Nasrin and the children out for lunch. Can you come back here tomorrow?" asked Haj Agha.

"Yes," said Hossein. "I just need to come up with an excuse for my mom to leave home. I am usually home on Fridays, studying for my examinations."

"Taking mom and the children for lunch is good idea, Dad," said Mahmood. "Hossein and I will take care of Hamid, and we will also go out for lunch after we are done."

Hossein proceeded to pull out a package filled with various tablets. "Hamid, here are the pills that you need to take. I have brought you a one-month supply of everything." He lifted each bottle, carefully showing the contents in each.

"This one is ferrous sulfate; you should take one of these pills two to three times a day. These two capsules are the antibiotics that you have to take. You take them twice a day. They can suppress your bone marrow and lower your retic count. Remember the retic count, Hamid?" asked Hossein.

Hamid blanked. He had never been good at remembering things.

"Just take the pills and capsules as Hossein is instructing you to. Don't worry about the retic count," interrupted Mahmood.

"And these smaller pills are your B12 and folic acid," Hossein said. "You take one of these each day. You think you can safely carry some of these with you to the military base and take them there?"

"Oh yes, I can," replied Hamid, eager to obey his careful instructions. "I can hide them in my stuff and take them when I go to use the bathroom."

"We don't want anyone to see you taking pills at the base. Do not trust anyone there. Do not share any of this information with anyone, even your most trustworthy friend. Okay, Hamid?"

Hamid nodded his head in agreement.

"Only take a one-week supply with you to the base. Hide them somewhere safe. If you notice any problems, just flush them down the toilet. We can always replace them." Hossein said.

Hamid nodded again.

"And if someone notices anything, or says something, what do you do?" asked Hossein.

"Deny. Deny. Deny," replied Hamid. "I don't know what you are talking about." Hossein smiled, satisfied with the correct response.

"Again, if anyone notices something, the first thing you do is to flush all these in the toilet. Okay?" Hossein knew he sounded patronizing, but it was vital that Hamid understood.

"Got it, Hossein," replied Hamid.

"Let's go down and have some dessert now," said Haj Agha, pleased the first part of the ordeal was over.

Together, united in their clever scheme, all of them went downstairs to join the rest of the family.

CHAPTER FOUR
THE MOTHER

Early the next day, Hossein woke, dressed in his warm clothes, and made his way to the garden at the back of his family's house. October was ending. The new chill in the air accurately reflected the time of year that had rapidly descended on Tehran. The trees had lost all their leaves; the only one that stood out from the rest was the persimmon tree bearing a few dozen fruits. Hossein had planted it there with his own hands when the family built the house. He loved the backyard; most of the trees and plants in it were there because of his own work. Hossein took his time walking slowly around the backyard several times, deep in thought about Hamid, his own future, and the risk they faced of being discovered—a risk that had suddenly become real.

What if Hamid is put under pressure and says something stupid to someone? That will be the end of my medical career…

Many thoughts were crowding Hossein's mind: his studies and coming examinations, his future career, and most importantly, his chances of leaving Iran for the United States. At the center of these thoughts, however, was Hamid and the challenges that came with his newly induced anemia.

Am I even doing the right thing here? Hossein asked himself again. *I think I am. Hamid is my cousin and we grew up together. We are like bothers. I even remember the day he was born. I have spent so many summers with him and Mahmood. I know I owe him this help and of course I want to give it to him, but it comes with so many risks to my own dreams. I could lose everything that I have ever worked for, all the years of studying hard, all the sleepless nights and cramming for examinations would be for nothing if we are caught. Will Hamid appreciate what I am doing for him? I hope he will. What will he do with the freedom we will secure for him? Will he do something good with his life?*

He slowly looked up and fixed his gaze at the puffs of cloud in the sky. *I must make sure that nothing goes wrong at any point in the plan, for Hamid's sake and my own. I also have to find a way to leave Iran. I need to identify a reputable smuggler to get me out of this place. I can't stay here for much longer.*

His thoughts began to speed up, spiraling and spinning from one idea to the next. *And my relationship with Afsaneh should not suffer. I have not spent enough time with her lately. Despite all the other things that I am juggling, I must not let my relationship with her suffer.*

A voice broke the tranquil silence of the garden as Hossein heard his name being called softly, bringing him back to reality.

"Oh, there you are! Good morning, Hossein."

It was his mother, Parvin. She walked purposefully toward him. When she reached him, Hossein kissed her in a genuinely affectionate greeting, and the two started walking across the garden together. Both Hossein and his mother considered this peaceful yet captivating garden to be best part of their home.

"You know, Hossein, I love this garden," said Parvin, soaking in and appreciating her surroundings as if it were the first time she had ever encountered the place.

"During the day, when you are at school, I come here often, reflecting on my life, just as you are doing now. I walk around this garden, weeding and cleaning, watering the potted plants, admiring the lovely trees, remembering what they looked like in the spring when they were in full bloom, and enjoying the silent beauty of the place.

"I know, Mom. I share your feelings," said Hossein.

Moving closer toward her son, his mother observed Hossein intently, with concerns clouding her expression. "You look preoccupied these days, Hossein." She remarked. "What is going on my son?"

"Nothing too serious, Mom. I have too many things in my mind. I am also bothered with the war," replied Hossein. "Its shadow is everywhere. Not a single day passes without us hearing the air-raid sirens, or seeing the impact of the war in Tehran. We lose electricity every night, even at the hospital. Iraqi planes are flying over our airspace daily, dropping bombs, completely at random! One hit a school near our hospital last week, in broad daylight. They brought many injured and several dead children to our emergency room. It was such a sad scene."

"I know, Hossein, I know," said Parvin. As a mother, she could more than sympathize. "But what can we do except take shelter in our basement when we hear the air-raid sirens? We are all hoping for the war to end soon."

"How did this war start, Mom? I hate Saddam Hussein."

Parvin sighed. She could not answer her son in the way she could answer his childish questions from bygone times. He was asking something she had asked herself many times before.

"Hossein, this is a complicated matter. It is not a simple war between two neighbors. It is an international game and we are the unfortunate casualties. It is much like World War II. Do you really feel like a history lesson now?"

"Yes Mom. I want to know. Tell me," said Hossein. "Do you remember when I was in middle school? You would sit with me and read me my history books. The way you told the stories made me understand. Remember, Mom?"

Parvin smiled fondly. "How could I forget?" said Parvin. "Well, do you remember your World War II history?"

"Some of it, Mom," said Hossein.

"Remember Hossein, at the onset of the World war II, Reza Shah declared that Iran will remain a neutral country and will not be a party to the war.

Over time, Hitler advanced all the way to the heart of Russia. Stalin's army could not withstand the German attack. Stalin needed support from the West. He sent a laundry list of war supplies, weapons, and heavy artillery that he needed to the United States. At the time, Iran was the only country with a railroad system that would connect the Persian Gulf to the Russian border, the best way to get the war supplies to Russia. Churchill, Stalin, and Roosevelt simply ignored the neutrality of Iran and decided that they will use Iran's railroad to send war supplies to Russia.

Parvin paused for a moment then continued. "Reza Shah rejected the allies' request and did not allow them to use our railroad. In response, the allies threatened the sovereignty and unity of Iran. The British army invaded our country from the south while the Russian army invaded Iran from the north."

She paused for a moment. Hossein fixed his eyes firmly on her, eagerly awaiting the next installment in the story. Parvin continued. "The British army was mostly interested in our southern oil fields and the affairs of British Petroleum Company. What do they call it now—BP? Reza Shah's army was defeated in both the south and the north. Then Reza Shah's son made a deal with the three superpowers. He allowed them to use whatever they desired, including the Iranian railroad, as long as, in return, they assured him the unity of our country, and that his father had a gracious way out. Reza Shah left Iran and remained in exile until he died.

"So, do you want to know why we are at war with Iraq now?"

"Tell me, Mom. I love your political point of view," said Hossein, genuinely fascinated by his mother's articulate account of their country's recent history.

"Well, no one knows the truths of this war," said Parvin, disheartened. "No one will ever know, at least for the next fifty years, until the Americans and the British unseal their secret files on Iran and Iraq. But I personally think it dates from World War II and the oil reserves of Iran. Iranians like you and me are the unfortunate victims of our natural resources and our geopolitical location in the Middle East. After World War II, the Shah tried to keep peace with the West. We sold our oil for low prices and the Shah led the country toward modernization. Look at your university and most of our hospitals; your own Western-trained professors are all good examples of how the Shah was bringing in Western technology and sciences, coaxing Iran forward to a better future by utilizing our natural resources."

She stopped again momentarily, ordering her thoughts, then continued by saying, "In 1954, the Shah entered into an agreement with the West to sell Iranian oil only at fair market prices. At that time, BP managed almost all our oil fields, and we never knew how much oil they extracted and shipped to the West. BP was simply paying close to nothing for our oil. The agreement was up for renewal in 1979. In 1973, the Shah declared that he would not renew this agreement in 1979 under any conditions. The primary reason for this inauspicious decision was that he wanted full control over the exploration and sale of Iranian oil. He wanted Iran to be the sole determinant of its oil price on the international market. But the West was more than a little displeased by his stance. This decision by the Shah was a complete reversal of his 1941 attitude towards the West, when Reza Shah went into exile. The West was not pleased with Iran's move towards full control of its oil."

After a short pause, Parvin continued, "As a result, we ended with a so-called revolution in 1979, the year that the oil exploration agreement was up for renewal. This so-called 'Islamic revolution' was little more than a game premeditated by the West. They no longer could set the stage for a *coup d'état* in Iran, as the army was backing the Shah. So they inflicted the *Islamic Revolution* on us. Counting on the strong and predictable religious tendencies of the Iranians, Western agencies, through the radio networks like the BBC, Voice of America, and even Radio Moscow, constantly broadcast false messages to Iran. And for their final trick, they chose a leader for the revolution. They arranged for Khomeini to go to Paris, where he was bestowed with all the media exposure he needed. He was on Western TV and radio daily, mobilizing the masses of people in Iran."

She sighed and said, "Naïve Iranians, not knowing what the heck was going on, fell for it. U.S. President, Jimmy Carter asked the Shah to leave, perhaps promising to return him to power soon, and shortly after that, we ended with this government. As you well remember, the first government after the fall of the Shah was very liberal, very westernized."

"Do you Remember Sadegh Ghotb Zadeh?" asked Parvin.

"Yes, Mom, I do. What about him?"

"He had spent much of his adult life in the United States and joined Khomeini in Paris. He then went up the ranks to become our first foreign minister. Soon thereafter, the leaders of the revolution did not approve of his controversial opinions, and had him executed for wanting to overthrow Khomeini's regime. Although Khomeini came to power with the help and support of the West, Iran took a path that the West did not like. Things got way out of control. If you asked me why Saddam Hussein attacked Iran, I would say that the West tried to overthrow Khomeini's regime, this time by way of Ghotb Zadeh. The mullahs uncovered his plot and had him executed. And then, Saddam Hussein felt encouraged to do the job, and he perhaps promised the West that he would overthrow Khomeini. The West supported him, yet he had no army to match Iran's manpower. Mayhem has been the result ever since. God knows what our future will be like."

Hossein carefully listened to all the information his mother was so fluently and knowledgably expressing.

"You are right, Mom. For a long time we have been subjected to intense manipulations from the West, whose only concern is to exploit our oil. It is all about exerting power to steal a country's resources. It happened with the French and British in Africa and everywhere else they went. The British army killed thousands of Indians and Egyptians simply because the poor people wanted sovereignty and independence."

"Anyway, enough about politics," she said. "What is new with you these days? How are your studies coming along?"

The swift change of subject disappointed Hossein, but he understood why his mother had done it. "Everything is fine, Mom. I am studying hard, very hard. I want to take the ECFMG examination next summer."

"Is that the examination that you have to pass to go and study in the United States?" asked Parvin.

"Yes Mom. I am preparing for it as much as I can. I am studying daily. I really want to pass this examination with high grades."

"So you're definitely going to the United States then? Have you figured out how?"

"I am working on that, Mom, but there is no easy way to get there. I will need to pass the ECFMG first, and then apply for postgraduate training. The problem is that I cannot take the ECFMG in Iran. I have to go to Europe for that."

"I see," said Parvin.

"I am really trying hard to find a way to leave Iran, to get out of this war, to find a safer place to live and to continue my education. Despite everything you said about the West, I think there are many excellent opportunities there that I may be able to take advantage of."

Parvin did not acknowledge his last point. It would only have ended in another political debate. Instead, she asked, "Have you found a trustworthy person to take you out yet?"

"Not yet, Mom," replied Hossein honestly.

Parvin saw the longing in her son's eyes and her heart ached. As much as she did not want him to leave, she understood his desire to get away.

"I feel very bad and sad for you," she said. "Life was much easier before."

"Leaving Iran is not easy, Mom. Going to the United States, although possible, is very difficult, but I am determined to do it. I want to become a hematologist. I will be wasting my time if I stay here beyond graduation. I know this is not easy for you, nor is it for me. But will you support my decision if I leave Iran in the summer?"

Hossein was wrong. He had no idea how difficult this was for his mother. The thought of him being so far away was almost unbearable, but the thought of him being unhappy for the rest of his life? Well that was even worse. For now, she decided to focus on the practicalities of the situation.

"Where will you go, Hossein? Have you thought about that? You have not yet done your military service, and you do not have a valid passport. On top of that, you can hardly get a travel visa these days. Leaving Iran and going to the United States is much like the *Haft Khane Rostam* for you."

"Yes, Mom, I know, I know. It is not going to be easy," said Hossein, remaining optimistic. He desperately wanted his mother's approval and encouragement. "A few of my friends have met with a guy, a smuggler, who guarantees that he can take people out of Iran to Istanbul for a fee of ten thousand U.S. dollars. He has already taken one person, the brother of one of my classmates, safely to Istanbul."

Parvin remained skeptical.

"And what will you do in Istanbul?"

"I don't know, Mom. I do not know. I have never been there. I do not know anyone there. I am not sure either if I want to go with this smuggler."

"Do you know what your friends will be doing in Istanbul once they get there?" asked Parvin. She knew he was utterly disappointed by her negativity, but her motherly instinct to protect was taking over. "I have heard many bad stories, and horrible things have happened to tourists there. Do you remember the movie we saw together? What was the title?"

"You mean *Midnight Express*," said Hossein with a sigh. "None of us is going to end in a Turkish prison, Mom. My classmates are smarter than that. Turkey will simply be a halfway house for us. Most of us want to go to the United States, and a few plan to stay with relatives in France or Germany. Before 1979, it was so easy for Iranians to go abroad to study. Half my hospital professors left Iran to study in the United States or Europe, and then returned home. That is what I wanted to do when I started medical school."

There was a moment of silence. The wind blew lightly. Hossein, aware of his mother's apprehension, slowly broke the quietness by saying, "Now, Mom, I just want to leave, and I don't know whether I even want to come back here. I cannot stand the current situation in our country. We did not need any of this. Who signed up for this chaos? Did you?"

"No, not this," Parvin replied slowly. These were the only words she could find.

"Mom, you won't believe how beautiful it was just after the fall of the Shah," said Hossein. "The spring of 1979 was so pleasant. I remember all the politically motivated students of Tehran University had set up bookstands on the grounds and courtyards of the university. There was complete freedom. All of us were friends. The communist students stood side by side with the religious students. Yet that amazing freedom lasted only for a few months, long enough to allow the *basijis* to identify and tag the politically motivated students."

Hossein took a deep breath and continued, "Soon after, the mullahs had all of them jailed and mostly executed, all to the chanting of the anti-American slogan, *Death to the Great Satan.* Then came the hostage crisis in November 1979. I think it lasted 444 days. The hostage-takers released their captives exactly at the moment of President Reagan's inauguration. Isn't that right, Mom? Someone coordinated the release of the hostages with the exact moment of Reagan's inauguration. What an effort. Can you believe it? Someone must have been watching the inauguration and talking to the people who were holding the hostages on the airplane while it was already on the runway, ready to take off as soon as Reagan took the oath of office as President of the United States. Why did we do that? We must have made some form of deal with Reagan. Right? Then we hear that the *Great Satan*, the United States, is our enemy. I cannot stand this, Mom." Hossein was becoming visibly agitated.

"I know, Hossein, I know," said Parvin in the soothing tone. "This entire thing must be very confusing for you. You want to be a doctor, so concentrate on studying medicine, and do not let anything else distract you from that. I want the best for you my son, so yes; I fully support you in leaving Iran. I am just worried. What you will do in Istanbul? How will you go the United States? Are there any other ways to get out of this country?"

"Mom, my passport is no longer valid. It expired last year," said Hossein. "I cannot get a new one unless I do my two years of military service. Then,

I will not get permission to leave Iran unless I do three additional years of civil service. And that holds true only if I survive the war. You know almost every medical school graduate ends up going to the front. I do not want to serve on the front lines of the war zone. I would rather take my chances in Istanbul."

"Going to Istanbul with no agenda is a much better alternative than going to the front. Yes I agree with that," said Parvin.

Hossein smiled as she nodded her head.

"Hossein, my wonderful son, the last thing I want to see is *you* being harmed. Talk to your friends and discover what they are going to do. Find a safe way of leaving Iran."

"Mom, I already know that the smugglers have taken several of our last year's graduates to Pakistan and Turkey," said Hossein.

"Don't ever go to Pakistan," replied Parvin.

"Why, Mom?" asked Hossein, slightly taken aback by his mother's serious tone.

"Just don't go there," she said, before adding: "I don't like what I hear about Pakistan."

"Okay, Mom, I promise I won't go to Pakistan."

Hossein could see tears of sadness pooling in his mother's eyes.

"Mom, another thing: wherever I go or however I get there, I *promise* that when I am settled in the United States, I will bring you there to live with me. Okay? I promised you that several years ago, when I was still in high school, and I still mean it now. I am a man of my word Mom."

For the first time since this topic took a hold of their conversation, Parvin smiled. "Okay, my love. I would love to join you in the United States."

For a few more silent minutes, the two continued to walk in the garden before Parvin suggested that they go in and get breakfast.

"Oh and Mom," said Hossein before they went inside. "I am meeting with one of my friends today for lunch. I will leave at about eleven and will be back about five or six tonight. We may also go to a movie. Just in case you wonder where I am."

"Okay my love."

soon. Okay? I promised you that some day, years ago, when I was still in high school, and I'm a man. I know I am a man now, and [illegible]."

Then the first time since the [illegible], a [illegible] of the [illegible] [illegible]. "Okay? [illegible] [illegible] to [illegible] the United States."

[illegible] [illegible] [illegible] [illegible] [illegible] [illegible] [illegible] [illegible] [illegible] [illegible] break [illegible].

"Oh, [illegible]," said [illegible] [illegible] [illegible] [illegible]. I am [illegible] [illegible] one of my [illegible] [illegible] [illegible]. I will [illegible] [illegible] [illegible] back [illegible] [illegible] [illegible] [illegible] [illegible] [illegible] wedding. [illegible]"

"Okay, [illegible]."

CHAPTER FIVE
TAXI DRIVER

Exactly as planned, at about eleven that morning, Hossein bid his mother farewell and left to visit Hamid for another blood-drawing session. He had to walk for several minutes to reach the main street where he could catch a taxi. Ambling down the sidewalks of his neighborhood, his thoughts turned to Hamid and how his plot would unfold; whether he will succeed or whether he would fail. The implications of the latter were too dire to think about. Determined to succeed, Hossein actively rejected each negative thought that dared to surface in his mind.

I have started this and I am going to finish it, he said to himself. *It is like being the pilot of an airplane. I have taken off, and no matter what, I must continue to my destination and land there safely. There is no room for a single mistake. I am not going to crash and burn. I will land safely.*

A taxi stopped for him at a busy intersection. He got in, and the same thoughts circled his weary mind as he rode toward Hamid's house. A welcome distraction came in the form of an additional passenger whom the driver had spotted by the side of the road and pulled over to let in his car. The new passenger, a young man in his twenties, got in and sat in the front seat.

"Thank you so much," he said to the taxi driver as he climbed in hurriedly.

Without minding the driver and the new passenger in the car, Hossein was again immersed in his thoughts. A short while later the passenger turned his head toward the back seat, and said, "How are you, sir? You look like a doctor."

He had obviously seen the distinctive medical bag by Hossein's side.

"I am fine sir, thank you for asking," replied Hossein. "Your keen observation was right. I am due to finish medical school in a few months."

"Which medical school?" the passenger asked.

Hossein was not sure if he wanted to engage in this conversation with a complete stranger, but the man seemed friendly enough, so he lowered his defenses and let the conversation flow.

"Tehran University."

"Woo. Good for you. I have a cousin who graduated last year from your school, and he is now in Pakistan trying to go to the United States."

This caught Hossein's interest. It seemed many people had the same idea as he did. Still, he resisted the urge to pursue questioning on the matter and remained quiet. The passenger continued his story.

"Much like many other medical school graduates, he left Iran to find a better place to live and study. This country is no place to live anymore. There was a time when we ruled the world, but now? Look at us. Our young men are dying by the thousands daily, our economy is in shambles, and we are forbidden to travel overseas. How quickly we downgraded from the glorious Persian Empire to the isolated Islamic Republic of Iran."

Hossein sighed, but nodded politely in agreement. Of course he felt the same, but it seemed his entire life centered on this conversation now.

The cab driver interrupted the passenger and said, "*Salavat befrest Agha*," meaning 'to say prayers, instead of bickering.'

"*Na baba*," said the passenger in Farsi, meaning "No way."

"I am serious," said the passenger, who was now on a roll, and Hossein's silence seemed only to spur him on. "You don't need to go far to figure this out. You, yourself," he said, pointing, somewhat aggressively, at the cab driver, "I bet you are working from dawn till dusk, driving this cab to make a living, and you still cannot make ends meet, can you?"

The driver, although used to passengers such as this one, found it a rather intrusive question from a stranger and chose not to respond.

"My uncle is a cab driver," continued the passenger. "I know a lot about this business. The best part of the job is that you meet different people and hear all kinds of stories. Well, I am going to tell you my story. Next summer, I will be out of this country. I cannot live here anymore. I do not want this war. I do not like the daily lies we are told. I do not like the dress code that we must abide by. I do not like the mullahs at all. There is nothing left here for me. So I am leaving. I am an engineering student at Sharif University, and you know what? I have been accepted to the Ph.D. program for structural engineering at a major university in the United States. Have you heard of MIT in Boston? Well, I am going there. But I cannot get a passport to leave Iran without going to war and serving two years of my precious life in the military. Do you think that this government cares about the youth and the intelligent people of the country? No. No, they do not. We are the future of this country; we are the future of the world. Well, I have said my goodbye to Iran. I want to get out of here, damn it."

"*Agha salavat befrest*," the driver repeated.

An uneasy silence filled the car. Everyone knew and was fully aware of the imminent issues that this passenger was talking about, but each was cautious about having anti-government discussions in public. After awhile, the driver broke the silence and said:

"I do know what you are talking about. My own son, my only child, is a law student at Tehran University. He is my life. He is everything I have. I have witnessed his dreams being shattered into a thousand pieces. He started law school before the revolution. They closed the university to purge the students and the faculty. When it reopened, they had a new curriculum that was solely concerned with the Islamic laws. Before all this, my son wanted to become an international lawyer, to work in other countries and travel the world. Now, he has to study this nonsense, the made-up law that the clerics are teaching. Almost overnight, the law school replaced its faculty with so-called professors, whose only qualification was graduating from *Hozeyeh Feizieh*, the religious school in the holy city of Qom. It does not take a genius to figure out why. Alas, there is no way around this. He cannot transfer and continue his education in a Western university. He is stuck now. You are an engineer. This other gentleman will soon be a doctor. You two can take whatever you learn here with you, go to the West, and continue your education there. My son cannot."

"I am sorry to hear this, sir," said Hossein. The sadness of their country's situation tightened its grip around his heart once more.

"Drop me off there, sir, near the pharmacy," said the other passenger to the driver. "I wish all the best to your son."

The cab driver pulled over to drop off the passenger. The passenger spoke directly to Hossein as he was getting out. His voice was hushed and loaded with conspiratorial intent. "You ought to leave Iran, too. They don't deserve us."

Hossein resisted the impulse to communicate his assent.

After the passenger had left, the taxi driver had no qualms resuming the conversation with Hossein:

"I feel bad for the intelligent youth of this country. I am sixty now, I have lived my life. But you are so young and so bright. My son is much like you, calm and thoughtful. But where can he go with a law degree from Iran?"

Despite his earlier desire to end the conversation, the taxi driver now seemed unable to stop speaking his mind.

"It was all the Shah's fault. It was all Jimmy Carter's fault. The United States, the United Kingdom, Russia, France—all of them wanted to topple the Shah's regime, because he said in one of his last interviews that he would not let blue-eyed, blond-haired people decide the price of Iranian oil. This was not a revolution. This was a modern *coup d'état*. The Iranian military was loyal to the Shah, so the United States could not initiate a *coup d'état* as they did in other countries. As a result, the Americans undermined his government by supporting Khomeini. I did not even know who Khomeini was until five or six months before the revolution. Did you?" asked the driver.

"No, sir. I did not know him, and I still don't know him," replied Hossein curtly. Although he agreed wholeheartedly with what the driver was saying, he had enough of talking about this today.

"He has become an iconic figure that you are permitted only to praise. You cannot say anything negative about him. The other day, at about six in the morning, I saw something that really bothered me. I was going down the

Takhte Jamshid Street. You know the big movie theater where there is a huge mural drawing of Khomeini on the sidewall of the theater?"

"Of course," replied Hossein.

"Well, I was driving towards the movie theater, and there was a body lying in the middle of the street, covered by a white cloth. Police and *basijis* were walking around it."

"I slowed down while passing the body," continued the driver. "One of my passengers pointed to the mural of Khomeini on the sidewall of the movie theater and noted that there was a large splash of red paint on it. He suggested that the dead person must have thrown a paint ball at the mural of Khomeini at the wrong time. A passing *basiji* must have seen the act, and shot him dead on the spot. No trials, no court hearing, none of that. A simple execution by a *basiji,* justified and supported by the Islamic government, because of an insult to the religious leader. Nowhere else in the civilized world would anyone be allowed to kill someone as they do here in Iran."

"*Agha salavat befrest*," said Hossein to the driver.

The driver took the hint. The cab ride continued another five minutes in pure silence. Upset and unhappy with the events that were happening around him in Tehran, Hossein gave himself again to the positive thoughts of leaving. When the taxi arrived at Hamid's house, he gave a large bill to the driver, got out of the car, stood next to the front passenger window to get his change, and only then, for the first time, did Hossein get a good glimpse at the driver's face. The driver had tears in his eyes. He did not make any eye contact with Hossein and simply passed the change to him, waved goodbye, and drove away.

Touched by what he had just heard in the cab, and suddenly feeling guilty for not contributing to the conversation, Hossein walked to Hamid's house to meet him and his brother. Hamid's father had taken everyone out, so Hossein could again take Hamid's blood in secret. He completed the procedure quickly and without complication. Once Hossein finished, the three left for lunch.

"Lunch is on me today," said Mahmood. "You have been so kind to come here today. I suggest we go to Tajrish for Chelo Kabab."

Hossein's mood brightened. "Good idea. I love Tajrish and the bazaar there."

The three got in Mahmood's car and drove away.

CHAPTER SIX
THE SMUGGLER

On the way to Tajrish Square for lunch, the three listened to their favorite music, which they used to listen to before the revolution, and they remembered the good old days that they spent together.

"So, Hossein Jaan, how long will it take for Hamid to become anemic?" asked Mahmood.

"If we keep up with the twice-a-week schedule of blood draws, as we did this weekend, in about three weeks, he will become anemic," said Hossein. "I will do a blood test on him the next time we take his blood. Once his hemoglobin level drops below ten, he should go to see the military doctor at the base. Normal hemoglobin is around fourteen. I forgot to ask you, Hamid, but did you take the medicines I gave you last night?"

"Yes, I did, last night and this morning, with food, as you instructed," said Hamid.

"Good, always take them with food, otherwise they can bother your stomach," said Hossein. "Iron pills can make you constipated and change your stool color to black, but it's nothing to worry about. Now keep in mind, we will need to fine-tune your treatments. Therefore, there will come a time when they may want to do a colonoscopy on you. We will have to stop the iron pills a few days before that. I will tell you when we approach that point."

"Okay, Hossein, whatever you say," said Hamid.

"We also need a backup plan," said Hossein, "just in case something goes wrong with our current plan."

"What do you mean?" asked Hamid.

"Well Hamid, try to imagine that the doctor at the base decides to admit you to the military hospital and keep you there for several weeks," said Hossein. "Who will be there to take blood from you every weekend? Your anemia will soon improve, and within a few weeks, you will be fit and ready for deployment to the front. It is a good idea to have a backup plan."

"What kind of backup plan are you talking about, Hossein?" asked Hamid.

"Leaving Iran," said Hossein. "Have you ever thought of leaving Iran, Hamid?" he asked.

"What? No. I have never thought of leaving Iran," replied a very surprised Hamid.

"Of course, we all hope that everything will work out the way we planned. But we can never be one hundred percent sure, though," replied Hossein. "Who knows what may go wrong with our plan. For all those unexpected reasons, it is a good idea to have a backup plan."

"You are right, Hossein. I agree with you," said Mahmood. "The only way Hamid can leave Iran these days would be by illegally crossing the border, right? With the help of a smuggler?"

"Correct, by working with a smuggler," said Hossein. "Smugglers can take you across the border, either to Turkey or Pakistan. And that is how I may be leaving Iran in the summer."

"Are you serious, Hossein?" asked Mahmood.

"I am very serious," replied Hossein. "There is no other way for me to leave Iran. As it stands, I am *mamnuol khorouj*. Most of my classmates are thinking of leaving Iran with smugglers. I am supposed to call and meet a smuggler today. Do you guys feel like meeting with him?"

"Meeting a smuggler, I have never done that," said Mahmood. "Be careful, Hossein. Most of those guys are sharks. They take your money, make plenty of promises, and at the end they disappear on you, either in Iran or in Turkey. I have heard so many horror stories."

"I don't like the idea of leaving Iran with a smuggler," said Hamid. "That is frightening for me."

"I understand, but how about we just meet and talk with him to see what he has to say?" said Hossein.

"Honestly, I am afraid of meeting a smuggler," repeated Hamid with a voice that was clearly shaken.

"This guy is highly recommended by one of my medical school friends," said Hossein. "He apparently took my friend's brother safely to Istanbul and set him up there nicely. He charges a lot, ten thousand dollars, but he seems to know what he is doing, and he does have good connections everywhere."

"Ten thousand dollars?" asked Mahmood with surprise. "That is a large sum, Hossein."

"I know, Mahmood," said Hossein.

The three drove for a while and discussed the pros and cons of meeting with the smuggler whom Hossein wanted to meet.

"Do you want me to stop somewhere near a public telephone booth?" asked Mahmood.

"Good idea, Mahmood," said Hossein. "Let me call him and find out if he can meet us today."

"Hey, there is a public phone over there," said Hamid. "Pull over, Mahmood."

Mahmood pulled over and parked the car near the public phone. Hossein got out, walked to the phone, and called the smuggler.

"*Befarmaiid*," said the person in Farsi, meaning "at your service."

"Good afternoon, sir," said Hossein. "Dr. Sadeghi gave me this number. May I speak with Mr. Jahangir?"

"Speaking."

"Dr. Sadeghi suggested that I speak with you about my travel plans."

"I see. Will you be traveling alone?" asked the voice on the phone.

"Well, sir, this is for two of us, me and my cousin. We want to travel early next summer," replied Hossein.

"Okay. I am going away tomorrow for three weeks. How about next month? Can you call me back then?"

"Mr. Jahangir, this is rather important to us. Is there any way that we can possibly meet with you today?" said Hossein. "I know it is Friday and it is your day off."

"What is your name?" asked the man on the phone.

"Hossein."

"Okay, Hossein Agha, where are you right now?" asked the man.

"We are in Narmak now, heading to Tajrish Square for lunch," replied Hossein.

"Tajrish Square, that is good," said the man. "I live five minutes away from Tajrish Square. Where are you going for lunch?"

"I don't know, sir, why?" replied Hossein.

"Okay. Meet me on the second floor of Hatam Kababi in Tajrish Square in exactly one hour," said the smuggler. "What do you look like? What are you wearing? How will I recognize you?"

"There are three of us. I am wearing a navy-blue jacket. Both my cousins are wearing dark jackets. One is in the military, and he has a short haircut. My other cousin wears eyeglasses."

"Okay. When you arrive at the restaurant, get a table for four people near the balcony on the second floor," said the smuggler. "Put a newspaper on the fourth chair. That is where I will sit."

"Thank you, sir," said Hossein. "And how will I recognize you, Mr. Jahangir?"

"Don't worry. I will be there. I will find you," said the man.

"Thank you, sir, see you shortly."

With that, Hossein hung up the phone and rushed back to the car.

"Go, Mahmood, go fast. We need to be in Tajrish in one hour. He will meet us at the Hatam restaurant," said Hossein.

"Wooo, Hossein, let's go," said Mahmood.

Mahmood drove as fast as he could. They arrived at Tajrish Square on time. Mahmood parked the car on a side street, and the three of them walked to the rendezvous at the Hatam Restaurant.

"Table for four, near the balcony please," said Hossein to the waiter. "One more person will join us in ten minutes."

The three sat down. Hossein frantically started looking for a newspaper.

"Do you have today's paper?" asked Hossein of the waiter.

"Sorry, we don't," the waiter replied.

Hossein ran out to the street, bought a newspaper, returned to the restaurant, and placed the paper on the chair they had reserved for the smuggler.

"This is the clue to Mr. Jahangir, the smuggler," said Hossein. "This is how he will spot us here."

"I see. He reads the newspaper too. Woo, what a literate smuggler," said Mahmood sarcastically.

"Guys, let us just be courteous when he joins us," said Hossein. "I do not know him at all. All I know is that he has successfully transported someone to Turkey. We are here to meet him and gather information from him, and he is here to meet two potential clients."

"Why two? Who is the second client?" asked Hamid.

"You are his second potential client," replied Hossein to Hamid.

Before Hossein had finished his last sentence, Jahangir appeared at their table.

"*Salam*," said Jahangir, meaning, "Hello" in Farsi.

The three stood and shook hands with him. Jahangir appeared in his mid thirties with short hair, dressed in a dark suit and carrying a briefcase.

"Thank you so much for taking time out of your Friday to meet with us. Do you have time to join us for lunch?" said Hossein to Mr. Jahangir as all four sat around the table.

"Thank you. I already ate at home. Why don't all of you go ahead and order your food," said Jahangir. "Unfortunately, I only have fifteen minutes to talk. We can meet again after I return. Let me give you a rundown of how I operate and what I can do for you. I take people only to Turkey. I stopped all travels to Pakistan a few months ago. Pakistan is rather unsafe these days. The trip takes about a week. You travel by yourself to a city near the border with Turkey, Orumieh, actually. You do not tell anyone anything. If you must say something, you say that you are there for vacation and visiting the thermal baths. We will set you up at a hotel there. You check in at the hotel. Someone will meet you at your hotel the day you arrive. You will leave the next day for the border in a group of three passengers and two guides. There will be some car rides, some horseback rides, and some walking. We travel at nights and rest and sleep during the day in our safe houses."

Jahangir paused and said, "We cross the border around midnight. On the other side, we deliver you to our Turkish guides, who will then take you to a safe house near the town of Van. In the morning, you will take the train from Van to Istanbul. Ten thousand dollars covers all your costs: meals, stays, travel, even the train ride to Istanbul and all the tips. We can also set you up in a hotel in Istanbul, or with an Iranian family until you find your way around there. That of course is extra. If you do not have a passport, I can make you a fake Iranian passport. That will be an extra five thousand dollars."

"So what do most people do when they are in Istanbul?" asked Mahmood.

"I cannot help you there," said Jahangir. "I just arrange for transportation. My advice would be to stay away from the Turkish police. Turkey is not a final destination for anyone these days. Most Iranians who go there apply for political asylum to various countries. You will have to explore that when you get there. Things are constantly changing. I don't want to give you false information."

"What are the risks? Have you ever had a situation when the police caught your people?" asked Hossein.

"Yes, that happened once. We paid off the local police, and that was the end of it. We have transported several hundred people safely to Turkey. I would say there is less than a one percent chance of something going wrong. For example, once someone got too sick. We had to take him to a hospital. On another occasion, someone got too frightened, and we had to send him back to Tehran. There are no refunds for such mishaps."

"How much advance notice do you need, and how do we pay you?" asked Hossein.

"There are two ways to pay us. You can pay me here in Tehran, or wire the money to our bank account in the United States," said Jahangir. "We ask for one-third up front, to put you on our waiting list, one-third one week before the trip, and one-third on crossing the border. For the last payment, you can pay us at the border, or your family can pay us here, whatever suits you best."

"When is the soonest that one can go?" asked Hossein.

"Right now, I have one opening for November, and three openings for December," said Jahangir. "If you are serious, you need to sign up and reserve your place. When do you want to go?"

"Early summer," replied Hossein.

"That is fine. We have plenty of time," said Jahangir. "Guys, I have to go now. If you are interested, bring thirty-three hundred dollars per person, and get on the waiting list."

"One last question, do you yourself take us across the border?" asked Hossein.

"I go every two to three months, to make sure everything is working fine," said Jahangir. "But you should not count on that. I trust my people. We have been doing this for a few years now. When it comes to taking people out of Iran, we are simply the best. People trust us. We are professionals at this. My suggestion to you is to figure out what you will be doing in Istanbul. It can be a rough place to live."

"Thank you, Mr. Jahangir. I will call you soon," said Hossein.

All of them stood and shook hands with Jahangir. As he was walking away, the waiter brought the food to the table.

"Do you trust this guy, Hossein?" asked Mahmood as they were eating their meals.

"He has safely taken at least one person whom I know to Turkey. Do you know any other smugglers that you trust?" asked Hossein of Mahmood.

"No, I don't, but I have never looked for one. I don't need to leave Iran," said Mahmood.

"Anyway, because we are working on getting Hamid out of the military, it is logical to have a backup plan," said Hossein.

"You are right, Hossein. We should look into this," said Mahmood.

"I don't want to go to Turkey," said Hamid.

"Where do you prefer to go? To Islamabad in Pakistan instead?" asked Mahmood of Hamid.

"I don't know, Mahmood. The idea of living in Istanbul by myself is very scary," said Hamid. "Hossein, will you come with me to Istanbul?"

"I may, Hamid," said Hossein. "I also am trying to leave Iran. That is why we met with this smuggler today."

"I will go to Turkey only with you, only if you also go," said Hamid.

"Sounds good, Hamid, but remember that leaving Iran with a smuggler is only a backup plan for you," said Hossein. "This is not our primary plan. Our primary plan is what we have already discussed, and we are already working on it."

"Guys, let's enjoy the lunch," said Mahmood.

Bon appétit," said Hossein.

CHAPTER SEVEN
THE PLAN

Saturday morning, Hossein went back to his hospital. While in the clinic, Hossein saw a patient whom he recognized from the past. The patient's name was Afshin. He was twelve, and undergoing treatment for acute leukemia at Hossein's hospital. Hossein approached Afshin, who was there with his father, Mr. Gohari.

"Hello Mr. Gohari, hello Afshin, how are you feeling?" said Hossein.

"I am feeling a lot better than when you took care of me a few months ago," replied Afshin.

"Have you gone back to school?" asked Hossein. "Remind me what grade are you in now?"

"I am in the sixth grade now," replied Afshin.

"How is school going for you?"

"Not so bad, but I am very behind," replied Afshin. "My leukemia, the treatments, and frequent hospital visits for chemotherapy, all that really affected my ability to study. I might have to skip school this year."

"I am sorry to hear that, but I am sure you will do just fine, Afshin," said Hossein. "You need to be focused and keep studying."

"Did you study a lot when you were in school?" asked Afshin. "You must have. You are a doctor!"

"Yes, I did, Afshin. I still do," replied Hossein.

"Can I ask you something? Do you think that I will be okay?" asked Afshin.

This was such a loaded question, coming from a twelve-year-old boy with a life-threatening disease. One hopes to never have to answer such questions, especially from a twelve-year-old child.

"Yes, Afshin, of course," replied Hossein. "I am certain that you will be fine, and before you know it, you will be back at school, studying to become a doctor yourself. As for your leukemia, Afshin, you have finished all your treatments now. The leukemia is in remission, and I am sure it will stay in remission permanently."

Mr. Gohari, the boy's father, interjected and said, "We are taking Afshin to England next month. Afshin is the love of my life. He is my youngest son. We are fortunate that we can take him to Europe for treatment. My brother lives in London and has made an appointment for Afshin to be seen at Royal Marsden Hospital."

"Great, I am happy to hear that," said Hossein. "I will be eager to know what they recommend."

"From the review of his medical records, they are thinking of possibly giving Afshin a bone-marrow transplant," said Mr. Gohari. "We might have to stay there for three or four months, or longer."

"So tell me, how will this work?" asked Hossein. "Who is going to be the bone-marrow donor?"

"Most likely my older son, Ehsan. He is in his last year of high school," said Mr. Gohari. "We are trying to get permission from the military and the health ministry to allow him to come with us. We sent blood samples from the whole family to London last month. Preliminary tests showed that Ehsan is a full match, and they can use his bone marrow for the transplant. They will need to run more tests on him once we reach London."

"I am glad to hear that he is a full match for Afshin," said Hossein.

"But the biggest problem we have now is getting Ehsan out of Iran," continued Mr. Gohari. "Like all other high school students his age, he is also *mamnuol khorouj* and will be drafted to go to war if he is not accepted at a university. Since the fall of the Shah, traveling out of the country has become a nightmare. I used to go to Europe and the United States all the time. I have an import-export business. I used to take my family with me whenever we could. Now, forget it. You cannot even get your passport renewed."

"I know. Things have changed a lot since 1979, especially for traveling abroad," said Hossein. "I am struggling with the same problem myself."

"The other day, we were at the passport office, inquiring about the rules that apply to Ehsan, and what we need to do to take him to London," said Mr. Gohari. "At the counter, there was a young *basiji*, taking the applications. Once we handed him Ehsan's application, he started reciting something from the Quran in Arabic, then he said:

'Lots of young kids like your son are going to war, sacrificing their lives for the country, and you are trying to take your son to London instead? Is his blood more precious than any of those who are fighting in the war as soldiers in Emam Khomeini's army, and dying for Islam?' This kid made me so mad. I was so upset that I wanted to punch him in his face. He was absolutely clueless as to what we have been through in the past year. He had no feelings for us whatsoever. I just kept quiet and ignored all he said."

"I am sorry to hear that," replied Hossein. "Many young and radical people like him have joined this government. We are at their mercy now."

"Do you know why?" asked Mr. Gohari. "This is all about money and nothing else. They use Islam as a cover. In the past, whoever who was with the Shah's government made a lot of money. Now the government has changed, the tables have turned, and it is time for another group to become rich. You will not believe what is going on in the country now. I am sure you know about the people trying to leave Iran, but perhaps you don't know about the influx of so many Iranians back into the country, or do you?"

"I don't know anything about that," replied Hossein.

"At the time of the Shah, many students would travel overseas to study," replied Mr. Gohari.

"Yes, I know that," replied Hossein. "In fact, several of my own friends did that right after graduating from high school."

"Around the time of the revolution, there was a major movement among Iranian students all over the world," said Mr. Gohari. "Students at every university abroad formed a local *Islamic Association*, attracting specific types of students. Since the revolution, many of these students have returned to Iran. Some of them have graduated with a degree from a respectable university and have taken important posts in the government, but most others have come back only to make money. Because they belonged to an Islamic Association overseas, they get preferential treatment from the government. Most of them get permission for import-export businesses. They get government loans to import various merchandise to Iran, and they share their profit with someone who is one tier above them. It is all about money. The closer you are to this government, the more money you can make. You will not believe how many people have become millionaires overnight. You have perhaps heard the term *'taahhod* versus *takhassos.'*

Mr. Gohari paused and said, "*taahhod* means commitment to Islam, more so to the current ruling clan in charge of our government. *Takhassos*, as you already know, means specialized knowledge. The current regime cares more about your commitment to them, and far less about your knowledge and skills. They select and empower only those committed to their ideology. Once you join them, you are set for life. It is entirely about making money now. Look at the cleric Mr. Rafsanjani now. He is a billionaire. How did he amass this wealth?"

"From the sale of pistachios, he claims," replied Hossein with a sarcastic tone.

"Yeah, right," said Mr. Gohari. "You remember the term *taghooti,* which they used for anyone connected to the Shah and had become very rich. Right now, there are people connected to this government richer than anyone at the time of the Shah. Remember, they criticized people who took their money and transferred it to Swiss banks; remember, they used to even publish their names and the amounts they transferred overseas. You will not believe how much money those tied to this government have transferred to Swiss banks. By their own definition of *taghooti,* there are far more *taghootis* now, connected to this government, than ever before."

Mr. Gohari paused and said, "I know you are busy and I don't want to get started on this topic."

"Not at all," replied Hossein. "All of this is very interesting to me. I never knew that so many Iranians were coming back from the United States. I never knew about the business dealings either."

"And currently too," replied Mr. Gohari. "None of this has ever been made public. You need to be with them to know these things. They are all in it to steal the wealth of the country. In every new project they start, there are several of their own people simply siphoning money into their pockets. A new highway costs several times more than it should. For any project, a large percentage of the budget goes into the pockets of modern middlemen rather than toward the actual expenditure."

"Getting back to Afshin, were you able to get a passport for him?" asked Hossein. "How long did it take?"

"We did, thanks to my friend," said Mr. Gohari. "One of my best friends is a high-ranking and well-respected army general now. I called him up. He made a few phone calls, and within two weeks, we had his passport. We are now struggling to get a passport for Ehsan, and once we have that, and once we go to England, I will enroll him in high school there and keep him there. I do not want him to return to Iran and have to go to war. Afshin's illness has been a major stress for us, but at least one good thing is coming out of it, and that is Ehsan will escape to freedom. I am sure you will keep this confidential."

"Of course I will," replied Hossein.

"Doctor, you have been very kind to Afshin," said Mr. Gohari. "I will never forget all the support you gave us when he was getting his chemotherapy at the hospital. You were always there, answering our questions. If you ever decide to leave the country, or need help getting a passport, call me, okay? That is the minimum I can do for you. Here is my business card with my phone numbers."

"Thank you so much," replied Hossein. "It has been my pleasure to take care of Afshin. You have a wonderful family. And I will take you up on your offer."

Ever since the clerics came to power, Hossein had been gathering information and planning for his soon-to-come departure from Iran. The idea of Afshin and his brother leaving for England sparked a new idea in his mind.

If Afshin and his older brother can get out of Iran on a medical leave, maybe Hamid and I can do the same. Maybe I can somehow make Hamid's illness so believable that he will get approval to go to Europe for treatment. With permission from the Ministry of Health, I might be able to go with him as an accompanying person. It was just a few months ago that another leukemia patient went to England for treatment. I need to research this more. This is a great idea.

During his lunch break, Hossein started drawing up a list of things that had to happen for this idea to succeed.

I must first make Hamid convincingly sick so that he will gain exemption from his military service. We then need to apply for Hamid to get permission to leave the country for medical treatments. I need to be qualified as an accompanying person to go with him. Hamid will need a passport and permission to leave Iran. I also will need permission to leave Iran and obtain a new passport. Hamid will need a formal invitation from a hospital in Europe, accepting him for medical care. We both will need visas to go wherever we will be going, and, finally, we will need money.

This is a complex plan, and we need also to consider what will happen once we leave Iran. We will need to live in Europe awhile. I will need to take my ECFMG examination and pass it with good grades. I will need to apply for, and be accepted into a residency program at a very good hospital.

With all these thoughts in his mind, Hossein walked towards the cafeteria.

Can I actually pull this off? asked Hossein of himself while standing in the lunch line. *Am I breaking the law now? Am I doing the right thing by making Hamid sick? Is this ethical? How will people in the future judge this? What would others think of me, when they learn parts of this story, or the whole thing? Will I ever become ashamed of this in maybe ten, twenty, or thirty years from now? And how will I judge myself when I grow old?*

Hossein did not have a single answer to any of these questions; neither could he discuss any of this with anyone else, even though he knew that several of his classmates were also planning to leave Iran.

The fact that I want to leave Iran, although it is against the existing laws of the country, is my own right and my own choice. Many people have already left Iran. I will not be the last to leave, either. Maybe the fact that the government has sealed the borders on us is against a higher law that governs humanity. I do not know what the United Nations is doing about Iran's repressive laws against its own citizens. The smuggler told us about Iranians applying for political asylum in Turkey. If indeed other countries are allowing Iranians to take refuge in their lands must mean that our government is doing something illegal or unacceptable by international standards. This has certainly been a brutal government, having executed thousands of youths just because they were leftist or they were questioning the legitimacy of the rule of Islam. Was it right for the young man who had thrown a paint ball at the image of Khomeini to be killed on the spot? Will there ever be any investigation of that? Will they ever question the basiji who pulled the trigger? Will they ever put him behind bars for murder? Where do we draw the line? Who is to say what is right or what is wrong? This country certainly has no respect for freedom of speech. No one can say anything against Khomeini or question his judgment. If you insult the man, they consider you an enemy of Islam, and execute you. If you are of the Baha'i faith, you are illegal and have no rights in this country. The situation in Iran is so messed up now. Mr. Gohari is right; it must all be about money. Be with them, steal the money, and enjoy the privileges that regular men and women of this country do not have. Well, my question should perhaps be, 'Am I doing the right thing under the circumstances, in Iran, in 1983, with this government in place?' They imposed all these horrible things on us.

Hossein could feel the answer in his heart: *Yes, you are doing the right thing, Hossein. I am going to make Hamid sick enough, not only to get him out of the military, but also get him out of Iran for medical treatment. I will accompany him to Europe. This is how I will leave Iran. Hamid will have a choice to leave Iran or stay. It will be up to him. I am not going to impose this on him. The fact is that he can help me get out of Iran, in much the same way that I am helping him get out of the military. This seems fair. This may be my only way, perhaps my best way out of Iran. The smuggler will be my backup plan. If the efforts to leave Iran with Hamid fail, then I will go the route of either escaping the county myself, or go with the smuggler.*

The idea of getting Hamid out of the military was farfetched enough; but adding this new aspect to it now, leaving the country with Hamid as his companion, resonated in his mind as a much bigger challenge and a more complex process.

I must talk to every patient who has gone or is going overseas for treatment, thought Hossein.

Thanks to his passion for hematology, Hossein had made a very good impression on his professors. After his lunch break, Hossein went to the hematology ward to talk to one of them.

"Hello, Dr. Nikbin, may I ask you something?" asked Hossein of his professor.

"Sure, Hossein. What is up?" said Dr. Nikbin.

"Dr. Nikbin, you know how much I love hematology," began Hossein. "I would like to continue my education in the United States, much as you did. Yet the situation now is very different, and it is much more difficult than it must have been for you."

"Yes, Hossein, that is so true," replied Dr. Nikbin. "In my time, I graduated from the same medical school that you are attending now, way back in 1969, almost thirteen years ago. Back then, at the time of the Shah, I took the ECFMG examination right here in Tehran while I was still in training. The results came in the mail a few months later. I sent several letters to various hospitals in the United States and to my surprise, two internal medicine programs—one at the University of Texas, and the other in Minnesota—accepted me. I went to Texas, simply because it was warmer. After a few years, I managed to do a fellowship in hematology and oncology at the MD Anderson Cancer Center in Houston. I then returned to Iran in 1976, and have been here since."

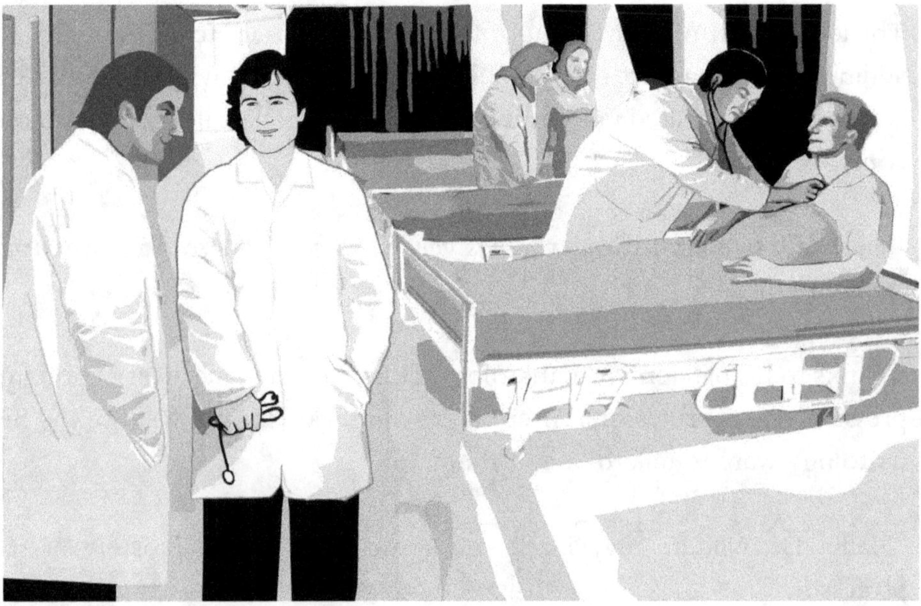

Dr. Nikbin paused and said, "Bright students like you deserve to go to the United States and study there. You deserve to have access to all the opportunities to advance your education, much like what I had. You simply do not get it here, because we are so far behind, and now with the new regime, it is going to become even worse. As you know, several of our good professors, those who had trained in the United States and Europe, have already left Iran. Just a few weeks ago we lost our last surgeon who performed kidney transplants. Therefore, that department does not exist here anymore. Then the nephrology department at Shariati Hospital closed, because they lost both their nephrologists, who left Iran. I am very concerned about the future of medical care and the future of medical education here. If I were you, I would do everything I could to leave this country and go to the United States. If you can, you should leave Iran. Do not even think twice about it. This government does not care about the quality of medical care that people get, or the quality of the medical education that you receive. They have a totally different agenda."

"I hear this from everyone these days. Everyone I meet is disillusioned with the government," said Hossein. "Even the cab driver I met last weekend was cynical."

"They have destroyed our international image," said Dr. Nikbin. "Once we were proud of our Iranian citizenship. But with all the rhetoric of Khomeini, all the 'Death to America' slogans, and the hostage crisis, our international image has been degraded."

"I have heard that the United States is hardly issuing any visas to Iranians, even if you make it to Europe or other countries where you can go to an American Consulate to apply," said Hossein.

"I know. Isn't that horrible?" said Dr. Nikbin. "There was a time that you could go to the American Embassy, here in Tehran, and get a visa to travel to the United States on the spot. Now, forget it. If I were you, Hossein, I would leave Iran and first go to Europe. Establish yourself there, and then try to find a way to go to the United States. Also, talk to Dr. Javan. Do you know him? He is a good friend of mine. He trained in Germany and worked there for many years before he returned to Iran. He may be able to give you some advice about studying and living in Germany."

"Thank you, Dr. Nikbin. I will talk to Dr. Javan. I know him very well. I worked with him during my surgery rotation."

"Also talk to Dr. Fathi; he studied in Paris," said Dr. Nikbin. "From all that I have heard, breaking into France's or Britain's medical system is much more difficult than Germany's. If I were you, I would consider Germany as my first step, and then work my way up to go to the United States. But first, talk to those guys."

Dr. Javan was a general surgeon at Hossein's hospital. Later that day, after Hossein finished his work and classes, he called the operating room and found out that Dr. Javan was still there in surgery. Hossein went to the operating-room area. He entered the surgical locker room. He changed into the operating-room uniform, put on a facemask and surgical hood, and entered the operating room.

"Do you know where Dr. Javan is?" asked Hossein of one of the nurses.

"OR Six, you can find him there," replied the nurse.

Hossein walked to operating room number six, greeted the surgeon, Dr. Javan, and with his permission, entered the room.

"Hey, see who is here. How are you, Hossein?" said Dr. Javan, both hands deep inside the patient's abdomen.

"Hello, Dr. Javan," replied Hossein. "I have some free time today and came over to see what is going on in here and learn a little. I miss being in the OR with you. I learned so much when I did my surgical rotation with you."

"You are always welcome to come and observe us here," said Dr. Javan. "Come over here and stand behind me. Let me show you something interesting. Look here. Do you see this large tumor? It is colon cancer. Fortunately, it does not seem to have spread anywhere. We are going to take this tumor out."

"Woo, very interesting," said Hossein.

Hossein stood on a stand, behind Dr. Javan, looking over his shoulder and between the arms of other staff in the operating room. After surgery, Hossein found an opportunity to talk to Dr. Javan.

"Dr. Javan, I would like to run something by you," said Hossein. "Do you have time to talk to me now?"

"Sure, you can talk to me," said Dr. Javan. "What is going on?"

"Dr. Nikbin suggested that I speak with you," said Hossein. "I am thinking of leaving Iran after I finish my studies here. I wanted to learn more about Germany's medical system and about living in Germany. You trained in Germany? Correct?"

"Yes, I did," replied Dr. Javan. "Germany is a great country. I was in Munich for about ten years. What makes you want to go to Germany?"

"If things work out, I will be leaving Iran this summer," replied Hossein. "My goal is to go to the United States and continue my studies there. But because I cannot get a U.S. visa here, I need to go elsewhere first. Dr.

Nikbin suggested that I consider Germany as a first step, a halfway home, then work my way up to go to the United States. This is what I wanted to talk to you about."

"Sure, I get the point," replied Dr. Javan. "I am sure you can get a very good training in Germany. The medical system there is a bit complicated, and not as straightforward as it is in the United States. Germany can be a good first place to go, to get yourself established a bit, so that you can ultimately go to the United States."

"If need be, would you be kind to write me a letter of recommendation, or contact someone where you trained, so that I can get through the door there?" asked Hossein.

"I will be happy to," replied Dr. Javan. "I know many people there, and have many friends who can help you getting settled there. If I were you, I would take the ECFMG examination in Germany. You should look into it."

"I am planning to take the next ECFMG examination in the summer," said Hossein. "I just don't know where I will be taking it yet."

"Why don't you visit the German Consulate in Tehran? I have been there many times. Germans working there are very pleasant and helpful. Talk to Herr Mueller if you can. Tell him that I suggested that you meet with him. See what he has to say."

"Thank you so much," said Hossein. "I appreciate the information and the help you provided me."

Hossein left the hospital that afternoon, brainstorming what his future might look like.

I have to first leave Iran, get a German visa, live there, and figure out how to reach the United States. This whole thing is becoming more and more complex. Well, nothing in life is easy. This is another hump that I have to get over.

Hossein's multi-step plan was indeed becoming more complex. Unforeseen challenges made it more difficult to pull off, and as his plan expanded, Hossein began to see many other things that might go wrong.

CHAPTER EIGHT
THE DRIVE

On his lunch break on Thursday, Hossein left his hospital to go to the German Embassy in Tehran. The embassy was on Ferdowsi Avenue, next to the Turkish Embassy, and across the street from Iran's Central Bank. The taxi dropped Hossein off in front of the bank.

I wonder how much money is being wired out of this bank to other countries right now, Hossein said to himself as he gazed up at the bank's imposing exterior.

He crossed the street and arrived at the German Embassy. The door was locked, but a sign on the door said that the working hours were from ten in the morning to two in the afternoon. So Hossein rang the bell, and the intercom crackled to life.

"Who is it?" asked a voice on the intercom.

"I am here to meet Herr Mueller," replied Hossein. "I have some questions about getting a visa to travel to Germany."

"Wait, please," the voice said.

After a few minutes, a tall man opened the door.

"Befarmaiid", or "Please come in," he said to Hossein in Farsi. "This way, please."

Hossein followed the man into the embassy. He led Hossein into a hallway and approached a teakwood door bearing the nameplate of Herr Mueller in gold-embossed letters. There were a few chairs in the hallway, apparently for visitors.

"Please have a seat here," said the man. "Herr Mueller will be with you shortly."

"Thank you," said Hossein and sat on one of the chairs.

The man walked away. Hossein looked around. He saw a few posters about Germany on the walls of the hallway as well as two security cameras, one at each end of the hallway, both facing him. Hossein was not sure whether the cameras were fixed in their positions, or if someone monitoring the cameras was actively watching him. He decided to test the cameras cautiously. He stood and walked toward a large poster on the wall opposite him. He looked at the poster for a minute, and then turned around to return to where he had been sitting. In doing so, he glanced at the cameras, and noted that they were indeed following his movements in the hallway. As he walked back to sit down, the door to Herr Mueller's office opened, and a tall blond man appeared in the doorway. He introduced himself as Herr Mueller, greeted Hossein, and invited him into his office. Hossein glanced admiringly around the office, tastefully furnished with, among other things, a wide glass-topped desk, plush leather chairs, and a beautiful Persian carpet. After they settled in their chairs, Hossein broke the ice by speaking first.

"Dr. Javan suggested that I meet with you," he said. "He is my university professor. I will be finishing medical school in about seven months. I am interested in taking a medical examination in Frankfurt during the summer, and I was wondering if I could get a visa to go to Germany to take this examination."

"I see. Can you tell me more about this examination?" asked Herr Mueller.

"I would like to go to the United States for my postgraduate medical training, and to do that, I need to take an equivalency test that is administered by an organization called ECFGM," said Hossein. "For obvious reasons, I cannot take the test in Iran. It is no longer administered here. Frankfurt is one of the test centers closest to me, and I would like to take this test there."

"My question to you is whether I will be able to obtain a visa to go to Germany if I choose Frankfurt as my examination site," said Hossein.

"Well, I think so," replied Herr Mueller. "We have not had this situation come up before, but if you provide documentation indicating that you are registered for the examination in Frankfurt, I am sure you will get a visa. We issue two-week visitor's visas, and one of those should be enough for you to go and take your test."

"What will you do in Germany after you take your test? Will you return to Iran immediately?" asked Herr Mueller.

Hossein did not see this question coming. He knew very well that he could not disclose anything more to Herr Mueller; neither did he want to jeopardize the possibility of getting a visa to Germany.

"As I will be going all the way to Frankfurt, I would like to travel a little in Germany, perhaps to visit the cathedral in Köln," replied Hossein. "I hear that it is a magnificent structure."

"Yes, it is indeed," said Herr Mueller. "All the best to you. Please come back when you have the confirmation and paperwork for a visa. My best regards to Dr. Javan."

"Thank you so much, Herr Mueller," said Hossein. "I hope to see you in a few months."

Hossein left the German Embassy and went back to his hospital. He remembered that Hamid would be home for the weekend, and it was time for him to have his third and fourth blood draws. When Hossein's workday was over, he called Mahmood.

"Is Hamid home yet? We need to meet today," said Hossein.

"He is home, but my mom has invited all the Niayesh family over," replied Mahmood.

"What? I had planned to come over to meet you and Hamid," said Hossein on the phone. Being afraid of bugged phone lines, Hossein could not speak freely to Mahmood

"What shall we do now?" asked Mahmood.

"Can you and Hamid come and pick me up from the hospital?" said Hossein. "I will think of something."

An hour later, Hamid and Mahmood arrived at the entrance gate to the Emam Khomeini Hospital. Hossein was waiting for them at the gate. He got in the back seat of their car.

Mahmood said, "Sorry for the mishap. What are we going to do now?"

"I don't know, Mahmood. I was planning to come to your home and to draw Hamid's blood there," said Hossein. "Let's drive around while I think of a plan of action. Remember that we need to repeat the blood draws twice per week, on Thursday nights and Fridays, the only time that Hamid is off the military base. We need to adhere to this schedule."

"Got it," said Hamid.

"So tell me, how was your week?" asked Hossein.

"Everything was fine, just as usual," replied Hamid.

"Did you feel weak, fatigued, anything like that?" asked Hossein.

"Yes, I did. Only on Saturday and Sunday," replied Hamid. "After that, I was okay."

"Okay, just be aware that next week, when you go back to the base, you may feel weaker and more fatigued, or you may develop shortness of breath," said Hossein. "With the next two sets of blood draws, you will become anemic. By the end of tomorrow, your body will have lost almost two liters of blood. That is a lot of blood, Hamid. So do not push yourself next week. If you feel weak, just go to your nurse's office, okay?"

"Sure, Hossein," replied Hamid.

"And the antibiotics and the iron pills, have you been taking them?" asked Hossein.

"Every day, on schedule," replied Hamid.

"Great," said Hossein.

"Where are we going?" Mahmood asked Hossein.

"I have no idea, Mahmood," said Hossein. "How about we go and sit somewhere and think? There is a delightful pastry shop not far from here. Let's go there. We can grab something to eat and think about where we can go to take Hamid's blood tonight."

Inside the pastry shop, the three sat near the window overlooking a busy street in Tehran. Men sat on one side of the pastry shop, and women on the other side.

"Look at the gender segregation here," said Mahmood. "I remember being in this exact place several years ago. What a change. This is simply bizarre."

"Let's order something to eat, and focus on where we can go to take Hamid's blood tonight," said Hossein. "Can you guys think of somewhere that we can go?"

"How about in a hotel room?" asked Hamid.

"I am not sure, Hamid," replied Hossein. "I have a bad feeling about doing this in a hotel room. I do not know why, but I do not like the idea."

"Why will three young men who speak Farsi without any accents, obviously from Tehran, go to a hotel and ask to rent a room there?" said Mahmood. "This will raise a lot of suspicions. Before you know, the hotel staff will call the *basijis* on us."

The waiter came and took their order. Hossein and his cousins enjoyed the tea and pastries they had ordered.

"Look outside guys, do you see all the cars?" asked Hossein of his cousins.

"Yes, there are a lot of cars out on the street," replied Mahmood in a tone of voice that indicated he guessed there was something behind what Hossein had just said, but that he did not quite realize what it was.

Hossein said, "We can do it right in the car. I will need longer tubes for this, so I'll have to go to the hospital to get some supplies."

"Do what in the car?" asked Hamid.

"I will take your blood in the car tonight," said Hossein to Hamid. "It is quite doable. I just need other supplies to do it. Let's go, guys. We have to go back to the hospital. I need to get a few more things."

Mahmood paid the bill at the pastry shop. The three of them returned to the car and drove back to Hossein's hospital.

"I will be back shortly," he said. "Just drive around awhile and be back here in ten minutes."

"Okay, whatever you say," said Mahmood.

Hossein got out of the car, went into the hospital, and took the supplies he needed. He came out in a short while and was pleased to see Mahmood just driving up. He got into the back seat of the car.

"Hamid, come and sit in the back with me, to my left," said Hossein. "Mahmood, let's get away from here."

Mahmood started the car and drove away from the hospital.

"Where should we go?" he asked.

"Let's try to find somewhere quiet," said Hossein. "Let's find a quiet alley where you can park the car for a few minutes."

Few minutes later, they were in a narrow street. Mahmood parked the car. On Hossein's instruction, Hamid took off his right shoe and sock, lifted his foot, and placed it on the back seat so that Hossein could work on it.

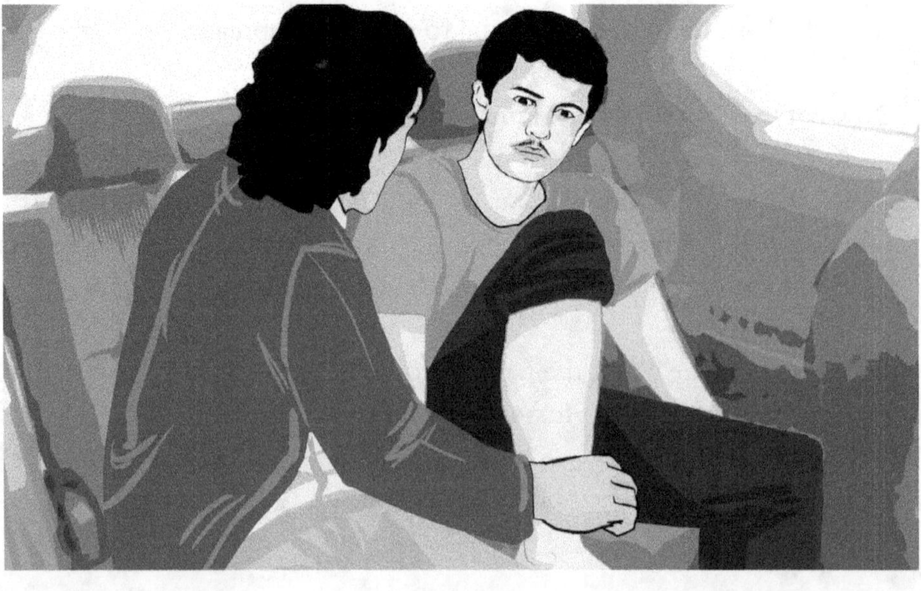

Taking out a butterfly needle, a connecting tube, and a vacuum bottle from his backpack, Hossein unwrapped the needle and the tubing, and connected the tubing to the needle. He then carefully inspected Hamid's foot and placed a rubber band around his ankle. Using an alcohol wipe, Hossein cleaned an area of the skin and inserted the butterfly needle into Hamid's foot, in the same spot that he had used last week. The blood started flowing into the tubing. Hossein connected the other end of the tubing to the vacuum bottle and secured the butterfly needle to Hamid's foot by winding adhesive tape around it.

"This is going to clot again, Hossein," said Mahmood.

"Not this time," said Hossein. "I have put enough heparin in the bottle. There's no chance of the blood clotting this time."

"What is heparin?" asked Hamid.

"Heparin is an anticoagulant," replied Hossein. "It prevents blood from clotting. Remember last week, the Coke bottles? Your blood clotted in them. I had a difficult time emptying the Coke bottles. This time, it will not clot."

"Okay, Hamid, gently move your foot down," said Hossein.

Hamid put his foot carefully down on the floor. The blood was flowing satisfactorily into the vacuum bottle.

"Okay Mahmood, drive," said Hossein.

Mahmood started driving the car while Hossein monitored the blood draw, controlling the flow rate and the volume of blood he was collecting with a clamp on the tubing.

"Mahmood, as you have guests tonight, why don't you just drop me off at my home?" said Hossein. "Meanwhile, let's plan where and how we will do this tomorrow."

Once Hossein had collected enough blood, he stopped the flow and asked Hamid to raise his foot. He took out the needle, put a Band-Aid on the wound, and wrapped Hamid's foot with a tight bandage. Hossein then capped the needle and put everything in a large red plastic bag.

"Keep your foot elevated, Hamid," said Hossein. "Keep applying pressure to the site of the needle prick."

"Okay, Hossein," said Hamid. He kept his foot on his knee and lay back in the car.

"Mahmood, in the future, if worse comes to worst, we can always do this in the car," said Hossein. "Think of quiet neighborhoods that we can drive to, where there is less traffic and the streets are peaceful. For tomorrow, we may be able to do this at my home. My mom and my sister may be going shopping, and I will be home alone."

"Okay, we can talk about that tomorrow," said Mahmood as he dropped Hossein off at his home.

The next morning, Friday, Hamid and Mahmood arrived at Hossein's house.

"Come on in, guys. No one else is here," said Hossein. "Let's go to my room and get this done as soon as possible. We will need to go to my hospital when we are done. I want to run some tests on Hamid's blood to see how anemic he is now."

"I am not used to being in your home with no one else around," said Hamid. "This is the first time. It feels very different."

"You're right, Hamid," said Hossein. "I feel the same. I have never drawn anyone's blood in here either. Come over, Hamid, lie on the bed. Let me check your foot."

After he had looked at Hamid's foot, Hossein said, "Everything looks great. We are fortunate that there haven't been any bruises, just the one tiny needle prick."

"That is great," agreed Mahmood.

"Let me check your blood pressure," said Hossein. "We could not do it in the car yesterday."

Hossein said Hamid's blood pressure was good, and then he asked, "Have you had any dizziness?"

"Well, overall I am fine, but this morning I felt a little dizzy as I was getting up from bed," replied Hamid.

"This is an early sign of anemia, Hamid," said Hossein. "You may feel dizzy more often; you may get lightheaded, or you may feel short of breath when you exercise or run. Over time, as I take more blood, these symptoms will become more noticeable and frequent. You will also notice that you have a lot less energy. I will run a blood test today, and I have a feeling that your blood count will be low enough for you to go to the clinic at your military base this week. Did you have a good breakfast this morning?"

"Yes, I did," replied Hamid.

"Mahmood, can you go to the kitchen and get us something to eat and drink?" asked Hossein. "Bring whatever you find. There is a piece of cake and some fruit there."

Mahmood nodded and went to the kitchen.

"I will also make us some hot tea, Hossein."

"Good idea, Mahmood," replied Hossein.

Hossein reached into his backpack, pulled out the supplies he needed, and started taking Hamid's blood. Mahmood returned with a tray. On it, he had placed some cookies, fruit, milk, and slices of cake.

"You have to eat something, Hamid," said Hossein. "After this blood draw, you will feel weak and fatigued."

"Thank you, Hossein, for going out of your way to help me," said Hamid. "I really appreciate all that you are doing for me."

"You are most welcome Hamid," said Hossein. "Now please eat something."

"Mahmood, can you play us some music?" asked Hossein. "I know that Hamid likes listening to Dariush. I have a few of his albums there, in the drawer, under the books."

Mahmood chose a tape, put it in the tape player, and adjusted the volume. Hossein got busy monitoring Hamid's blood draw. The golden voice of Dariush singing his famous *Booye Gandom* song, "The Scent of the Wheat Farms," filled the room. Hossein carried on with the blood draw as the three listened to Dariush's songs and ate cake and cookies.

"I will get the tea," said Mahmood.

"Great, we are almost done here. Let me also take some blood samples in test tubes," said Hossein. "We will go to the hospital after we drink our tea."

Shortly thereafter, the three left Hossein's house and drove away in the car.

"Mahmood, drop me off over there," Hossein said, pointing to a side entrance of the emergency room of the hospital. "I need to get rid of all these needles and syringes here. You guys go for a drive around the area and come back to pick me up in half an hour, and think of a good place to go for lunch."

Mahmood dropped Hossein off and drove away. Hossein walked through the emergency room into the hospital complex. He first went to his on-call room and put his white lab coat on. He then got the plastic bag that contained all the tubing and needles he had used for Hamid's blood draw. He walked down the hallway, took the elevator, and got off at the internal medicine ward. He greeted the on-call nurses. The unit was very quiet. He entered the medical supply room and quickly dumped the contents of the bag inside the medical waste container. He then walked over to the laboratory, where he met the on-call technician.

"I did not know you were on call today. How can I help you?" said the lab technician.

"I need to run a hemogram on a sample," said Hossein. "May I use the Coulter machine?"

"Of course, you may," replied the technician. "You know the machine well. Let me know if you need any help."

"Could you do me a favor and run a manual retic count on this sample?" asked Hossein, as he handed him one of the test tubes containing Hamid's blood.

Hossein removed the plastic top from the test tube of Hamid's blood, placed it inside the machine, and pressed the "Run" button. Within a minute, the machine printed the results. Hossein glanced at the printout and was happy to see that Hamid was now anemic.

"Retic count is one percent," announced the lab technician.

That was exactly what Hossein was hoping for, a low retic count. Hossein quickly disposed of his test tube of Hamid's blood sample, as well as the retic count slide and tube of blood that he had given the lab technician.

"Hey, thank you so much," said Hossein.

"Anytime," replied the lab technician.

Hossein walked back to the on-call room, changed, and left the hospital. Outside, Mahmood was waiting for him in the car. Hossein got into the car.

"Let's go, guys," said Hossein. "Good news! Hamid is truly anemic now. His hemoglobin is ten now, and that is before we see the effect of today's blood draw."

"Is this good?" asked Hamid. "What is a normal value for hemoglobin?"

"Yes, Hamid, this is very good," replied Hossein. "Normal hemoglobin for you should be around fourteen. You can now go to the clinic at the base. We are on now, full steam ahead. Mahmood, let's go somewhere pleasant for lunch."

"What did you mean when you said that his hemoglobin is ten before the effect of today's blood draw?" asked Mahmood.

"I took this blood sample at the end of the blood draw today," replied Hossein. "His body had not yet adapted itself to the blood draw of today.

If we were to run the same blood test tonight, his hemoglobin would be lower. It would be near or even below nine."

"So should I go see the doctor in the clinic tomorrow?" asked Hamid.

"Yes, Hamid, you should," answered Hossein affirmatively. "Tomorrow morning, while you are doing your regular physical exercises, tell your supervisor that you don't feel good. Sit somewhere. Tell him you feel very weak and exhausted. These are signs of anemia, and you will feel them tomorrow as you run and do push-ups."

"I am a bit nervous," said Hamid.

"I fully understand, Hamid," replied Hossein. "I would be too. I can only imagine how frightening this must be for you. Just be natural and do not worry too much. Let them do their job and figure out what is wrong with you. All you have to do is to tell them that you are not feeling well. Don't say anything else."

"Okay, Hossein. I will do my best," said Hamid.

Then, the three went out for a late lunch.

CHAPTER NINE
THE FATIGUE

The next morning, soon after Hamid arrived at his camp, he joined the other soldiers for the morning march.

The sound of marching soldiers, mixed with the daily reading of Quran verses in the background, filled the cold early-morning air. The group sergeant was yelling, "One, two, three, four, turn about! One, two, three, four, one, two, three, four…"

Until this morning, Hamid had not fully understood what Hossein meant when he told him about the symptoms that he would experience because of the anemia. Now, as he was marching, Hamid suddenly felt very weak, and nearly fainted. He stepped away from the group, and sat on the ground. His sergeant noticed that Hamid had stepped out, and he walked over to him.

"Hey, soldier, are you okay?" asked the sergeant.

"No sir. I feel weak. Very, very weak," replied Hamid.

"Oh my God, you are so pale and sweating. Lie down on the ground. Bring me a stretcher, NOW," yelled the sergeant.

Four soldiers carried Hamid on a stretcher to the base's clinic. They put him in a small room with another soldier. The base's nurse came to see him as soon as he arrived.

"What happened to you, soldier?" asked the nurse. "What is your name?"

"I am Hamid," he replied. "I just felt very weak. I had to sit down. My heart was pounding in my chest and I felt extremely out of breath."

"Your pulse is very fast. Let me check your blood pressure."

The nurse checked it and said, "Your blood pressure is very low. Let me get the doctor."

Shortly thereafter, the doctor walked in.

"Hello, I am Dr. Bashiri. How are you, son?" said the doctor.

Dr. Bashiri, unlike the previous doctor whom Hamid had once met, was a tall man with a happy and kind face. He wore a white coat on top of his military uniform.

"I am feeling better now. I felt very weak as we were marching out there," said Hamid.

"Has this ever happened to you before? Do you have any medical issues?" asked the doctor.

"No, doctor, never," said Hamid. "I have always been healthy."

The doctor looked at Hamid's chart and examined him. He looked at his eyes, checked his neck, listened to his heart and lungs, and felt his abdomen.

"Well, Hamid, I think you may be dehydrated," said the doctor. "I want you to take it easy today. Just go to your dorm and rest. No marching, no classes, just rest. Read a book. I hope that this is just dehydration. Drink plenty of fluids today. We will see how you feel tomorrow. If you feel the same way again, come back here. I will do a more thorough workup. For now, rest is all you need."

"Thank you, doctor," said Hamid, and he walked to his dormitory. On the way, his sergeant intercepted him.

"Are you feeling better now?" asked the sergeant.

"Yes, sir, I am much better now, but the doctor told me to relax for the rest of today and see how things go tomorrow," replied Hamid.

"I agree with the doctor," replied the sergeant. "You were very pale when I saw you and that frightened me. I am glad you are feeling better now. Go to the dorm and lie down. Report to me tomorrow morning. Stay well, soldier."

"Thank you, sir," replied Hamid, and with a military salute to his sergeant, walked away to the dorm.

Now I get it. This is what Hossein was talking about, thought Hamid. *I felt very weak this morning, but I am a lot better now. I wonder if this will get any worse.*

The next morning, Hamid ate a good breakfast at the base and attended his military strategy class. In the class, the teacher was lecturing the soldiers on how to set up military traps and select targets to destroy. After the class, all the soldiers went to the practice ground. The sergeant came to Hamid.

"Hamid, how are you today?" asked the sergeant.

"I am fine, sir. Ready to serve my country, sir," replied Hamid.

"Okay, but just don't push yourself, especially if you feel weak."

"Okay, sir."

The march started, and within ten minutes Hamid had to walk away and sit on the ground again. The sergeant quickly came to check on him.

"What happened, son?" asked the sergeant.

"Same thing as yesterday, except that I did not push myself as I did yesterday," replied Hamid.

"You are pale again. Sit here and rest," said the sergeant. "Once you feel better, go to the clinic."

The sergeant turned and yelled, "Get him some water immediately."

Two soldiers ran to get Hamid some water. A few minutes later, Hamid could compose himself and walked to the clinic.

"You are back again. Your name is Hamid?" said the nurse.

"Yes, I am Hamid," he replied.

"Why are you here today?" asked the nurse.

"For the same problem as yesterday. I am so weak that I cannot run," replied Hamid.

"Sit down here," said the nurse. "Let me check your blood pressure and pulse."

The nurse checked his vitals and said, "Your blood pressure is fine, but your heart is beating too fast. Come with me to the examination room."

Hamid followed the nurse.

"Sit on the examination table. The doctor will be right with you," said the nurse.

Dr. Bashiri walked in with Hamid's medical records in his hands.

"Hello, Hamid. What happened today?" asked the doctor.

"I just felt very weak again," replied Hamid. "I could not run. I had to sit down."

"Okay. Your pulse is fast," said the doctor. "Let me examine you."

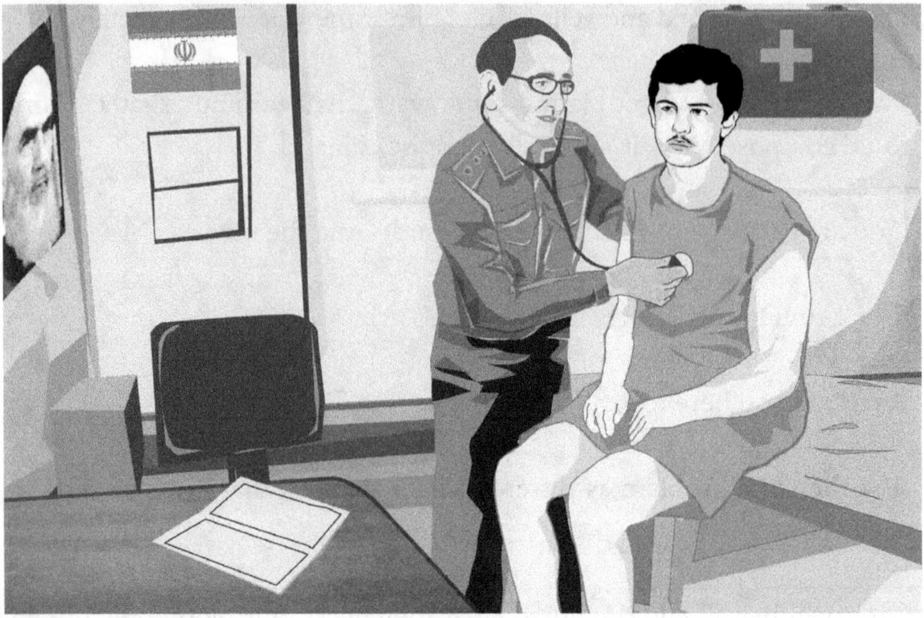

Dr. Bashiri listened to Hamid's heart with his stethoscope. He examined his lungs, looked at his eyes, and pulled down his lower eyelids to look under them. He then asked Hamid to show him his hands, which he did.

"I think I know what may be wrong," said the doctor. "You look pale. You may be anemic. I am going to order some blood tests."

Hamid was unsure of what he should say or how he should react. With the prior knowledge that he was anemic, he wanted to act in a way that did not raise any suspicion, so he said, "What does anemic mean, doctor?"

"Low blood count," the doctor replied. "Let's do the blood tests first. Then we will talk more about it tomorrow. It may not be anemia. I do not know. Let's wait for the blood results. For now, I am going to inform your sergeant that you should not do any running or physical activities until we know what is going on."

"Thank you so much, doctor," said Hamid.

"Nurse, please draw Hamid's blood and send it in for hemogram and chemistry," said the doctor.

Hamid rolled up his left sleeve, and the nurse drew two tubes of blood.

"Okay, Hamid, all done," said the nurse. "You can leave now. Go to your dormitory. We will talk to your sergeant."

Hamid walked to his dormitory. He lay on his bed, staring at the ceiling.

I wonder how this plan will unfold, he thought. *This is just the beginning of a long road. I hope this will get me out of here. God, if you are up there, please help me. Please make this work for me. I do not want to die. I do not want to go to war. Help me, God.*

As he was praying for himself, his sergeant walked in.

"How are you doing, my son?" asked the sergeant.

Hamid liked his sergeant, as he was a very pleasant man. He truly cared about every soldier who worked under him.

"I am okay. I just don't have much energy," replied Hamid.

"Listen, Hamid, I am sure the doctor will help you," said the sergeant. "For today, just stay here and rest. I do not want you to do any work today. Go to the library. Read a book. You can skip classes this afternoon too. I spoke with Dr. Bashiri. He will know more tomorrow. See him tomorrow, and we will take it from there."

"Thank you, Sergeant," said Hamid. "You are very kind."

The sergeant left. Hamid stayed in his bed until lunchtime. At lunch, he joined his group in the cafeteria. It was a busy scene with hundreds of tired soldiers. Hamid brought his lunch tray and sat with his friends.

"Hey, Hamid, how are you?" asked a friend. "What is going on with you?"

"I feel tired all the time," replied Hamid. "I just don't have the energy to run or do any of my normal tasks."

"All of us hope that you get better soon," said the friend. "Don't worry. You are healthy. This must be the flu or something. It will pass."

"Yes, I know. I hope it passes soon," replied Hamid.

"I hate this food," said one of Hamid's friends. "What is this garbage they feed us?"

"I can't wait for the weekend to get home and eat my mom's cooking," said another soldier.

"Don't complain, guys," said a soldier walking by and overhearing the conversation. "Next month, you will all be at the front, eating canned beans three times a day."

"Thank you for the information," said Hamid's friend to the passerby.

"What do you think Emam Hossein fed his army in Karbala?" asked the same soldier. "We are at war, and all you guys do is complaining about the food you eat. Shame on you."

Hamid and his friends looked at one another. They knew this guy must be a fanatic. They ate their lunch in silence until the soldier walked away. They waited until he was out of sight, then all of them burst into laughter.

After lunch, Hamid returned to the dormitory. He lay on his bed, staring at the motionless fan on the ceiling. In the quiet of the empty dormitory, Hamid fell asleep, and an unpleasant dream resurfaced as Hamid's sleep deepened.

Hamid saw himself at the front, hiding in a ditch. Bombs were dropping, bullets were flying, and flames were erupting all over the place. He knew that his family was watching him all the time from a safe place nearby, as if they were watching a movie in which Hamid was a soldier. Hamid got out of the ditch and fired shots at a slew of enemies, and in doing so, he heard his mother scream, "Nooooooo!" and as he turned back to look at her, he was shot in the back.

Hamid awoke sweating and afraid.

"Are you okay, Hamid?" asked a young soldier who was in the dormitory sitting in his bed, not far from Hamid. Half the soldiers had already come back to the dormitory, as the working day had ended and they were getting ready for dinner.

"I am okay," said Hamid. "I just had a nightmare."

"Who doesn't? All of us do," said the soldier. "I have nightmares every night. Ask around. I bet there is not a single soul who does not."

"Are you new here?" asked Hamid.

"Yup, just started my service last week," said the soldier. "My name is Keyvan."

"I am Hamid. Pleased to meet you, Keyvan,"

"Are you from Tehran, Hamid?"

"Yes I am,"

"Same here, I am from Tehran too. So many of us who did not make the *Konkoor* now have to go to war."

"Careful about what you say, Keyvan,"

"Why?" Keyvan laughed.

"Too many fanatics here in the base," replied Hamid, "Before you know it, they will report you. Today at lunch, there was this guy talking about Karbala and Emam Hossein."

"I didn't think of it that way," replied Keyvan. "And you are right. I will be careful. You are not a fanatic, are you, Hamid? You don't look like one."

"No, don't worry. I am not," replied Hamid.

"It is dinnertime, Hamid," said Keyvan. "Shall we go to the cafeteria?"

CHAPTER TEN
THE DEBATE

The next morning, Hamid put on his army uniform and walked to the clinic.

"Good morning, Soldier Hamid," said the nurse.

"Good morning," replied Hamid.

"Dr. Bashiri is expecting you. Follow me," said the nurse.

Hamid followed the nurse into the doctor's office. Dr. Bashiri was sitting in his office, behind a desk, with a stack of medical records. He was busy writing notes on one of the charts.

"Good morning, son," said the doctor.

"Good morning, Dr. Bashiri," said Hamid.

"Listen, I got your blood work back, and you are very anemic, Hamid," said the doctor. "Your hemoglobin, the index we look at, is 9.2. That is too low. The normal range for you is about thirteen to fifteen. Have you ever been anemic before?"

"No, sir, never," replied Hamid.

"Anyone in your family ever had anemia?" asked the doctor.

"Not that I know of, no," replied Hamid.

"Well, Hamid. We need to run a few more tests to better understand the nature of your anemia," said the doctor. "I am also going to refer you to the medical clinic at the army hospital next week. I want you to see a specialist there."

"Thank you, sir," said Hamid. "I appreciate all your help. Can I get a copy of my blood tests to show my parents?"

"Sure," said the doctor. "I will have the nurse give you a copy of the results."

"I need to tell my parents about this," said Hamid. "They may want to take me to see our family doctor. Is that okay?"

"Sure, Hamid," said the doctor. "That is fine; there is no problem with you seeing someone else privately. However, we also need to follow our own procedures around here. We just want to get you better, discover why you are anemic, and treat you. In addition, with the degree of anemia you have, you cannot be running out there, nor doing what other soldiers do. I will have you transferred to a different division. You can do either office-based work, or something that does not involve much physical activity."

"Sure, whatever you say, doctor," said Hamid.

"So, more blood tests for you," said the doctor. "We will check your iron level and vitamin levels. Also some stool tests to make sure you are not bleeding into your stomach."

"Thank you, sir," replied Hamid.

"Nurse, come here," shouted Dr. Bashiri.

The nurse came in, and Hamid followed him to another room, where he drew more blood from Hamid and handed him a pack of three cards.

"These are stool-sample cards," said the nurse. "When you go to bathroom, place a little of your stool, using these wood sticks, on here. Seal the packs and bring them back to me."

"Do I bring them all together?" asked Hamid.

"Yes, do all three, on separate dates, and bring them in next week. From here, you should go to see Sergeant Nazari. His office is in the administration building. He will assign you a new post."

Hamid left the doctor's office and went to the base's administration building.

"I am here to see Sergeant Nazari," said Hamid.

"Follow me," said the guard at the door. He took Hamid to the office of Sergeant Nazari. As the sergeant approached, Hamid offered a military salute.

"Come to my office," said the sergeant. "Dr. Bashiri tells me that you have anemia and that you should be excused from physical work and daily exercises for now, until they figure out what is going on with you, and you are all better. Is that correct?"

"Yes, sir," said Hamid.

"Okay, I am transferring you to the registrar office," said the sergeant. "The office keeps track of all the soldiers arriving or leaving this base. All your duties will be behind the desk. You think you can handle that?"

"Yes, sir," said Hamid. "I will do my best."

"Very well," said the sergeant. "I will take you upstairs."

Hamid followed Sergeant Nazari to the second floor of the administration office, where the sergeant showed him his new desk and cubicle.

"You will be stationed here," said the sergeant. "You will report to Sergeant Esfandiari. Well, here he comes."

The three exchanged military salutes, and Sergeant Nazari introduced Hamid to Sergeant Esfandiari.

For the next few days, Hamid worked in the administration office. Thursday afternoon, Hamid left the base to go home. While at home, he discussed the events of the previous week with Mahmood and his dad.

"We need to let Hossein know," said Mahmood. "I spoke with him last night. We should go to his hospital now and get him. Let's go, Hamid."

Mahmood and Hamid drove to get Hossein from his hospital. Hossein was waiting at the main gate.

"Hop in, Hossein," said Mahmood, and Hossein got in the back seat.

"Hello, guys. Hey, Hamid. How are you?" said Hossein.

"I am fine. I have lots to tell you," replied Hamid, and he updated Hossein about the events of the week.

"From this point on, we must be very careful," said Hossein. "The plan is working well. They transferred you to a different department. That means no front for you while we keep you anemic. But we want to get you out completely."

"That will be very nice, Hossein," said Hamid as he handed his lab results to his cousin. "I knew you would want to see these."

"Good thinking, Hamid," said Hossein. "Your hemoglobin is 9.2. We need to continue the blood draws, but we can relax a little and take less blood this time. Each time anyone does a test on you, get a copy of the results. Tell them that your dad wants a copy of all your lab results. Now, they are sending you to a specialist, most likely an internist. I do not think that they will be sending you to a hematologist yet. They will be running more tests, and perhaps they will do some procedures, such as an endoscopy or colonoscopy. You have to let them do whatever they want to do. Okay?

"Okay. I will," said Hamid.

"One more important thing you need to keep in mind," said Hossein. "At some point, you may be asked to give a sample of your urine for a urine test. Once that happens, you will be collecting a urine sample in a cup. If you do it in a bathroom, with no one around you, get a sharp thing, like a needle, the pins of your hat, whatever, and poke a tiny hole on the tip of your finger and drop only one drop of blood inside the urine cup then urinate on it. Okay?"

"Why do I do that?" asked Hamid.

"When they test your urine, they will detect blood in it, which you normally don't have," said Hossein. "Blood in the urine will confuse the hell out of them. They will have to somehow link it to your anemia. Also, stop taking the iron pills, but continue the vitamin pills, and antibiotics that I gave you."

"Sure, Hossein, got it," said Hamid.

"Listen guys, I have a very busy weekend before me," said Hossein. "Let me take your blood right now. I have all the supplies with me. I have to be somewhere in about an hour."

Again, Hossein repeated the blood-drawing procedure in the car as Mahmood was driving. This time, he used Hamid's arm and inserted his needle into the exact site where Hamid had his blood drawn in the clinic at the base.

"Mahmood, can you please drop me off on Karimkhan Boulevard, near the Armenian Church on Vila Street?" asked Hossein.

"Sure, Hossein, but I was hoping that we could go for dinner after this," replied Mahmood.

"Thank you, Mahmood, but I cannot do it on nights like this anymore," said Hossein. "I am studying German now. Last week, I signed up for German-language classes at the Austrian Cultural Institute. I have a class at seven tonight."

"Why are you studying German?" asked Mahmood.

"Long story. I will tell you next time we meet," replied Hossein.

"Are you thinking of going to Germany?" asked Hamid.

"Yes, Hamid. I am," replied Hossein.

"Woo, Hossein. When did this happen?" asked Mahmood.

"Last week," replied Hossein. "It is a long story. I will tell you all about it the next time we meet and have time. Drop me off right here please. Let's talk tomorrow. Maybe we can have lunch and talk then."

Hossein turned to Hamid. "And you keep taking your pills," he said.

"Bye, Hossein," said both Hamid and Mahmood, and they waved goodbye to him.

Hossein walked into his German class just on time. His girlfriend Afsaneh had kept a seat next to her for him. After the fall of the Shah, the Iranian government segregated men and women everywhere. Unmarried men and women were not to sit next to one another or be together in public. The German classes offered at the Austrian Cultural Institute did not have to honor this rule, as they were technically taking place on another country's sovereign property.

"*Salam,* Afsaneh," said Hossein.

"*Salam,* Hossein," said Afsaneh. "You are so late. Where were you?"

"Sorry, Afsaneh," said Hossein. "The last person I had to attend to took a lot longer than I expected."

"The German language is harder than English, Hossein," said Afsaneh. "Are you sure this is a right choice? You persuaded me to take this course with you. When I told my parents, they were shocked that I wanted to study German and not French. My mother sensed that it must be because of you."

"Oh, okay," said Hossein. "And how was your day? How do you like your pediatric rotation?"

"Good, I like it," replied Afsaneh. "But I am not sure if I want to become a pediatrician. I like radiology a lot better."

"Afsaneh, are your parents okay with you leaving Iran?" asked Hossein.

"Yes, they are," replied Afsaneh. "We have several relatives in Paris and in the United States. And guess what? No one in Germany, my dear. No one! And you have no one there, either. I still do not get it. Why do we need to study German?"

"Afsaneh, although you can take your examination in France, going to Germany seems to be my only option." said Hossein. "Last week, I visited the French Embassy, inquiring about getting a visa to take my ECFMG in Paris. You know the French. The clerk at the embassy told me that they no longer issue visas to young Iranians. So many Iranians have gone to France on a visitor's visa and applied for political asylum that they no longer allow us to go there. "

"I also visited British Embassy," continued Hossein. "They did not even allow me inside the embassy. They gave me some crooked answers on the intercom as I was talking to them from the street. On the other hand, I do have a good chance of getting a visa to travel to Germany. I went to the German Embassy and spoke with someone."

"I can take my ECFMG examination in Frankfurt and live there until I can travel to the United States. I know that you have relatives in Paris and you are lucky to have a multiple-entry visa for France. I do not have that."

"You know where I will be taking my examination." said Afsaneh. "In Paris."

The teacher walked in as the two were talking, and began the class.

At the break, Hossein and Afsaneh found a quiet corner to talk.

"I want to leave Iran after we are done with our internship. That is in July. If I do not leave Iran, I will have to go to the front. I do not want to do that either. Naturally, going to a country like Germany can be a next stop for both of us."

"True. But how about Paris? How about London?" asked Afsaneh. "I have relatives in all those places, but no one in Germany."

"Well, if we study German, we can also go to Vienna," said Hossein.

"How about France or England?" asked Afsaneh.

"I already researched this. I went to both embassies," said Hossein. "Perhaps you can try as well. You are a woman, they may respond to you differently."

"Okay. I may do that," said Afsaneh. "What are you doing tomorrow?"

"Studying," replied Hossein.

"How about we study together? Would you like to come to our house?" said Afsaneh. "My father is out of town, and my mother will be in and out. She enjoys cooking for you."

"Let me see how my day evolves tomorrow," said Hossein. "I might have to visit a relative in the morning. I will call you tomorrow. Perhaps I will stop by in the afternoon."

"Try to come. Okay, Hossein?" asked Afsaneh very persistently. "That will make my mother happy."

"Okay, Afsaneh, I will," replied Hossein.

Hossein spent much of his Friday morning at home, studying, and in the late afternoon, he went to Afsaneh's house for dinner.

CHAPTER ELEVEN
THE BRAVE

On Saturday morning, when Hamid returned to his training base, he had a note on his desk to report to the medical clinic.

"Good morning, Hamid. How are you?" asked the nurse.

"Very much the same, thank you." replied Hamid.

"We have made arrangements for you to go to the medical clinic at the military hospital," said the nurse. "You can take the shuttle to the hospital. Your appointment is at ten this morning. You better go now."

Hamid left the room and took the shuttle to the hospital.

The Shah's government had established a military hospital system to provide medical care to all active-duty military personnel and their family members. Since the war broke out in Iran, the military hospital had become the principal trauma center to attend to all army personnel injured in the war. The majority of patients admitted to the hospital were young Iranian soldiers who had sustained combat injuries, mostly having lost arms or legs. As Hamid entered the hospital, he saw many ambulances, each bringing two to three injured soldiers. The operating room of the hospital was active twenty-four hours a day. Most physicians at the hospital were either orthopedic or general surgeons. At the military hospital, almost everyone was dressed in an army uniform.

Hamid found the medical clinic and signed his name on the list of patients awaiting attention. After a short wait, the receptionist called his name, and he went in to see the doctor. The nurse took Hamid to an examination room and had him sit on the examination table. The doctor came. His ID tag read, "Dr. Parsa, Internal Medicine."

"So you are here for an evaluation of your anemia problem," said the doctor.

"That is correct," replied Hamid.

Dr. Parsa asked Hamid several questions about his anemia; he then examined him and reviewed the lab results from the military base.

"To determine the cause of your anemia, we need to perform a detailed medical workup," said the doctor. "We are actually going to admit you to the hospital today, so we can do the entire workup quickly and get you out in a few days."

"That means that I have to stay here?" asked Hamid.

"Yes, you have to stay at the hospital," replied the doctor. "You can call your parents and inform them, so they won't be worried. You will be out before the weekend. We discharge all patients such as you to go home on Thursday evening."

"Thank you, doctor," replied Hamid.

"A few more things," said the doctor. "We will need to draw more blood from you today. We will do a urine test, a cardiogram, and a chest X-ray. You will not be eating anything after ten tonight; you will have two major studies tomorrow morning, a gastroscopy, and a colonoscopy. With the gastroscopy, we send a tube from your mouth into your throat, your esophagus, your stomach, and then your small intestine. You will also have a colonoscopy; that is to look inside your large bowel. The nurse will explain all these to you. You will have to take a preparation for the colonoscopy later today."

"This is all overwhelming for me," said Hamid. "I need to talk to my parents."

"That is a good idea," said the doctor. "You can use the public phones we have here to call home. Your family can also come here to visit you."

Hamid was taken to the medical floor, and he was put in a large ward that had several beds, most of which were occupied by young soldiers with war injuries. Shortly after his arrival, his nurses walked in and provided him with the in-patient hospital clothing. Hamid changed and lay on his bed. Then a lab technician came to take blood from his arm. After the blood was drawn, the technician gave Hamid a cup for a urine test and gave him instructions on how to use it. Hamid got out of his bed and went to the bathroom to provide the urine sample.

He remembered what Hossein had asked him to do. This made him somewhat nervous. The bathroom had a window to the outside courtyard of the hospital. He looked around for a sharp object and noticed that the corner of the small window of the bathroom had a very pointy and sharp edge. He rubbed his right index finger on that corner until he punctured his skin. He dropped a small drop of his blood into the urine cup. He wiped his hand with toilet paper and then urinated in the cup. He placed the cap on the urine cup, flushed the toilet, washed his hands, left the bathroom, and handed the urine cup to the lab technician, and then he went back to his bed to lie down. An hour later, he went for a chest X-ray and a cardiogram.

Later that afternoon, Dr. Parsa came to visit Hamid.

"How are you, Hamid?" asked the doctor.

"I am fine, Dr. Parsa," said Hamid.

"You already know that the hospital is serving the victims of the war," said the doctor. "We need to expedite your workup. We are expecting fifty new patients tomorrow, so I am trying to organize your tests so we can get you out of here tomorrow afternoon."

"I understand. Whatever you think is the best for me and for the hospital," said Hamid.

The next morning, Hamid was taken to the procedure room. He underwent a gastroscopy and a colonoscopy. Dr. Parsa met him in the recovery room.

"Your gastroscopy and colonoscopy were both normal," said the doctor. "You have some blood in your urine. I have discussed this with our urologist. He will be coming by to see you. He told me that you might need a cystoscopy. Once that is done, you will be free to go."

"Thank you so much," replied Hamid.

Dr. Parsa left, and a short while later, another doctor came to visit Hamid.

"Hello soldier, my name is Dr. Tabrizi," said the other doctor. "I am a urologist. I specialize in the diseases of the urinary system. Dr. Parsa asked me to see you because you have blood in your urine. With you being anemic, we need to make sure that you do not have something unusual in your bladder or kidneys. As you are already in here, we may as well do a cystoscopy and look in your bladder."

"What is a cystoscopy, doctor?" asked Hamid.

"We use a rigid steel tube that is about a foot long and insert that inside your penis, and we advance it into your bladder and look in there," said the doctor.

"In my penis?" asked Hamid as his face turned white. "Oh my God, can we do something else instead?" Hamid said.

"Well, Hamid, we do this procedure under sedation," replied the doctor. "We will give you some potent intravenous sedatives that will put you to sleep, and you won't feel anything. The good thing is that you will go home soon after we are done with the procedure today."

"Is it possible to do something else instead?" asked Hamid again, hoping that the doctor might change his mind. "I don't like the idea of the rigid foot-long tube going inside my..."

"No, Hamid, this needs to be done," replied the doctor. "You have blood in your urine. You are anemic. The source of the anemia may be in your bladder."

"Okay then, whatever you say, doctor," replied Hamid.

Deep in his heart, he cursed Hossein. *See what you are putting me through?* said Hamid to Hossein in his heart.

Shortly thereafter, Hamid went to the procedure room for a cystoscopy. This was not a procedure for which Hamid had signed on, but he knew that he had to simply go with the flow.

After the procedure, Hamid went to the recovery room. He spent a few hours there. The recovery room was a large unit with some twenty beds in a long hall, lined up side by side. Next to Hamid were two other young soldiers. The one to the right of Hamid was still asleep with anesthesia. Both his legs were in traction and elevated from his bed. His right arm was in a cast.

To the left of Hamid was another young man who had lost both his legs. He was wide awake and started a conversation with Hamid.

"What happened to you, brother?" asked the solider.

"I just had a cystoscopy; they looked in my bladder," said Hamid. "What about you? What happened to you?"

"I just had my third surgery," said the soldier. "I stepped on a land mine."

"I am so sorry to hear that," replied Hamid. "When did this happen?"

"Two weeks ago," said the soldier. "We were making advances on the Iraqis. We were able to push them back about two kilometers. Apparently as the bastards were heading back, they were planting land mines."

"Do you remember what happened, or how it happened?" asked Hamid.

"I don't know how it happened," replied the solider. "I only remember an explosion and fire. Apparently, I lost consciousness after the incident, and my comrades came to my rescue. They carried me on their backs for about half a kilometer, where they intercepted an ambulance. They took me to the nearest military hospital. I woke the next day, without my legs. They had cut off both my legs above the knees. My wounds became infected, and they sent me here. I have been here for a week now. Today, I had another surgery."

"Oh my God, I am so sorry to hear that," said Hamid. "I am sure you will be up and moving around soon."

"God willing, I should have my artificial limbs in a few months," said the soldier. "I am determined to get on my new feet and learn how to walk and run with them. I want to go back to the front, but they won't let me."

"I am sure you will find a way to fight the Iraqis," replied Hamid.

"I will, and I will stay in the military until we beat and defeat the bastard, Saddam Hussein," said the soldier. "He can take my legs from me, but he cannot take my soul from me. We are not going to let him take our country. We will win this war."

"*Enshallah*," or "God willing," said Hamid. "We will win this war. Saddam is a monster."

As the two were having their conversation about the war, Dr. Tabrizi and Dr. Parsa both came in to talk to Hamid.

"Well, the procedure went well. But I did not find anything that would explain the blood in your urine," said Dr. Tabrizi. "For now, we can watch this problem, continue the workup for anemia, and if needed, I will see you again. In the future, Dr. Parsa will take care of you."

"Thank you, doctor," replied Hamid.

"Our workup so far has not revealed a cause for your anemia," said Dr. Parsa. "We will need to send you to a hematologist, a blood specialist, who can further assess your anemia. We are going to refer you to the hematology clinic at Emam Khomeini Hospital. My office will arrange this for you. We will be in touch with you and tell you what to do next. Your hemoglobin is about 9.5, so you can go back to your base and take it easy. Let's hope that the hemoglobin remains the same. You can either spend the night here tonight, or go back to your base. I leave it up to you."

"I prefer to go back to the base, doctor," said Hamid. "Thank you so much for all the care and attention. I feel fine, and I know that you need the beds for the wounded soldiers coming from the war. I don't want to occupy a bed that someone else may need."

"That is very thoughtful of you, Hamid," said the doctor. "I will arrange for the transportation back to your base. I wish you the best. We will be in touch."

Shortly thereafter, a nurse came and led Hamid to his hospital room, where he changed into his military uniform. The nurse then accompanied him to the shuttle. While in the shuttle, Hamid's mind could not stop thinking about the soldier who had lost his legs.

I did not even ask what his name was, thought Hamid. *What a brave person. He has lost both his legs, but has no doubt in his mind that he has to keep fighting in this war, a war that I don't believe in, a war that I am trying to escape from. Maybe I am wrong. Maybe I should also be fighting in this war. Why should he lose his legs, and I walk out? Am I doing the right thing? Who is right? Maybe I am dead wrong in what I am trying to do. Maybe Hossein also is wrong by doing what he is doing for me. Clearly, what we are doing is totally illegal according to the current beliefs of all those who go to war, all those who lose their lives. What would they think about me? Will I ever be able to keep my head up and tell someone else what I am doing now? Should this story be forgotten? Should this story never be told? Will I ever be able to discuss what I am doing now with someone else? With my future wife? Will I tell my children about this? But then again, maybe I am not wrong. Could dad be wrong? Could Mahmood be wrong? I know many others who would not want to be where I am, and would not want to be a soldier. I know many who have already escaped Iran. I am not sure what is right or wrong anymore. That soldier certainly messed me up. Until this afternoon, I had never doubted my beliefs, but now I doubt everything. Maybe I should give my life to my country and go to the war and fight like that other soldier. Is there a heaven? I think there is.*

With that, tears filled Hamid's eyes. He looked outside to the street and the crowded sidewalks of Tehran.

I don't know anymore, said Hamid to himself. *I wish there was a way for me to distinguish right from wrong. I wish I could just step out and ask those people out there walking on the street. Ask them to help me solve this quandary. In all my life, I have never had to cope with anything as serious as this. I have involved myself in something that is way above me, way beyond my ability to judge its correctness. God, please help me make the right decision. Please talk to me. Tell me what is wrong and what is right.*

Soon the shuttle arrived at the base and Hamid stepped out. He was in a different state. His mind filled with all the philosophical and ethical questions that were germinating in his head since his encounter with the soldier who had lost his legs. His young mind was challenged for the first time; challenged to find answers to series of questions that no one has the right answer for. Hamid was facing the biggest challenge of his life, one that had almost brought him down to his knees and numbed all his senses.

With all these somber thoughts, Hamid walked to the cafeteria of his base. Soldiers had lined up to get their dinner.

The next morning, Hamid returned to his cubicle. On his arrival, he stood and saluted his sergeant.

"Good morning, Sir," said Hamid with a firm military pose and gesture.

"Good morning, Hamid," said the sergeant. "How are you feeling today?"

"I am fine, Sir, ready to serve my country, Sir!" replied Hamid.

"Okay, Hamid," said the sergeant. "I heard from the military-hospital doctor that you need to see a hematologist. They are setting that up for you. As for working here, your duties are very light. We will keep things easy until they figure out what is going on with you and solve that problem. *Enshallah*, everything will be fine, and you will fully recover soon."

"Thank you, Sir," replied Hamid.

"Here is what you need to do today. We need to make a list of outgoing soldiers and take it to the central command office by Thursday afternoon. The rough number of this group is about 450 soldiers. You need to transcribe this list, in alphabetic order, and rewrite it on this form. Also, use this book, and include all addresses, home phone numbers, and parents' names."

"Yes, Sir," replied Hamid.

Hamid sat at his desk in a cubicle near a window on the second floor of his building. He had a view of the ground, where soldiers were marching and practicing battle scenarios. From his window, Hamid could see his old sergeant, his team, and his friends on the common grounds of the base.

On Thursday morning, Hamid finished his assignment and delivered the list to his sergeant.

"Hamid, we received good news for you today," said the sergeant. "The military hospital has made arrangements for you to go to Emam Khomeini Hospital and see a specialist there. Report to the base on Saturday. I will have the shuttle take you to the hospital. Here are your referral papers and your medical records. You need to take all these with you and be there at eleven in the morning. Good luck."

"Thank you, sir," replied Hamid.

At the end of the day, Hamid left the base for home. As he walked outside the base, he saw his brother Mahmood waiting for him in his car. With a smile on his face, Hamid got in the car.

"So many things happened this week," Hamid said.

"You have to tell me all about that," said Mahmood. "By the way, we are picking up Hossein from his hospital, and we are all going to his home for dinner."

"Oh nice, I love Hossein's family home," said Hamid.

Hamid told Mahmood all about the events of the week as the two were driving to get Hossein from his hospital. As Hamid was relating all this, Mahmood understood how touched Hamid was by his conversation with the soldier who had lost his legs. Hamid also talked about all the unsettling thoughts he had after meeting that young soldier.

"Mahmood, I am so confused," said Hamid to his brother. "Do you think that we are doing the right thing? Our country is at war. Thousands of young men have died in the war and here I am, trying to escape from it. How do you think we will be judged for the actions we are taking now?"

"Listen, Hamid, there are always two sides to every story," replied Mahmood. "Do you know why we are at war with Iraq? Do you know who is supporting Iraq now? Do you think Iraq invaded our country without consulting the United States, Britain, and Russia? This war is too complicated. Moreover, our army is not what it was at the time of the Shah. Why did Saddam not attack Iran when the Shah was in power? Instead, he chose to attack us after the fall of the Shah. He is the enemy of our country, and we love Iran, but there comes a time when each Iranian must make the right decision for himself. The right decision for the soldier who lost his legs was to go to war; the right decision for you is what we have already discussed, and we need you alive. We do not want you to die. You know that going to the front is a death sentence. We are trying to avoid that. Furthermore, you are not alone in wanting to avoid the war; tens of thousands of young Iranian men do not want to go to war either. Thousands have already left Iran. Hossein wants to leave Iran too. You already know these things."

Mahmood paused for a while and then continued, "Hamid, I fully understand your situation. You are the one who will ultimately decide what to do. If you genuinely want to serve this country, you can, and I will support that decision. I do understand where you are coming from, but I hate to see you go to war. Mom and dad have lost sleep because of your situation. God forbid, you go to war and something happens to you, or you suffer like the soldier who lost his legs; can you imagine what mom will do? That will simply shorten her life by ten years."

Hamid listened to Mahmood quietly. He had no answers to any points that Mahmood had raised. The rest of the drive to get Hossein continued in silence as the two brothers kept their thoughts to themselves. The silence broke as they arrived at Hossein's hospital.

"Hi, Hossein," said Mahmood, his voice sounding from the inside of his car, and mixing with the noise of a busy Tehran street corner—the roar of the cars and wailing of ambulance sirens.

Hossein got in the back seat of the car, and Mahmood drove away.

"I have to tell you something, Hossein," said Hamid. "This idea of yours, the thing with a drop of blood in urine, I did not know what consequences it would have. I just went ahead and did it."

"Okay, and what happened?" asked Hossein.

"Have you ever had a foot-long, rigid metal pipe shoved up your penis?" asked Hamid.

"Oh my God," said Hossein. "I am so sorry, Hamid. Did you have a cystoscopy?"

"Yes, Hossein," said Hamid. "That is exactly what they did to me. This was a mental and physical torture for me."

"Oh my God, I am sorry to hear that. Are you okay now?" asked Hossein.

"Yes, I am fine now," replied Hamid. "This was quite an embarrassing and painful experience."

"I know, I know," replied Hossein. "I am sorry to hear that, Hamid. What else did they do?"

"I had two endoscopies, upper and lower, plenty of blood tests, a cardiogram, and at the end they set me up to come to your hospital for a consultation with a hematologist," said Hamid. "Here are my medical records."

Hamid handed Hossein a folder containing the medical records that he was supposed to take with him to the hematology consultation. Hossein started reviewing the records.

"Well, they did a thorough workup and could not find the cause of your anemia," said Hossein.

"No wonder," commented Mahmood.

"And you will be seeing Dr. Etemadi," continued Hossein. "I know him well. He always devises the weirdest diagnoses for every patient. I will be curious to see what he will devise for your anemia."

"Hossein, I have a basic question for you," said Hamid. "I was touched by a conversation I had the other day with a soldier who had lost his legs in the war."

"I am sorry to hear that, Hamid. Was he okay?" asked Hossein.

"Yes, he was okay," said Hamid. "I was touched by his devotion to the war and to our country. Do you think we are doing the right thing here, Hossein? Is this the right thing? To mess up the system to get someone out of the military?"

"Woo, Hamid, that is a loaded philosophical question," replied Hossein. "I don't know how to answer that."

Hossein paused for a minute, to think of a proper way to respond to Hamid. He then said, "Let me answer your question this way. The other day, after I was done with my work, instead of taking the usual path I walk home, I took a different path. From a distance, I saw a very bright thing, and as I walked toward it, it became obvious to me that it was a shrine."

"Someone had died and there was a funeral in the neighborhood," continued Hossein. "As I got closer, I noticed that this was a shrine for someone who had just died in the war. These days, you see so many of these shrines; they are all over the place, in practically every neighborhood and in front of every mosque. I usually walk by them and do not pay any attention. This time, however, as I was walking by the shrine, I looked at the picture of the deceased, and to my surprise the person looked familiar. It was as if I knew that person. This caught me up short and I decided to see whether I knew this person. I stopped to read obituary posted on the shrine."

Hossein had to pause for a few seconds, as relating this encounter had made him quite emotional.

"Hamid, I knew that person," continued Hossein. "His name was Javad. He was one of my high school classmates. I remembered that in 1976, at the time of the Shah, after we graduated from high school, he went to the United States to study. Learning about his death made me extremely sad.

On the spur of moment, because the funeral was in progress right there and then, I decided to go in and pay my respects. Although I knew Javad, I did not know any of his family. They were holding the funeral in their home. The doors were open for visitors. I could hear verses of the Quran read aloud. A few men were standing at the door, greeting the visitors. I introduced myself. One of the men was Javad's brother. He accompanied me to their family room, where men were sitting on the floor, leaning against the four walls of that room. From a distance, I could hear the cries of several women in another room. Javad's brother introduced me to his father and I sat next to him. I talked to him for a while, and told him who I was and how I knew his son.

"'My son Javad loved his country,' his father said to me. 'He went to study in the United States. For the past year, he always wanted to come back and go to war and fight Saddam Hussein. I insisted that he should stay in the United States, but he argued every time and wanted to return to Iran and serve his country. I persuaded him at least to finish his studies, which he agreed to. He got his masters in civil engineering. He returned two months ago, and the next day he went to sign up to join the Army Corps of Engineers. With only one month of training, he went to the front, and then last week he died when a bomb hit their shelter.'"

"His father could not stop crying, Hamid," said Hossein. "Can you imagine being a father, raising a son, sending him to the United States so he gets his masters in engineering, then losing him like that? What a loss that is. Hamid, I felt so bad. I held back my tears until I got home that night and was alone in my room. I knew this person. He was my high school classmate. Whom can we blame for his loss? I do not know. Is there anyone to blame? Does any of this matter anymore? He is dead, gone, and does not exist anymore."

"I think about these issues slightly differently," said Hossein. "I am studying medicine so that I can save *lives*, a very simple principle. Therefore, I will never bear a weapon; I will never fire a bullet at anyone, even if it is the enemy of my country. I also love Iran. Iran is my country too. I was born here. I have roots here. I have family and friends here. But I think that a person who is alive can help Iran more than a dead person. I have simplified this for myself. I do not want to kill anyone; I do not want to be killed. I want to become a doctor, an exceptionally good one, so that I can help people. If I am in Iran, I will help my own compatriots. If I happen to leave Iran, and even if I never return to Iran, I will help whomever who may be ill and whomever I can heal. Don't all of us remember what our epic poet, Saadi said?" Hossein recited the poem.

Human beings are members of a whole,

In creation of one essence and soul.

If one member is afflicted with pain,

Other members uneasy will remain.

If you've no sympathy for human pain,

The name of human you cannot retain!

"This is what our beloved poet Saadi wrote several centuries ago," continued Hossein. "It is natural for us to feel the pain and suffering of others. What you felt was a pure sense of compassion for someone your own age who had sustained serious war injuries. Do not forget, we are all human beings, and we all have emotions. I have my own emotions. I have my own feelings. But how do we make sense of all this? How do we put things in perspective and decide what is right or wrong? I think, somewhere up in our brains, sitting next to our emotions and feelings, there must reside our logical being, our common sense, our ability to see reality clearly and to bring some degree of clarity to our lives."

"My logical being tells me that I should become an exceptionally good physician, so I can help people and save as many lives as I can," continued Hossein. "To that end, the reason that I decided to do what I have done for you thus far, is to simply save another life—in this case, your life. Hamid, regardless of how others judge us, no matter what others may think about our actions, if we succeed in what we are doing, we will save your life. To me, going to war is like developing a life-threatening disease, like having a heart attack, which can kill you. You should think this through, and if you genuinely want to go to war, I will support that decision. If, on the other hand, you chose to pursue what we have already started, I will be glad to help you with that as well."

Hossein paused for a minute, turning his head to look out the window of the car. Gazing at people walking on the sidewalks, Hossein started thinking.

Woo, why did I agree to do this? I have far too many things to worry about, and now I have to cope with all the emotional difficulties. Well, nothing big ever works perfectly. Hamid is so young. He is just out of high school. He is quite stressed and nervous. I am not sure what he will decide, but I will not back out on him. I will stay the course. If he chooses to continue this plan, I will help him. And if he chooses to go to war, which is certainly his prerogative, I will have to stay out of that. That will be between him and his family. To that end, I will just extend my help, as I have already done. It will be up to him to accept my help. I will not impose anything on him.

The three remained silent for a while. Mahmood was driving through the busy streets toward Hossein's House. After a short while, Hamid burst into tears and said:

"I do not know, Hossein," as his voice was shattered with emotions and cries. "I am sorry for all this. You are a great person, and I know that you want to help me. And I do not want to die. I am so depressed and confused now."

"Hamid, we are all here to help you," said Mahmood. "No matter what you decide, we will support you, but as your older brother, I think what we started with Hossein is the right thing to do. Do not let anything derail you from the path we chose several weeks ago. In the future, and as you grow older, you will come across many more situations like this. Just stay the course, Hamid. Okay?"

"Okay, Mahmood," replied Hamid.

Halfway to Hossein's house, Hamid broke the heavy silence and said, "Hossein, when can you do my next blood draw?"

"How about right now, as we have done before?" replied Hossein.

Mahmood's face brightened as he heard the conversation between Hamid and Hossein. He pulled over on a quiet side street. Hossein pulled out his needles and vacuum bottle. By the time they arrived at Hossein's house, they had completed everything. Hossein had drawn the blood, and Hamid was feeling a lot better emotionally. They entered Hossein's house together. Hamid's parents were already there. Everyone greeted the three men. Hamid's dad hugged his two sons and Hossein, and he kissed them on their cheeks. All of them sat as Hossein's mom served tea for everyone.

"Dinner will be ready in about half an hour," Hossein's mom announced.

"Haj Agha, let me show you our garden," said Hossein. "Our persimmon tree is full of ripe persimmons now."

With that, Hamid, his Dad, and Mahmood walked out with Hossein to enjoy the garden.

"Haj Agha, I just wanted to update you about where we are with Hamid," said Hossein in the privacy and quiet of the garden. "He is doing well, and everything is going smoothly. On Saturday, Hamid will be coming in to my hospital for a hematology consultation. I think it will be a good idea for you to come in and be there with him, meet with the hematologist, and show that you are concerned about his health. Ask the doctor all kinds of questions; what he thinks is going on, what is the prognosis, what kind of treatments Hamid may need, and so on. I know the doctor Hamid is going to see. He will most likely want to do a bone-marrow test. He does this on almost every patient. So be ready for that, Hamid."

"What is a bone-marrow test?" asked Hamid.

"Bone marrow is the organ that makes blood," replied Hossein. "It is diffusely spread and located inside the bones, mostly in your pelvic bones, spine, ribs, and skull and so on. A bone-marrow test is done by taking a sample of bone marrow from the pelvic bone."

Hossein pointed to his own back and said, "From here, Hamid."

"Will that hurt?" asked Haj Agha.

Hossein turned to Haj Agha and said, "Hamid will see Dr. Etemadi. He is quite good at doing this procedure."

Hossein turned back to Hamid and said, "He uses plenty of anesthetics, so you will have very little discomfort. I think this will be your last procedure. I cannot think of any other procedures that anybody would want to do on you. I will try to be in the clinic when you are there. But I think our risk will be less if we do not show that we know each other, so please act as if you do not know me at all. Come in as a regular patient. I will try to stay out of your sight, so you do not have to see me, but I want to know what Dr. Etemadi will think about your anemia. Okay?"

“Okay, Hossein Jaan. We don’t know you at all,” said Haj Agha. “At least this Saturday.”

“Let’s pick some persimmons and take them inside,” said Hamid, and with that, he reached out and picked a few of the bright orange fruits from the tree.

CHAPTER TWELVE
THE PATIENT

Saturday morning, Hossein went to the hospital early, finished his morning rounds, and went to the hematology clinic of Dr. Etemadi just in time for Hamid's appointment. The clinic was a busy place, with several residents, interns, and medical students wandering around and seeing patients. Afsaneh also was in the clinic.

"Hey, what are you doing here, Afsaneh?" asked Hossein.

"My uncle is a patient of Dr. Etemadi. He is not doing well. I have brought him here to be seen today."

"Is he okay?" asked Hossein.

"He is quite anemic," said Afsaneh. "He is not eating well. His internist wanted him to come back and have Dr. Etemadi see him."

"Let's go and find him," said Hossein.

Afsaneh and Hossein spotted Dr. Etemadi as he walked out of a consultation room with a group of residents. Hossein discretely looked in, and saw that Hamid and his father were there. Dr. Etemadi pulled all the interns and residents aside in a corner of the hallway. Hossein and Afsaneh approached Dr. Etemadi and greeted him.

"Good to see you two. Want to join us in our discussion?" asked Dr. Etemadi. "We just saw a young person with an interesting clinical picture."

"Yes, Dr. Etemadi," said Hossein.

"Please give us a summary of this case," said Dr. Etemadi to one of the residents.

"This is a nineteen-year-old male, recently diagnosed with anemia," said the resident who had seen Hamid with Dr. Etemadi. "He has had a negative workup, including gastroscopy, colonoscopy and a cystoscopy. He is here for a hematology consultation. His physical examination was negative. His blood count today shows hemoglobin of 8.5 with a low retic count of 0.5 percent. Iron studies, vitamin B12, and folic acid are normal."

"Nice summary," said Dr. Etemadi.

"What is your differential diagnosis?" asked Dr. Etemadi of the resident. With that, Hossein's heart started racing and pounding. He could not wait to hear the conclusions that they had reached.

"I am not sure—there is no bleeding, the iron studies are normal, the retic count is low, and his white-blood cell count also is on the low side," said the resident. "So I think this young man may have a primary bone-marrow disorder."

"Very good, I am impressed," said Dr. Etemadi. "Any ideas what he might have? How would you work him up? We need an answer for him. He is young," said Dr. Etemadi.

"I think he needs a bone-marrow test," replied the resident.

"And your working diagnosis is?" asked Dr. Etemadi.

The resident remained silent. He could not answer. Hossein's heart was pounding. Afsaneh was silent.

"I don't expect you to know this, but this young man most likely has *myelodysplastic syndrome*," said Dr. Etemadi. "I am fairly sure that this is what he has."

Hearing the diagnosis, Hossein was relieved.

This will work, Hossein thought. For a moment, he separated himself from where he was, and started thinking about the next steps to take.

"What is myelodysplastic syndrome?" whispered Afsaneh in Hossein's ear, breaking Hossein's chain of thought as he was brainstorming his next several steps.

"I will tell you later," replied Hossein. "Let's listen to Dr. Etemadi."

"Let's get a bone-marrow tray," said Dr. Etemadi to the resident. "Let's do his bone marrow and get him out of here."

"Hossein, you are very good at doing bone marrows. Would you like to perform the aspiration and the biopsy on this patient?" asked Dr. Etemadi.

Hossein's heart started racing again. The idea of him doing a bone marrow biopsy on Hamid was simply not acceptable to him. In a fraction of second, he had to come up with at an excuse not to do the procedure on his cousin.

"I would love too, but this may be a good opportunity for someone else to practice the procedure. I have done plenty of bone marrow biopsies."

"Good point Hossein. Who wants to do this bone marrow?"

"May I do this procedure?" replied one of the residents who had seen Hamid with Dr. Etemadi.

"Sure. Go right ahead, and let me know if you run into any issues," said Dr. Etemadi to the resident who had volunteered.

Hossein knew that Hamid would curse him once again because of the pain and discomfort of the bone marrow biopsy. This was another painful procedure that Hossein was putting Hamid through. Hossein knew, though, that not only was it necessary, it also was the most crucial procedure for the success of his plan. Hamid's release from the military, his own travel outside Iran, his future career, and everything that he had dreamed about depended on this one particular test. There was no way around it. Deep in his heart, he just hoped that Haj Agha would object to the resident doing the procedure, and would demand for Dr. Etemadi to do it. But he had no way to relay this to Hamid and Haj Agha.

"Who is the next patient?" asked Dr. Etemadi.

"Dr. Etemadi, my uncle is your next patient," said Afsaneh.

As Afsaneh was talking to Dr. Etemadi, Hossein saw Afshin, the young leukemia patient who was going to England.

Hossein said, "One of my patients is here. May I be excused for fifteen minutes to see this patient?"

"Of course you may," replied Dr. Etemadi.

Hossein walked over to Afshin, who was there with his father.

"Hello Mr. Gohari, hello Afshin. How are you?" said Hossein.

"Hello, doctor, I am fine," replied Afshin. "We are here to see Dr. Nikbin one last time before we go to England."

"So everything worked out?" asked Hossein.

"Yes, we are all set," said Mr. Gohari, Afshin's father. "We have all the passports and visas that we need. We will be leaving next week."

"I am glad to hear that. Do you mind if I ask you some questions?" said Hossein to Mr. Gohari.

"Of course you may."

"I am curious to know how long it took for the health ministry to approve your application," said Hossein.

"We put in our application about three months ago, and got all the approvals about one month ago," said Mr. Gohari. "And for the medical expenditure, they allow us to get ten thousand dollars at the bank's exchange rate, which is about half the rate on the street. If we need more money to exchange, we will have to send them the medical invoices. The central bank will then allow us to wire the funds to England."

"Thank you so much. I wish all of you the best and hope to see all of you well and healthy in a few months," said Hossein to Afshin and his father.

"All the best to you too doctor. See you in few months," replied Afshin.

Shortly after his visit with Afshin, Hossein joined Afsaneh and Dr. Etemadi. The visit with Afsaneh's uncle had concluded, and Dr. Etemadi suggested that the residents and Hossein to go to the laboratory and see the bone-marrow samples taken from Hamid.

"Who did this bone marrow?" asked Dr. Etemadi as he was looking in the microscope.

"I did, sir," replied the medical resident who had performed the procedure.

"This is a good specimen," said Dr. Etemadi. "You did a good job. Look. Do you see these cells in the middle? These are red blood cell precursors; there are far too many of them there, and his retic count was low. Correct?"

"Yes, 0.5 percent," replied the resident.

"Look at the margins of the red cell nuclei," said Dr. Etemadi. "The nuclear margins are slightly abnormal. This patient has myelodysplastic syndrome. All of you should look at this bone marrow, and then read about it. Let me write my report for him. Where is his paperwork?"

"Here, sir," replied the resident.

"How do we treat this disease?" asked Dr. Etemadi.

There was a moment of silence among the residents.

"We don't have any treatments for this disease," said Dr. Etemadi. "Some of these patients end up developing leukemia in a few years. If he is lucky enough to go overseas, he can be considered for a bone-marrow transplant. For now, however, while his hemoglobin is above eight and he is not symptomatic, we do not do anything. If his hemoglobin drops below seven, we will transfuse him."

"Okay, guys, let's go and talk to him. I feel sorry for his father," said Dr. Etemadi. "All of you let me do the talking."

"May I be excused, Dr. Etemadi?" said Hossein. "I have to attend a noon lecture now."

"Oh please," replied Dr. Etemadi. "All of you who have noon lectures may go. Thank you for attending the clinic today. We indeed saw several interesting patients."

Hossein left the clinic on purpose, simply because he did not want to be in the room with Hamid and his father. Afsaneh was walking in the distance, in front of Hossein, accompanying her uncle to the main lobby of the hospital. Hossein followed her and waited for her to say goodbye to her uncle. In the minute or two that Hossein was waiting for Afsaneh, his mind was busy thinking about Hamid.

Woo. Myelodysplastic syndrome, thought Hossein. *That is a good one. With this, we will get him out of the military with no problems. We can also get him permission to go overseas for treatment. We just need to keep up with the weekly blood draws and keep his hemoglobin between nine and ten. That way, he will be fine and won't have too many symptoms, and if someone checks his hemoglobin, he will be anemic until his military-exemption card is issued and is in his hands."*

"You look so thoughtful, so concerned. Are you okay, Hossein?" said Afsaneh as she approached him in the main lobby of the hospital.

"Yes, I am fine, Afsaneh," replied Hossein. "I am glad to see you. I wanted to talk to you."

"Sure, what's up?" asked Afsaneh.

"Have you completed your ECFMG examination application?" asked Hossein. "We need to mail them soon."

"No, I have not," replied Afsaneh.

"Are you going to?" asked Hossein. "I am going to the bank first thing tomorrow morning to exchange money and get a check in U.S. dollars for the examination's registration fee," said Hossein.

"Can you also get me a bank check?" asked Afsaneh.

"Will be happy to," replied Hossein.

"Hossein, how about you come to our house tonight for dinner?" asked Afsaneh. "My mother likes you so much and will be happy to make you your favorite dish. We can complete the applications together, and I can give you money for my application fee," she said.

"Sure, Afsaneh, how about seven tonight?" asked Hossein.

"Seven sounds good. See you then," replied Afsaneh.

Later that night, Hossein went to Afsaneh's home. He rang the bell, and Afsaneh opened the door for him. She invited Hossein to come in, showing him the way to the dining room.

"Thank you, Afsaneh. How was your day today?" asked Hossein.

"It was good until you left. Come inside. I will tell you all about it," said Afsaneh.

"What happened?" asked Hossein.

Hossein and Afsaneh sat at the dining-room table. Soon after, Mrs. Borhan, Afsaneh's mother, came in. Hossein stood to greet her.

"Hello, Mrs. Borhan. How are you?" said Hossein as he extended his hand to her.

"Hello, Hossein Jaan, welcome to our home. How are you doing today?" asked Mrs. Borhan as she firmly shook Hossein's hand.

"I am fine, Mrs. Borhan, thank you for asking," replied Hossein.

Hossein sat next to Afsaneh and her mother at the dining table.

"So how are your German studies coming along, Hossein?" said Mrs. Borhan, with a gentle smile on her face. With that comment all of them laughed.

"Coming along fine, Mrs. Borhan," replied Hossein, as he was trying to control his own laughter. "Mrs. Borhan, for many Iranians, life in the past few years has become more difficult. I am sure you already know that Afsaneh and I both intend to leave Iran in the summer. Afsaneh has told you that already."

"Yes, she has," replied Mrs. Borhan.

"And how are you going to leave Iran?" asked Mrs. Borhan.

Hossein had to pause for a minute. He could not disclose details of his plans to Mrs. Borhan.

"I have talked to a smuggler who can take me out of Iran," replied Hossein.

"A smuggler will take you where?" asked Mrs. Borhan. "You will go to Turkey or Pakistan, correct? And how will you reach Germany from there?"

"With the paperwork for the examination, I will be able to get a visa to go to Germany," said Hossein. "I have already discussed this with the German Embassy here."

"Are you sure, Hossein?" said Mrs. Borhan. "This sounds rather risky."

"Very true, Mrs. Borhan," replied Hossein. "I just cannot stay in Iran, get drafted into the military, and go to war. I must leave Iran. Fortunately, the story is different for Afsaneh, as women are exempt from military service. She already has a passport with a valid French visa. She can also easily get a visa to Germany and fly nonstop from Tehran to Frankfurt."

"We are also going to look into England and France," said Afsaneh.

"Anyway, you two are adults," said Mrs. Borhan. "You know what you are doing. I support both of you in your endeavors and wish you the best of luck. Let's eat dinner. Mr. Borhan will be coming home late tonight."

"Mom, let me tell you what happened today at the hospital." said Afsaneh. "Hossein and I were talking in the lobby of the hospital, and apparently two of the very devout female interns, members of the Islamic Association, saw us. Do you know how they dress, Mom?"

"Yes dear, I can imagine how they dress," said Mrs. Borhan. "A tight black scarf covering their hair, and a long brown coat, and perhaps a white lab coat over all that."

"And a pair of dark eyeglasses," added Hossein.

"They came to talk to me right after you left," said Afsaneh as she looked at Hossein. "They told me that it is not proper for me to be talking to you in public. They told me that they knew that you and I have something going on, and that all public interactions between men and women have to be limited to work and nothing else."

"I cannot believe this," said Mrs. Borhan.

"Are you serious, Afsaneh? They told you that?" asked Hossein.

"Yes and even more," continued Afsaneh. "Get ready to hear this Mom. One of them said that talking to Hossein about non work-related matters would seriously jeopardize my chances of getting into a residency program here in the next year. That is, if they see me in public with him, as they saw us today."

"Who are they?" asked Mrs. Borhan.

"They are members of the medical school's Islamic Association," said Afsaneh. "They are the most devout group of Muslim students, and have gained a lot of power now."

"And what did you tell them?" asked Hossein.

"Nothing, I just walked away," replied Afsaneh. "I would not talk to those people. What would you have told them if you were in my position, Hossein?"

"I don't know," said Hossein. "Their male counterparts once came to talk to me as well."

"Really?" asked Afsaneh.

"You know this tall skinny guy, who talks with a thick *Esfahani* accent?" said Hossein.

"Yes, I think I know who you are talking about," said Afsaneh.

"The other day, after the last lecture of the day, he came to talk to me," said Hossein. "I have never, not even once, had any form of conversation with this guy. He hangs out with his own clan. He caught up with me as I was leaving the hospital. He first recited some verses from the Quran and then said to me, 'Listen up, you wise guy, you have to clean up your act. You must act in a more Islamic manner. You laugh too much,' he told me, and he said that I didn't have respect for the Islamic Association."

"And what did you tell him?" Mrs. Borhan asked.

"I told him, 'I don't know what you are talking about. I do not laugh. I fully respect everyone's views, and all I care about are my studies and nothing else. I don't belong to your group in much the same way that I don't belong to any other groups.' He continued his nonsense for a while, and at the end, he told me that, if necessary, he would be the one who will bring in a G3 semiautomatic rifle and cleanse the University of bad and corrupt people. Mrs. Borhan, at that point, I simply said goodbye to him and left. This is why I want to leave this country. These guys think that by growing a beard and looking dirty and unclean, they can rule everyone. This guy is presumably a future physician of our country. I am becoming a physician to save lives, and he talks about bringing in a G3 semiautomatic weapon to kill. This is simply sickening."

"I totally understand you, Hossein," said Mrs. Borhan.

"I have said my farewell to Iran," said Hossein. "I am leaving this country. I only hope that Afsaneh will be able to come along, and I hope that we can share a life together."

"Afsaneh, what do you think?" asked Mrs. Borhan.

"I am not happy with the situation either," said Afsaneh. "I would love to continue my studies elsewhere. Leaving Iran for me is a lot easier. I feel bad for Hossein, because leaving Iran for him is lot harder than it is for me."

After dinner, Mrs. Borhan kept herself busy in the kitchen. Hossein and Afsaneh reviewed their applications, laughed, joked, and talked about what their future might be like.

"Hossein, if all goes as planned, how soon you think we will be able to start our residencies in the United States?" asked Afsaneh.

"I am not sure, Afsaneh," replied Hossein, "because there are so many steps between where we are now and where we want to be. If all goes well, it will be about a year and a half, July 1984, when you and I will be able to start our residencies in the United States."

"That is such a long time," said Afsaneh.

"But that is our only real chance to succeed in life and get somewhere," said Hossein. "The alternative for me is to stay in Iran and serve in the military for two years. If I survive the two years, then I will have to do three years of civil service in a remote location in Iran. It is only then that I can do my residency training here. So for me, if I stay in Iran, I will start my residency five and half years from now, and if I leave Iran and go to the United States, I have a chance to start my residency in one and half years. Indeed, I will have finished my internal-medicine residency in the United States when our male classmates will just be starting their residencies here in Iran. And I am sure that you know what I would prefer to do."

"Very true, Hossein," said Afsaneh.

"But you can start a residency here if you like," said Hossein to Afsaneh.

"I don't know," said Afsaneh. "I am confused. On the one hand, I would like to leave Iran; and on the other hand, I may be able to continue my training here without too many interruptions. Lately, there has been talk about female graduates such as me having to do civil service in remote areas too. If that becomes mandatory, I will also have to work in a village for at least two years before I can start a residency here."

"That is very true," said Hossein. "You need to take that into consideration. Do you still want to register for the examination?" asked Hossein.

"That, I want to do," said Afsaneh, with tears forming in her eyes. "But living in Germany for a year is difficult for me to conceptualize now. You know, Hossein, I love you, and I want to be with you, and I certainly do not want to stand between you and your education."

"Since you have a valid visa to go to France, I suggest you choose Paris as your examination center," said Hossein. "I chose Frankfurt, and hope that I will be able to reach Germany in time to take the test. No matter what, we will reunite in Europe. Either I will come to Paris to be with you, or you will come to Germany. Let's worry about that later. At this point, our postgraduate training takes precedence over love."

"I would be happy if we were to stay here and live together, no matter what, no matter how I must dress," said Afsaneh.

"Let's talk about this another time," said Hossein. "I don't want to see you getting all emotional over this. We cannot make all the decisions in one night. We will have plenty of time to decide what we want to do with our lives. Worse comes to worst, we will both stay in Iran and do what everybody else does. But for now, we both need to focus on the most important things. We have examinations coming up in a few days, so please do not become emotional over anything. Also, let's get these applications in the mail as soon as we can."

"Are you going to the bank tomorrow?" asked Afsaneh.

"Yes, first thing tomorrow morning," Hossein replied.

"Here is the money for my application," said Afsaneh. "Thank you for doing this for me Hossein."

"Before we can mail these, there is one more thing we need to do," said Hossein. "Our signatures need to be notarized by an official agency recognized by the United States."

"Who or where can we take these applications to get them notarized?" asked Afsaneh.

"Here are the instructions," replied Hossein. "Applicants living outside the United States must sign here before a notary at a U.S. consulate in their home country."

"Let me read the section," said Afsaneh, taking the application. "Well, it does not say anything about applicants who live in countries where the United States does not have an embassy or consulate. What should we do? Where do we take this for notarization? They don't make it easy for us Iranians, do they?"

"First thing tomorrow morning, on my way to the bank, I will stop at the old U.S. Embassy complex to inquire about this," said Hossein. "Outside the doors, there are usually plenty of Islamic guards and *basijis*. They must know."

"Are you serious, Hossein?" asked Afsaneh in a surprised manner. "Wasn't the U.S. Embassy taken over by the students? Have you forgotten the hostage crisis already? What are you thinking, Hossein? The guards there are all anti-American. They will shoot you there."

"Okay, okay, Afsaneh," smiled Hossein. "That was just a joke, my dear."

"I heard it too," said Mrs. Borhan. "That was a good one, Hossein."

All of them laughed and laughed.

"You, Hossein," said Afsaneh. "*Naa-mard*. For a second I took you seriously. I am so used to taking everything you say so seriously."

"Anyway," said Hossein. "The only place I can think of is the embassy of Switzerland. The Swiss represent U.S. interests in Iran. That is the only place we can take these forms to."

"I did not know that," said Afsaneh. "Do you know whether Iran also has a similar representation in the United States?"

"Yes, we do," said Mrs. Borhan, as she overheard their conversation and laughter.

"Our interest section in the United States is in the Embassy of Pakistan."

"Remember when we were in high school, when we had to take the logical-reasoning quizzes?" asked Hossein of Afsaneh. "Something like the relationship of a circle to a sphere is like a square to a …? The answer was a cube. Want to hear a new one?"

"Yes, I remember that," said Afsaneh. "Tell us."

"The relationship of the United States to Switzerland is like relationship of Iran to…" said Hossein.

"The answer is… Pakistan," said Afsaneh.

They all laughed, and enjoyed some tea and dessert.

"When do you think we can go to get these notarized?" asked Afsaneh of Hossein.

"Tomorrow I will be going to the bank, how about Thursday at lunch break?" replied Hossein. "I will call them tomorrow to see if they can do this for us."

"With all those Islamic guards and the student Islamic Association, it is best that they don't see us leaving the hospital together," said Afsaneh. "Let's go there separately and meet there."

CHAPTER THIRTEEN
THE SARRAF

Early the next morning, Hossein was at the doorstep of Tehran's Central Bank, where he found himself in a growing line of people waiting to get inside. The bank doors opened promptly at eight a.m., at which point the previously orderly single-file line rapidly transformed into a boisterous and chaotic mass of people rushing to get into the bank ahead of everyone else. The Central Bank of Tehran had a spacious rectangular lobby with several counters, separated by wide Roman columns. Once Hossein was inside the bank, and the initial hurried commotion had subsided, he joined the line in front of the counter that handled foreign-currency transactions. With several others in front of him, he knew he would be waiting awhile. A painfully slow hour passed until finally it was his turn.

"What do you need?" the bank clerk asked abruptly. He was a relatively young, thin, dark-skinned man, with a huge beard and darkened glasses. He eyed Hossein suspiciously, in the same way he had to the customer before him, and the customer before that. It was as though he assumed everyone he encountered was attempting to commit some form of crime.

"I need two certified checks, each in the amount of 250 U.S. dollars," said Hossein.

"Who are you sending the money to?" asked the bank clerk, still regarding him uneasily.

"To ECFMG, the Educational Commission for Foreign Medical Graduates, to register for a medical examination," replied Hossein calmly, undeterred by the clerk's direct questioning.

"So this is going to the United States?" asked the bank clerk.

"Yes, sir," said Hossein.

"We cannot do that," said the clerk dismissively. Hossein said nothing. After few seconds of silence, the clerk sighed. "Wait here for a minute. I will ask my supervisor."

Hossein watched as the bank clerk walked to a middle-aged, bearded supervisor pacing behind the counters. After a dubiously short conversation, the clerk returned.

"As I said, we cannot do this."

"Why not?" asked Hossein.

"We are not authorized to issue or transfer funds to any entities in the land of the Great Satan, the United States."

Hossein chose not to argue with the clerk. It was pointless. He simply said, "Thank you" and "Goodbye" to the clerk and quietly left the bank. As he was walking along Ferdowsi Avenue, not far from the bank, Hossein noticed several *sarrafis*, private currency exchange agencies that work independent of the banks. He walked across the street and entered the first *sarrafi* he saw. Hossein had never dealt with such agencies before, but he knew their purpose. *Sarrafis* were private entities that were in the business of exchanging Iranian Rials for foreign currencies. They dealt mostly with cash. Naturally, the exchange rates these dealers offered were more costly to their customers than the bank's. The Central Bank of Iran had extremely tight limits on the amount of foreign currency an approved traveler could purchase. International currency markets did not accept Iran's currency, the Rial, so Iranians planning to travel abroad had to exchange their money in Iran, before they left. Depending on the purpose of the trip, the bank would exchange only between five hundred and three thousand dollars per traveler. Travelers requiring a larger amount had no choice but to do business with a *sarrafi*.

The *sarrafi* had a normal-looking storefront, its wide windows opening directly onto the street. Hossein walked in and the *sarraf*, or currency dealer or storeowner, greeted him. The *sarraf* was a middle-aged man wearing a dark-grey suit, sitting behind a desk sparsely adorned with a black rotary phone and a calculator.

"Hello, sir. I was wondering if you could help me with a currency exchange matter," said Hossein.

"Sure, what do you need?" answered the *sarraf*.

"I need two checks, each for 250 U.S. dollars, written to an entity in the United States. Can you issue checks in U.S. dollars?" He asked, unable to disguise the hopefulness from his voice.

"You need two checks?" asked the *sarraf*.

"Yes, two checks," replied Hossein.

"Please have a seat," said the *sarraf*. "Allow me to make a phone call."

The *sarraf* picked up the handset of his old-fashioned phone and deftly dialed a phone number he had clearly committed to memory. A short conversation took place entirely in Armenian, and seemed to end abruptly. The *sarraf* replaced the receiver and regarded Hossein with a smile on his face. This looked much more promising.

"Today is your lucky day," he said. "I can get you the checks you need in ten minutes. The charge for each is twenty-five U.S. dollars. Your total will be $550. I assume you will be paying in rials?"

"Yes, sir," replied Hossein.

Hossein paid the sum as requested and watched intently as a young man walked in and handed two typewritten checks to the *sarraf*, each for 250 U.S. dollars. The *sarraf* instructed Hossein on how to fill in the blanks. Happy with his completed transaction, Hossein left the *sarrafi*, caught the attention of a dozing taxi driver parked on the street, and made his way to his hospital.

On his lunch break that Thursday, Hossein left his hospital in a taxi, and went to the Swiss Embassy. Afsaneh had already arrived and was waiting for him by the entrance.

The embassy was relatively quiet, with few people at the door. Hossein and Afsaneh talked to the guards and showed them their papers. Once the guards were satisfied with the presented documents, they escorted the two of them into the complex without further questions. The embassy was in a modest, three-story building in a suburb of Tehran, on the northern side of the street. Hossein and Afsaneh obediently and silently followed the escort inside the embassy, passing through the front courtyard and entering the office building. Walking briskly, the escort led Hossein and Afsaneh down a corridor and into a waiting area.

"Please have a seat here," said the escort. "Someone will be with you shortly."

The waiting area served several rooms. One of the doors had a sign on it that read, "Foreign Interest Section." Since the United States and Iran had abandoned their diplomatic relations, the Swiss government was acting, through its embassy in Tehran, to serve and protect the interest of the United States in Iran. The embassy's foreign interest section provided consular services to U.S. citizens living or traveling in Iran. Most visitors to the foreign interest section, however, were Iranians who also held U.S. citizenship.

After a few minutes, a young, blue-eyed and blond Swiss man entered the waiting area and greeted Hossein and Afsaneh in Farsi.

"*Salam*, my name is Peter Werner," said the man. "What brings you here today?"

"Good afternoon Mr. Werner. We are planning to participate in an American medical examination," said Hossein. "Our application forms need to be signed before a notary. Would you be able to notarize our signatures on these two forms?"

"Of course," said the Mr. Werner. "Please follow me to my desk."

Hossein and Afsaneh followed Mr. Werner to his office.

"Please have a seat here. I will be right back," said Mr. Werner.

Hossein smiled politely, his plan was finally coming together. He and Afsaneh took their seats and waited.

As opposed to the rest of Tehran, the Swiss Embassy was a peaceful and civilized place. Just a few yards away from this building was a bustling and oppressed city under daily attacks from Iraqi warplanes and long-range missiles. Inside the embassy, however, there was an indisputable feeling of peace, comfort, and freedom. Being there felt to Hossein and Afsaneh as though they had somehow been transported away from the anarchy and oppression of Tehran and delivered into a true European environment. Female staff members were dressed in Western clothing, as is common of all women in modern societies, strikingly different from the Iranian women living just outside the walls of the embassy. The Islamic government of Iran enforced a dress code for all women, ordering them always to cover their hair and bodies using plain and muted fabrics of gray, brown, black, or dark blue. No woman could dress in yellow or light green, for example. But inside the embassy, there was no trace of this dress code.

"Look, Afsaneh," said Hossein. "The Islamic laws certainly are not enforced inside the walls of this complex. Here, we are in Europe; outside we are in Iran. This is freedom; this is what our life should be like."

"Yes, I did notice that," said Afsaneh, smiling and scanning the room again. "Let's get our signatures notarized and go back to the hospital. Where did he go?"

Shortly thereafter, Mr. Werner returned with a box that contained his notary stamp.

"Please sign here, on this dotted line," said Mr. Werner to Hossein.

"You too, please," said Mr. Werner to Afsaneh.

"Thank you so much," said Hossein to Mr. Werner. "We appreciate your help. Is there a charge for this service?"

"You are most welcome," replied Mr. Werner as he handed the notarized forms back to Hossein and Afsaneh. "There is no charge for this service. I wish both of you the best. Study hard to pass this test on your first attempt. Good luck to both of you."

Hossein and Afsaneh got their papers back from Mr. Werner, said goodbye to him, and walked through the corridor toward the exit sign.

"On the way back to the hospital, I will stop at the post office to send these out by certified mail," said Hossein.

Afsaneh stopped for a moment, looked at Hossein and said, "Thank you for all your help, Hossein."

Hossein simply nodded. They continued walking toward the door and into the open-air courtyard at the front, which separated the main building from the entrance gate.

The two took their time walking slowly toward the gate. They had felt and smelled the air of freedom within their oppressed country, and this offered them a momentary taste of what life could be like. They were enthused and inspired by an unfamiliar feeling of liberty, unobstructed by the laws in effect just a few yards away, outside the embassy walls. Relaxed and carefree, they held each other's hands and walked with smiles on their faces, feeling safe and wrapped in a comfort and freedom that would last only until they reached the front doors once more. To them, this moment, the freedom to hold hands, something that they could never do in a public place, was so precious. The desire to prolong the moment was strong and caused them to walk slowly, languishing in the comfortable unfamiliarity. But both knew that this feeling was fleeting; reality was waiting for them just outside the embassy walls.

The door loomed menacingly ahead. As they got closer, Hossein and Afsaneh hesitantly released the grip they could have held for hours. They grimaced as they physically distanced themselves from each other. Before they reached the door both replaced their expressions with impassive countenances that allowed them to blend in with all the others out on the street. Their faces no longer represented their inner beings; instead, they were merely masks that hid a secret whose revelation would provoke negative consequences. They knew that the key to survival in that environment was assimilation. They had to stop smiling, had to stop feeling free, and had to act and look as if they were also two depressed human beings, deprived of their basic rights. It was only with that appearance that their immediate society would accept them. Any open display of happiness, including showing affection in public, had been seized from Iranians, to be replaced only with sadness, emptiness, and a sense of loss.

As the two stepped outside the embassy, Afsaneh walked faster to get ahead of Hossein. She got into a taxicab and went to the hospital. Hossein, although he was going in the same direction, took a separate cab. In his heart, he felt happy and content with his life; his multi-step plan for freedom and academic success was working. Hamid's medical condition had taken a reasonable course. He could see him becoming exempt from the military following a diagnosis of myelodysplastic syndrome. Hossein had done his research. He knew that Hamid had a good chance of getting approval to go to Europe for medical treatment. The main question now was whether *he* would be able to obtain government approval to accompany Hamid on his trip. He knew immediate family members could accompany a patient, but a cousin, he was not sure.

There is only one way to find out, thought Hossein. *Hamid would need to apply and pose the question to those who are in power.* For now though, he knew he needed to keep drawing blood from Hamid to keep him anemic. *I am sure time will reveal the answer.*

On his way to the hospital, with myriad thoughts racing through his mind, Hossein stopped at the post office and mailed both his and Afsaneh's applications.

CHAPTER FOURTEEN
THE RELIEF

Hamid continued working in the registrar's office at the base, maintaining the list of soldiers due to go to the front lines soon. One morning shortly after his arrival at work, his sergeant called to inform him that he needed to report to the clinic and meet with his doctor. Hamid took his military hat and walked there confidently, purposefully.

"Please have a seat, Hamid," said Dr. Bashiri. Despite his formal tone, Dr. Bashiri was already familiar with Hamid. "We received a notice from the hematologist at Emam Khomeini Hospital, where you went for a consultation. Did they tell you the results?"

"I am not sure if I understood it correctly, but they told me that there is something wrong with my bone marrow," replied Hamid.

"That is correct," replied Dr. Bashiri. "Honestly though, we don't know exactly what is going on in your bone marrow yet. You will need to follow up with the hematologist there. The reason I wanted to talk to you, however, is that the degree of anemia you have prevents you from performing your military duties. The military hospital has already begun the process of issuing you an exemption from service. This process usually takes about two months. If in the next two months you cannot work every day, we can make arrangements for you to work only half days." It took all the willpower Hamid could summon not to smile.

"Thank you, sir," replied Hamid. "These days, I feel very tired every day. It is difficult for me even to climb stairs." He hoped his voice had not betrayed the immense feeling of relief he was experiencing.

The doctor nodded solemnly in agreement, "I understand."

"Because you are so anemic, I am going to change your status to part-time, office-based duty, with privileges to go home every day. I will let your sergeant know. This will be effective as of today. I will ask you to come to the clinic once a week, so I can document your condition and your progress. Good luck. I wish you well, Hamid."

Hamid's homecoming that day was a pleasant surprise for his parents and his brother Mahmood. There was a sigh of relief from Hamid's father. He was happy that his son had made it through the first part of the process. An incredible feeling of relief washed over him, knowing that he finally had his son back, a son whom he could have easily lost to a war that was not his, was not Hamid's, and was only the consequence of a complicated series of international events. Hamid was ecstatic. After months of fear, and weeks of stress and inflicted fatigue and weakness, he now knew that Hossein's plan was working.

Hamid's mother, Nasrin, had been kept in the dark. She did not know what was happening to her son. She was very worried about Hamid's health, and wanted to know what was wrong with him. Hamid's father responded tactfully to her queries about his health and the treatment plans that Dr. Etemadi had in mind for him.

"We are going back to the university hospital next week to talk to the doctor about treatments," said Hamid's father softly, but dismissively, to Nasrin.

"We should go and see Hossein," whispered Mahmood to Hamid and his father. "He needs to know this." Mahmood called Hossein's house. His aunt Parvin said that she expected him to be home at about seven that night. Hamid and Mahmood got in the car and drove to Hossein's house. Once they arrived, Hossein opened the door for them.

"Hamid, what are you doing here?" exclaimed Hossein, clearly surprised by his cousin's presence. "Aren't you supposed to be at the base?"

"That is the reason we wanted to come and talk to you," said Hamid.

As they entered, Parvin greeted them. Together the three walked hurriedly into Hossein's favorite part of their home, the backyard garden.

"What is going on, Hamid?" asked Hossein. "What happened? I know that they decided on a strange diagnosis, which I actually like."

"Yes," replied Hamid. "The doctor at the base wanted to see me today. He told me that they started the process to get me an exemption from military service. This will take about two months. From today, I am working there only on a part-time basis. I can come home every day now."

"That's terrific, Hamid!" said Hossein, not even attempting to hide the sense of accomplishment he was feeling. "I am so happy to hear that. Still, we do need to continue the blood draws, all the vitamin pills, but we should stop the antibiotics now. That way, you will remain anemic; you will look and feel the same. We have achieved so much so far, and we don't need to do anything different that may raise questions."

"I agree, Hossein," said Hamid. "When will we take more blood again?"

"From this point on, we will take your blood only once every two weeks," replied Hossein. "I will run tests on your blood each time. You also need to continue visiting the hematology clinic at the hospital. Once you have your exemption card in your hands, we have hit a home run. But until then, we still need to be careful."

"I agree, Hossein," said Hamid earnestly.

"So have you thought about what you will be doing once you get your military-exemption card?" asked Hossein.

"I'm really not sure yet, Hossein. I am so excited because I will be out of the military soon. I will be partying a lot, I would say."

"Are you interested in going to college and studying something?" asked Hossein.

"Of course I am, but I could not pass the entry examination," Hamid replied dismissively.

"How about studying abroad?"

Hamid raised an eyebrow inquisitively. "Why do you ask that?"

"Remember the smuggler we met a few weeks ago?" said Hossein, his voice becoming increasingly serious, gaining a conspiratorial edge. "I told you then that you should have a backup plan to leave Iran if things didn't go well. I am glad that things are going well now, but I want to tell you about a plan I have, a plan that, if successful, will allow both of us to leave Iran. I know we have not talked about this before, but I think that, with the diagnosis they made at the Emam Khomeini

Hospital for your anemia, we have a good chance of getting permission from the Ministry of Health to take you to Europe for treatment. With that approval, they will allow another person, a family member or a relative, to go with you, to accompany you on your trip. I could be that person."

Hamid paused for a second. It was a lot to take in, but the idea seemed promising to him nevertheless. He cautiously replied to Hossein. "I like this plan a lot, but I need to think about it," then as an afterthought he added, "I also need to talk to my dad about it."

"Of course," said Hossein. He had expected this reaction.

Mahmood was thoughtful but extremely happy. In his heart, he cheered wildly that his brother had now escaped the potential death sentence of going to war, but he was nevertheless concerned about the rest of Hossein's plans, which included Hamid's departure from Iran. He loved his younger brother, and so did not want Hamid to leave Iran. On the other hand, he knew that Hamid had not passed the university entrance examination and could not study in Iran, leaving him with limited options. Despite his selfish desire for his brother to remain close by, he did want him to gain access to higher education and to succeed in life, something that the circumstances in Iran made impossible.

Mahmood spoke up and said, "Hossein, I tell you this, despite not having discussed it with our dad yet, I know we will all do whatever we can to help you leave Iran. Without your help, Hamid would have been serving at the front now, and maybe would have already been killed or horribly wounded. You have no idea how thankful and indebted we are to you. As a family—my dad, Hamid, and myself—we are all eternally indebted to you. Put simply, you saved Hamid's life. We will do everything to help you achieve your goals."

Hossein was genuinely moved by Mahmood's heartfelt promise and the purpose of his plan seemed clearer, his need to achieve it rapidly growing in intensity.

"Thank you," Hossein said. "I am confident that we will be able to get Hamid an exemption from his military service. When we started down this path, getting him out of the military was our only goal. But now, I see this as the beginning of a new chapter in his life. Getting an exemption is only one step in the process. Taking him overseas, to Europe at least, and maybe even to the United States, will provide opportunities he simply would not have in Iran. That also is the reason that I want to leave Iran myself."

Mahmood nodded fervently in agreement. "I think Hamid should take this rare opportunity to do something with his life." He turned and asked encouragingly to Hamid, "What do you think?"

"Honestly, I have never thought about leaving Iran," replied Hamid. "My mind has been so preoccupied with the military service and the war, and more recently with the anemia. I have never really been able to think about my future, and until now, I never really wanted to. But now that I can see an end to my military service, I can begin to look forward to my future and make some serious plans. I want to get this right. I love the idea of going to Europe or the United States to study, and I am positive that this is the right thing for me to do. I know it is an amazing opportunity for me, especially as it would be impossible for me to gain admission into any university here in Iran."

The conversation was becoming more animated and picking up momentum as the initially muted and formal conversation grew increasingly elated.

"I agree with both of you," said Hossein. "I always try to think several steps ahead—several months, even several years ahead. By foreseeing your possible future, you can start shaping it now, to mold it toward the ideal you want it to be. We should think ahead, and make decisions today that will affect and improve our tomorrows. We have all worked hard trying to secure a proper future for Hamid, and look at what we have achieved so far. But this is just the beginning. Achieving overall success in life is a far bigger task. Hamid, you should take maximum advantage of the situation. If all goes well, and if Haj Agha agrees, I think we will both be able to leave Iran in the summer, in about six months."

Despite his earlier request for time to think about the proposal, Hamid realized he had already made his decision. It was impossible not to let the positive momentum carry them away.

"Hossein, I will come with you wherever you go," said Hamid. "You have helped me so much. I know you want the best for me. I will work hard. I will study hard. I will do whatever I have to, so that I can get into a good university."

Hossein always had been a good communicator. He knew Hamid was one-hundred percent sold on the idea.

"That is wonderful, Hamid," he replied. "I don't want us to get ahead of ourselves and spend too long dreaming about the possibilities that lie ahead, but I so think that we may be able to establish a life in the United States one day. So work with me, and I will help you as much as I can."

Hamid suddenly felt overwhelmed. Gratitude to the man who stood before him, talking about a future far beyond even his wildest dreams, consumed him.

"I know you will, Hossein," he replied. "How can I ever thank you enough? I feel so indebted to you. You have saved my life."

Unable to control his emotions any longer, Hamid started crying. It was a cry of happiness, a cry of thankfulness, a cry coming from deep in his heart. He could not suppress it; he did not want to—he truly appreciated all that Hossein had done for him. The two men embraced. Mahmood, also touched by the situation, walked quietly away from Hossein and Hamid. Unlike Hamid, he was not comfortable sharing the newly formed tears that had unexpectedly sprung to his eyes.

"Hamid, together, we are going to succeed in life and have a great future," whispered Hossein as he hugged Hamid. "Your future is in your hands; it's up to you to shape it. You can write the story of your life and your future however you wish. I am confident that with some hard work, you will be a successful person and live a wonderful life. One day we will both go to the United States. That is a promise, Hamid. I will do my best to get you to the United States. The rest will be in your own hands."

⋆ ⋆ ⋆

Over the next three months, Hossein continued to draw Hamid's blood every two to three weeks, monitoring his blood count to keep his hemogram values at a steady, low level. Hamid continued going to the military base and working there on a part-time basis, visiting the doctor once every week without fail, and attending every one of his hematology clinic appointments. He had a newfound determination to realize the potential future Hossein had shown him. At the end of winter—the end of the calendar year in Iran—the military granted Hamid an exemption from service.

CHAPTER FIFTEEN
CHAR SHANBE SOORI

The Persian calendar year begins on the first day of spring and ends with the last day of winter. On the eve of the last Tuesday of the year, Persians bid farewell to the year that has passed with their thousand-year-old ceremony of *Char Shanbe Soori*. "*Char Shanbe*" means "Wednesday" in Farsi and "*Soori*" means "red." When night descends and smothers the world in a blanket of darkness, Persians light bonfires in ritualistic celebration. Fire lines the streets in rows, illuminating backyards, and blazes boldly in open public places. Persians will customarily jump over the fire singing, "*zardi-ye man az to, sorkhi-ye to az man.*" Which means, "My sickly yellowness and paleness be yours, and your fiery red color become mine," words that simply represent the age-old concept of exchanging the enervated *old* with the promise of the *new*.

The morning of *Char Shanbe Soori* was another regular working day for Hossein. He was in the middle of his usual patient rounds at the hospital when he caught sight of Afsaneh. She seemed to glide toward him, a smile rising subtly on her lips.

"What are you doing tonight?" she asked, her voice usually hushed, an almost playful whisper. She leaned closer toward Hossein, reaching up to speak directly into his ear. "Can you come to our house tonight for *Char Shanbe Soori*?"

Something about the tone of her voice roused a familiar intrigue from deep within him.

"I would love to," said Hossein. He looked at her for a moment, trying to read the unfamiliar expression, but her eyes gave nothing away. "What time would you like me to arrive?"

"Be there at six," said Afsaneh, her response instantaneous, the smile refusing to disappear from her mouth.

Later that evening, just as instructed and as punctual as ever, Hossein arrived at Afsaneh's home. The neighborhood was full of the heady atmosphere of *Char Shanbe Soori*. Teenagers ran around, delighted to be engaging in the festivities of this portentous occasion. One could hear firecrackers even before sundown. Some youths had succumbed to their impatience and were already leaping over prematurely lit bonfires in their front yards.

Hossein rang the bell on Afsaneh's door. Seconds later, she greeted him with a beaming face.

"Hello, Hossein. Welcome, come on in," she said hurriedly. "I have good news, Hossein." She paused for a moment, in an attempt to build some tension in the conversation, but she was simply too eager to share the news. The words tumbled out of her mouth, "You will not believe this, but today I got a letter from the ECFMG, confirming that I will be taking the examination in Paris. Everything is set for July. I am so excited, Hossein. I can finally see us getting out of here!"

"Oh Afsaneh!" said Hossein, deeply moved by her news and by the uncontrolled enthusiasm her delicate body radiated. "I am so happy for you, for us, for both of us, Afsaneh. Let me see the letter!"

Afsaneh practically ran down the hall to her room, picked up the letter from her desk, and handed it to Hossein who followed close behind. The two sat down on the edge of her bed. Hossein started reading its contents aloud.

"Dear Afsaneh, this is to confirm that you have been registered to take the ECFMG examination in Paris, France. Please arrive at the examination center by eight a.m., and ensure you bring with you two forms of picture ID."

Afsaneh watched Hossein as he continued reciting the letter. She was overflowing with excitement and exhilaration. She had never felt like this before. Unexpectedly, Afsaneh turned her body toward him. She placed her hands gently on either side of his face, and started kissing the man with whom she hoped to share her future. Intoxicated with anticipation and desire, she kissed him passionately and deeply. Hossein, taken aback, put the letter aside and wrapped his arms around Afsaneh, returning her desire. The passion between the two lovers intensified.

Afsaneh caught her breath between kisses just long enough to whisper, "You know, we are alone for the next two hours."

Hossein felt his excitement build rapidly, understanding the suggestion.

"Are you sure?" he asked softly. He wanted this to happen with every fiber of his being, but he respected the beautiful woman who looked longingly into his eyes. He had to know she was really ready.

"Yes, I am," replied Afsaneh, nodding her head and smiling seductively. She felt alive, all her senses heightened with excitement.

Afsaneh was ready to make love with Hossein. It was an act she had considered, and even imagined several times, but had told herself she would wait until the time felt right. And now, in this moment, she knew unequivocally that this beautiful man who sat beside her was the right person with whom to share her love. Although she was not completely sure if they would ever marry, she felt comfortable enough to allow this to happen, to allow Hossein to enjoy her, and for them both to enjoy the intimacy that their bodies had desired for so long. She was eager to surrender herself to him.

A small moan escaped unbidden from Afsaneh's lips as Hossein trailed kisses down her body. She loosened her clothes, slowly exposing more skin, revealing herself inch by flawless inch. Hossein was entranced.

"You are so beautiful Afsaneh." He whispered as they lowered themselves onto the soft white linen sheets.

An hour had passed. The two lay entangled still in each other's bodies, lost in the intimate moments they had just shared. It was Afsaneh who broke the silence by suggesting quietly, "Come on Hossein, let's go and set up some fire and celebrate."

The two dressed quickly, and shared one more affectionate kiss before walking together to the backyard of Afsaneh's house. Afsaneh could not stop smiling. She felt as though she were walking on air.

High walls surrounded the backyard, providing privacy. By now, the sky had turned a deep indigo and the sound of firecrackers assaulted their eardrums from every direction. Although they could not see anyone, they could clearly hear the laughter and the cheerfulness of neighbors. Happiness filled the air, and lifted everyone who breathed it in. Afsaneh's parents arrived just as they were setting bonfires in their backyard. Within minutes everyone was jumping over the fire, shouting and singing, *zardi-ye man az to, sorkhi-ye to az man!*

People rejoiced long into the night, until one by one, the fires of *Char Shanbe Soori* burned down to embers and the exultation slowly drifted away. Hossein, Afsaneh, and her parents left the backyard to sit in the dining room and have dinner. Mrs. Borhan played her favorite music, Johannes Strauss's waltz, *On the Beautiful Blue Danube*. She hummed the familiar melody absentmindedly. At the dinner table, there seemed to be only one topic of conversation: the life and future of Afsaneh and Hossein outside of Iran.

"I am sure that you two will do well," said Mr. Borhan, Afsaneh's father. "You are bright, young, intelligent and capable individuals. I have a great deal of respect for both of you. I have faith that wherever you go—whether to Germany, France, or the United States—you will succeed and live happy and successful lives. Just believe in yourselves and work hard."

Hossein saw the pride in Mr. Borhan's eyes as he gazed at his daughter.

"Thank you, Mr. Borhan," replied Hossein, "That means a lot to me, to us both".

Mrs. Borhan brought tea and a large serving plate of dried nuts and dried fruit, an array of food typical of *Char Shanbe Soori*. Hossein, however, could not calm down. A thought was niggling at the back of his mind, refusing to let him fully relax and enjoy the evening.

Where is my letter?

After dessert, Hossein decided he could wait no longer. He needed to go home and check his mail.

"It is getting quite late," said Hossein. "I should go. And as always, I appreciate your wonderful hospitality. It was my honor to share this perfect evening with all of you."

Hossein caught Afsaneh's eye as her father walked him to the door. They shared a secret smile and both knew the other was recalling the intimate events they had shared so recently. Afsaneh dropped her head and blushed when her father looked in her direction.

An hour later Hossein arrived home.

"Hello, Mom. Did you check the mail today?"

"Yes dear. Something came for you. I put it on your desk," said Parvin.

Hossein's heart leaped. He rushed to his room, and sure enough there it was, exactly what he had been hoping for, the same letter he had read aloud while perched on Afsaneh's bed earlier that day.

"Mom, come and see what I got!" shouted Hossein, jumping to his feet, unable to exhaust the adrenaline that coursed through his body.

"It's the confirmation for the examination in Germany this summer!"

"Well there you go. You got your New Year present, my son," she said warmly. "This is God's New Year gift to you."

"Yes, Mom," said Hossein. "I am so happy about this. Let's have tea and something sweet in celebration."

Hossein sat with his mother in their dining room. The two drank tea with Persian pastries and cream puffs, two things that Hossein was unable to resist.

"Mmm… cream puffs, my favorite. Thanks Mom." said Hossein.

"*Nooshe Jaan*, Hossein," said Parvin, meaning, "Enjoy them."

But sadness rapidly replaced her cheery façade. "Hossein, soon it will be the New Year, and I have a feeling that this will be the last New Year that we will spend together for a long time."

Hossein fell back into his multiple inner conflicts once more: the desire to succeed coupled with the pain of leaving his mother alone versus remaining in the company of his loved ones but nothing to pin his future dreams on.

"I know, Mom. I love you so much, and you will never know how much it will hurt me to leave you, but this is something I *must* do to succeed in life. Without this, my future is so bleak."

"I know that dear," replied Parvin. "I fully support your academic achievements. You must go. And you should go."

His heart physically ached at the thought of saying goodbye to his mother.

"Mom, remember I will take you with me wherever I go," said Hossein. "And once I am settled in, you will come and live with me. Deal?"

"Deal, my love, deal," said his mom with tears running freely from her eyes. "Oh Hossein, my dear, dear son, please believe me, these are tears of happiness. I am truly pleased for you. You deserve the best, the best education you can get and the best life ahead of you. I know you will be an amazing doctor and I support you on your journey. One day I will see it for myself; I will see you change the lives of your patients with my own eyes. I look forward to that day."

"Thank you, Mom," said Hossein, his voice more choked and high pitched than he had expected.

"It is late, my son" said Parvin, standing up. "Go to bed. Get some well-deserved rest."

CHAPTER SIXTEEN
NEW YEAR'S DAY

The Persian New Year begins at the exact moment of the spring equinox, which naturally can deviate by as much as six hours from year to year. This special time, marked by the ceremony known as Norooz, is poignant for all Iranians, who do their best to spend it with the immediate family. Symbolism, as true of many cultures, plays a huge part in Iranian traditions, and to symbolize the new year, the change of season, and life as a whole, Iranians set a table with at least seven items. The seven items, however, have one thing in common: their names all start with the letter S of the Farsi alphabet. Persians refer to the finished table setting as *Haft Seen*. *Haft* in Farsi means "seven," and *Seen* is the name of the letter S.

Just before the year officially changes, the family gathers around the *Haft Seen* table, and meditate together in quiet reflection and patient anticipation. In contrast to this calm welcome to the New Year, the days immediately preceding it are busy with preparation for a week of merriment and visits from family and friends. In the final hours of the year, everyone takes time to look back and reflect on the past year. Each individual contemplates his or her achievements, large and small, and begins setting goals for the fresh New Year ahead.

This New Year was extra special for Hossein and his family, because each of them knew that he was planning to leave Iran in the summer. All were acutely aware that Hossein had become a serious and determined young man, intent on matching his achievements to his admirable capabilities. An unsettling mood of impending loss overwhelmed the room, as they all knew that this would be the last time he would sit around *Haft Seen* with them in Iran to welcome the New Year.

It pained Hossein to witness the sadness painted on the faces of those he loved so dearly, particularly his mother's. Parvin, the ordinarily cheery, upbeat woman appeared uncharacteristically thoughtful and apprehensive. In her heart, she was deeply saddened at the thought of losing Hossein, and concerned about her youngest son's future. The love of fathers and mothers for their youngest child, the one who will always be their baby no matter how old the child becomes, is a special kind of love. There is a unique and unbreakable bond, a bond impervious to distance. Hossein felt privileged and blessed to be the youngest child of such genuine, loving parents.

The equinox this year was due to take place in the early morning of March 21, 1983. The television broadcast the countdown for the beginning of the New Year. At their house, Hossein and his family members each meditated in his or her own private way. Parvin opened the holy book of Quran and started reading, whispering a verse in a voice so quiet it was almost inaudible.

Hossein, while simultaneously listening to his mother, was thinking and making a wish, as many do at this exceptionally sacred moment. The idea and the thought of not being with his family next year, around the *Haft Seen,* was bothering him more than ever before. He chose to focus on his confidence in the promise he had made to his mother years ago. The thought of bringing her to the United States after he got himself settled brought him a great deal of comfort. It was how he steeled himself against the consuming emotions associated with leaving his loved ones behind. Hossein could easily imagine that just in a few years, he would be with his mother again. Time goes by so quickly; it would not be long before he was sitting around the *Haft Seen*, ready to welcome another spring equinox in the company of his mother. But next time, it would not be in Iran.

Despite all his reservations about leaving his dear family, Hossein was happy for this to be his last *Haft Seen* in this oppressive country that threatened to stifle his dreams. The need to succeed in life, the need to achieve a better education, the desire to survive, the fear of a war still continuing at that exact moment—all that would be alleviated the moment he left Iran. He was satisfied with what he had achieved so far, but he was ready to leave his birth-country in his past and take a leap of faith in search of a better future, yet he knew there were still several major obstacles he had to overcome during the next few months.

Hossein's wish was a simple and predictable one. *I hope that all goes well with my departure plans.*

Excited sounds filled the room. Not from the voices of those around the table, but of the countdown coming from the television set. "Thirty seconds to the beginning of the new year… Twenty seconds… Ten seconds, nine, eight, seven, six, five, four, three, two, one!" And so began the solar year, one thousand three hundred and sixty two.

The whole family hugged and kissed each other, and wished the best for each in the New Year. Mother opened the Quran to the page that contained several new thousand-rial notes. It is a Persian tradition to give the gift of money to everyone at the dawning of the New Year. This money is thought to be blessed, symbolizing wealth and ease in life.

As the first few moments of 1362 ticked by, each member of the family discussed his or her personal hopes and wishes for the coming year. Parvin wished her son all the best in his studies and in becoming a good doctor, and she openly acknowledged, again, that this might be the last New Year they were around the same *Haft Seen*. She was unable once more to prevent the tears in her eyes from spilling down her cheeks. Hossein and his siblings hugged and kissed their mother, trying to comfort her.

The New Year marks the beginning of the two-week long stretch of holidays and celebrations. Everyone in Iran gets involved. The country virtually shuts down for the first week; schools close for both weeks. This is a momentous and joyful time that Iranians use as an opportunity to go and visit all their relatives, close and distant, and their friends as well. For the first few days of the New Year, the youngsters go to visit their elders, and a few days later, the elders pay the youngsters a visit—another typical Iranian tradition.

Iranians have a unique respect for guests in their homes, in which most keep a special room for visitors, the *Mehman Khane*. Translated, *Mehman* means "guest," and *Khane* means "home." This special room of the house is the one that is the most beautifully decorated and the one that contains the best furniture. Persians traditionally keep this room for the exclusive use of guests, separate from the day-to-day activities of the family.

In preparation for the imminent arrival of guests, Hossein's family had ensured their guest room was pristine. In its center sat a large coffee table, adorned with a beautiful tablecloth. A large and sparkling crystal bowl, placed precisely in the middle of the table, was full with the juiciest of fresh fruits. Several trays surrounded the center bowel, each possessing a specific type of New Year confection. Parvin had also lit two candles, which were burning slowly, bathing the room in a rich aroma and homey warmth. To finish, she had placed a big crystal bowl of roasted almonds, pistachios, hazelnuts, and Hossein's favorite pumpkin seeds on a side table. Parvin left to do a last-minute check, and make sure that the table was properly set and the room was completely ready.

Within the first few hours of the onset of the New Year, the first group of guests arrived, naturally Hamid's family. Hossein opened the door to greet them. Haj Agha, Nasrin, Hamid, Mahmood, and their younger brothers and sister all walked in. Everyone hugged and kissed and exchanged their New Year's wishes in the hallway. Hossein's family eagerly ushered them into the *Mehman Khane*.

Everyone took their places. Hossein sat next to Haj Agha. After several minutes of general chitchat, Hossein's mother and sister left the room to bring fresh-brewed hot tea for the guests. Nasrin and her daughter closely followed Parvin to the kitchen. Hamid's younger brothers soon ran out to watch the television in another room. Hossein's brother followed them. Haj Agha took advantage of the privacy and whispered into Hossein's ear the news his nephew had been hoping to receive for some time: "Hamid finally got his exemption card; thank you, Hossein, and congratulations."

Hossein's adrenaline spiked again, registering his elation.

"Oh wow, I am so happy to hear this," he grinned. "That is truly the best New Year's gift that anyone could have asked for. Hamid, I am so happy for you."

"Thank you, Hossein, for all you have done for me," said Hamid, his eyes brimming with gratitude.

"You are most welcome, Hamid," said Hossein. "That is the first step we successfully completed, but we have a lot more to do. Soon after the holidays, we need to start the application process to get you out of Iran."

"I fully support that," said Haj Agha. "Hossein Jaan, please continue to do your best for my dear son. Look after him and take him with you, wherever you end up. He will have a much better future in Europe or the United States. If you could get him established in either place, I would be forever in your debt."

Before Hossein could reply, Parvin entered with a tray of tea served in the most beautiful china teacups. Nasrin walked in behind her. Everyone drank tea, and savored the delicious Persian candies and fruit. Happiness and joy filled the room once more. Hamid was especially joyful. He treasured being with his family on this New Year's instead of being at the front.

"Let's go for a walk in the garden, guys," said Hossein to Hamid and Mahmood once the tea was finished. "Spring has already touched our garden, and we have plenty of flowers in bloom. We should take time to appreciate them."

The air in the garden was fresh with a gentle spring breeze. The trees and all the plants of the garden displayed tender, small buds, and the promise of new life. The air was no longer cold.

"This year will be memorable for all of us," said Mahmood. "I hope that you two will be able to leave Iran. It will be a completely life-changing experience for both of you."

"It is the next step in our lives, Mahmood," said Hossein. "Hamid, it is important that you stay focused on the practicalities. Once the holidays are over, you and Haj Agha must go to the Health Ministry and apply for permission to leave Iran for medical treatment. We are going to reduce the blood draws now, so you feel better, but we cannot stop altogether, because we do not know how they may rule. They may ask for a second opinion, or they may want to see you. I simply don't know what exactly will happen, and don't want to risk anything."

"I agree with Hossein," said Mahmood. "We don't know how the Health Ministry will handle your case."

"Okay, guys, enough talk of sickness," said Hossein. "Smell these rosebuds; you can already detect their fragrance. Spring is in the air."

"Do you remember our summers at the Caspian Sea?" Mahmood asked.

"How can I forget?" replied Hossein. "Those were some of the best days of my life."

"Those days will never be repeated," said Mahmood. "We must keep the memories fresh, and not let them fade. In the past five years, our lives have changed immensely. God knows where we will all be five years from now. But I know one thing for sure—I will never forget our walks on the hiking trails of Ramsar, the beaches there, the smell of citrus trees in the air. Those things, all the tiny details, are etched into my memory for eternity."

Hossein smiled and silently thanked his parents for allowing him to experience those precious carefree days, the days he missed so very much.

CHAPTER SEVENTEEN
THE FLIGHT

"Hossein, I need to talk to you," said Afsaneh one morning when she was working with Hossein in the clinic. "Can you come to our home tonight?"

Something in her tone of voice made Hossein feel very uneasy.

"Tonight? Is everything okay, Afsaneh?"

"Yes, tonight," she replied, puzzlingly avoiding eye contact with Hossein. "This is very important, but I cannot talk about it here."

"Okay. I will be there about seven," replied Hossein. With that, Afsaneh made her excuses and hurried away, offering no further explanation.

Hossein was anxious and agitated for the rest of his shift. He could not stop picturing the vexed look he had seen on Afsaneh's face; something was deeply affecting her. He hoped she had not had a change of heart about their future plans. In all the years he had known her, he had never seen her so nervous, so tense. That they had become so close lately made her shifting mood even more perceptible to Hossein.

After what seemed like a very long day, he went to Afsaneh's home as he had promised. He arrived early, eager to learn the secret behind what was troubling the woman for whom he cared for so deeply.

"Hello, Hossein, please come in," said Afsaneh quietly. Her eyes were tinged red, her face ashen. It took one glance at her distressed face for him to realize the gravity of the situation. Whatever she was getting ready to disclose was very serious.

Hossein followed Afsaneh to her room. She closed the door behind her and for a short while silence ensued. Hossein was desperate to discover the source of this beautiful woman's inner turmoil, but he waited patiently for her to volunteer it without prompting. Then Afsaneh opened her mouth to speak, but it suddenly became too much for her; seeing Hossein's face swathed in concern had weakened her. She broke down; tears flowed freely from her eyes.

Hossein walked over, cradling her in his arms "My God, Afsaneh, what is it? What is wrong? Why are you crying, my love?"

Afsaneh tried to talk, choking on her words between the sobs that she was unable to control. She leaned into him, allowing herself to take comfort from his strong arms, arms that promised to protect her.

"Hossein… I am… pregnant," she eventually managed to say.

Hossein felt his heart stop momentarily. He could not respond. For the first time in his life, words had forsaken him.

Afsaneh continued, picking up the pace, trying to explain the situation quickly, before more sobs consumed her throat and lungs once again.

"I missed my period last month. With the stress of the war and work and examinations, I did not think too much of it, until last week when I started feeling… different. My breasts were swollen and I knew what the symptoms pointed to, so I did a urine pregnancy test and then repeated it yesterday. They were both positive." What am I going to do?"

Afsaneh looked up desperately at Hossein; searching his eyes for a solution that would make the problem go away, make everything better.

"This is entirely my fault. I should have been much more careful," were the only words he said.

"No, Hossein, it is not your fault. Remember, it was I who started this on *Char Shanbe Soori*. You never forced or insisted on sex with me. It was all me, I wanted it so much. Then, we kept repeating the events of that night, indulging ourselves whenever we could, and yes it was wonderful, it felt perfect, but look at us now. We are in so much trouble, Hossein. What about our future?"

Afsaneh's tears refused to stop flowing. They soaked through Hossein's shirt, dampening his shoulder. The news stunned him. He could barely stand on his own two feet, but he knew what he had to do. He was the man, he was her man, and he had to be strong. Hossein gently lifted Afsaneh's chin upwards so she was looking at him. The delicate skin around her bloodshot eyes was red and raw. She was distraught. A wave of love and sympathy gushed over him as he tried to compose himself.

"Afsaneh, listen to me, and listen carefully. We are in this together. Please do not think that this is just your problem. This is also something for which I take full responsibility. We enjoyed each other, we shared so many wonderful moments together, and now, we share this issue, and together we will figure something out. It will be okay, I promise. Afsaneh, look at me. I love you. Together we will fix this, okay?"

In fact, he had no idea how he would fulfill this promise, but he knew it was up to him to find a way. He could not bear to see Afsaneh like this, it was breaking his heart.

"Okay, Hossein," she replied tentatively as she wiped hot tears from her face. Just hearing his simple reassurance had helped alleviate some of her fear.

"Have you talked to anyone about this?" he asked, stroking her hair softly.

"No, of course not. How could I? I cannot tell my parents. I cannot tell any of my friends. You are the only person who knows, the only person I want to know."

"My love, come and sit here next to me," said Hossein lowering himself onto the bed.

Afsaneh did as she was told, placing her head on his shoulder once more, looking down to the floor, and crying. The two sat there for a long while just staring blankly ahead and holding onto each other.

"Have you thought about what you may wish to do, my love?" Hossein asked cautiously.

"I just do not know," replied Afsaneh. "I cannot think clearly. There are so many implications; a whole web of issues surrounds whatever decision we choose to make. I am so, so confused."

"How about we review the options we have, and decide what the best course of action is," said Hossein. The logical part of his brain, the part that would make him such a great doctor, had kicked in. "Certainly, this is not something that we can ignore."

"I know," replied Afsaneh. "But I cannot make this decision on my own, it is too hard" she whimpered, her voice trailing off. "What do you think I should do?"

"I know, I know, shhh. We'll do this together" he soothed, cradling her.

"The way I approach this may be different to how you approach it, but please let me explain my thoughts," said Hossein. "I am going to run through several options, and then we can see which might work best. Okay. Option one: we marry and keep the baby. I am not sure what your parents will think, but this is one option." He waited, trying to gauge her response.

"I don't want to impose this on you," replied Afsaneh. "And anyway, it would be impossible for us to have a quick wedding. My parents have always wanted a huge ceremony for me. I promised them that. How can I now tell them that we need to marry next week? Even if we plan for a proper wedding, it would not happen for a few months from now, and by then everyone will know that I am pregnant. That is not going to work. And Hossein, aside from all that, I really am not ready to have a child right now. I need to finish my studies; I need to leave this country. Marrying and having a child will mess everything up for both of us."

She looked exhausted. Hossein took a deep breath before verbalizing option two, although they both knew what option two was.

"What about... an abortion?" asked Hossein. He considered himself a logical and practical man, but the values of Iranian society had made their mark even on him, and just uttering the word left a sour taste in his mouth.

"Of course I have thought about that." replied Afsaneh steadfastly, sighing. "I think that is what I want to do; what we have to do. The timing is all wrong. This is not the right time for us to marry or have a child." Despite her innate maternal instinct and the inner conflict she faced, it was clear she had already made her decision.

"But how will you get an abortion in this country?" said Hossein. "You know the new Islamic laws do not allow elective abortions. They allow abortions only if the pregnancy is endangering the mother's life. All terminations of pregnancy must be reported to the authorities, and can be done only in specific hospitals."

"Yes, I know all that," replied Afsaneh. "But you know as well as I do that there are doctors still performing abortions here, illegally."

"My dear, this is such a risky thing to do," said Hossein wearily. "You are already aware of all the things that can go wrong after an abortion. If you develop an infection, or must go to the hospital for excessive bleeding or other complications, you will end up in jail and God knows what else they might do to you. What do you think your parents would do, or how they would feel then?"

"I know, I know, Hossein," replied Afsaneh, her voice quivering, the sobs threatening to make a grand reappearance. "I am well aware that performing abortion is a crime against Islam, punishable to the maximum extent allowed under the Islamic law: execution. I know that they equate abortion with manslaughter."

"None of the gynecologists who used to perform abortions are performing them now," said Hossein. "But there must still be a few who do it for money."

"Do you know of anyone?" asked Afsaneh hopefully. "Do you know anyone who performs abortions these days?"

"I will have to research it. I will ask around. But I cannot think of anyone right now."

Afsaneh looked dismayed. "Will you promise to look for me? For us?"

"Of course I will," said Hossein. "I promise you that. But listen to me Afsaneh, we need to do this in complete secrecy, without anyone *ever* discovering. That is the hardest thing."

With that, their conversation ceased again as they became embroiled in their own individual thoughts.

Again, it was Afsaneh who broke the silence.

"Hossein, if we cannot find anyone to do it, can you do it for me?" she asked meekly.

Hossein was taken aback. "What?! Afsaneh I cannot!" he stammered, struggling to comprehend the enormity of the task that had just been asked of him. "You want *me* to do this? I have never done this procedure, not even once."

"But you have observed it," said Afsaneh.

"That is true, I have seen it done, and I have read about this procedure," replied Hossein. "But where would we do it? With what equipment? And have you thought about the consequences if anything was to go wrong?"

Afsaneh dealt with each question in turn, trying desperately to remain calm. "We can do it right here, in my room. I could get the supplies and equipment we need from the hospital. One thing we would need is a medical suction machine, and that we can buy from a medical supply store in Naser Khosrow Street."

"Afsaneh, I'm sorry, I want to make this right, I really do, but I do not feel comfortable doing this, especially in here in your own home. What if I get something wrong? What if you bleed badly? What do we do then? Do I take you to our hospital? Before you would even have recovered from the bleeding, I would be jailed, and perhaps killed! This is not a good option Afsaneh."

His response was more than she could deal with.

"Please Hossein! Please help me! I do not know what to think, I do not know what to do, I am going crazy! We live a in a society that does not accept our situation. We live in a country where getting an abortion is illegal and has a death sentence tied to it." She was becoming hysterical.

"Shhh, calm down my love, calm down," he whispered into her ear, clasping her hands tightly. "The best option for us at this moment in time is to find someone who does the procedure and go for a consultation," said Hossein.

"But you just said you don't know anyone!" said Afsaneh. "We cannot go to any of the gynecologists who work at our hospitals, or who are in any way affiliated with the University."

"Yes, that's very true," replied Hossein. "But I will find out who still does abortions in Tehran, just give me a day or two. You should try to research this too, see if you can locate someone who does it."

Afsaneh seemed to accept this. "Okay Hossein, I will," she promised.

An hour and several more comforting embraces later, Hossein left to go to home.

What a mess, he said to himself as he got into bed. *This should have never happened. At this stage of my life, there is no room for such a mishap. I cannot believe I let this happen. How is she going to get an abortion? And where? And who could do it? It is almost impossible under the circumstances.*

After a sleepless night, the next day Hossein went to work at the hospital as usual. All day, he was unable to get Afsaneh out of his thoughts. When he was not thinking about her, or recalling her heart-wrenching display of misery and anguish, he was considering how he should go about finding a doctor who still performed abortions.

That evening, preoccupied with thoughts of Afsaneh, Hossein walked to the emergency room to start his night shift there.

Hossein knew all the nurses who worked there well, and had developed trusting friendships with several of them. He waited until past midnight, when things had settled down, to find an opportunity to speak with senior nurse Moniri, whom Hossein had known for four years. He knew it was a risk talking to her, but he felt he could trust her.

"Hello Ms. Moniri, can I talk to you about something?"

"Well of course, Hossein, what is it?"

"I need some help with an important matter."

"Okay," said Ms. Moniri. "Fire away, I'll help you the best I can." She sensed an unfamiliar seriousness in Hossein's voice.

"Ms. Moniri, I need to find a gynecologist who performs abortions. Someone I know is trying to find a doctor who still does the procedure. Do you know of anyone?" He dropped his eyes, unable to deal with the nurse's inquisitive gaze.

"Umm, let me think," said Ms. Moniri. She raised one eyebrow as she spoke to him. "I am sure you know about the newly enacted laws, penalties, and punishments for doctors who perform abortions?"

"Of course I know," Hossein said dismissively. "I just need to find someone, who, despite all this, still does perform abortions. My… friend… is desperate."

Hossein hoped he was not giving too much away. Intentional dishonesty was never one of his skills.

"Okay," said Ms. Moniri. "First of all, tell your friend to be ready to pay a hefty fee. When the punishment for the doctor is execution, the rare few who still do it want substantial compensation for taking the risk."

"I kind of assumed that would be the case," replied Hossein. "But the crucial thing right now is to find a doctor. We… my friend… will worry about the cost later."

"I will have to ask around," said Ms. Moniri. "The last doctor I knew left Iran for the United States a month ago. He was completely disheartened with the system. Almost all gynecologists have stopped performing abortions now, because of the potential consequences and penalties."

"But you will ask around for me?"

"Yes, I will, but give me a few days," said the nurse. "How pregnant is she?"

"I am not certain, but perhaps about ten weeks," replied Hossein matter-of-factly.

"Okay, well at least she has a few weeks to take care of this," replied Ms. Moniri. "I will be working here again the day after tomorrow, on the morning shift. Come and see me then. I will let you know if I found anyone."

Two long and stressful days later, Hossein went to the emergency room to find Ms. Moniri. It was probably the busiest Hossein had ever seen the department. He looked to the waiting area and saw a crowd of several *basiji* soldiers milling around.

"Hello Ms. Moniri," said Hossein. "What on earth is going on? What are all these *basijis* doing here?"

"Follow me and I will show you," said Ms. Moniri, standing up. "Just be prepared for a less-than-pleasant sight."

Hossein followed Ms. Moniri to the Code Blue room of the emergency department. A group of interns walked out of the room just as they approached it, looking decidedly uneasy. Just then, Hossein saw the body. Its lifeless form lay supine on the only examining table in the room. Another nurse walked briskly past them and turned off the bright light above the body.

"They pronounced him dead a few minutes ago," she said matter-of-factly before turning on her heel and leaving Hossein and Ms. Moniri alone with the body.

It did not matter how much training he had, or how many dead bodies he witnessed, being this close to one still affected Hossein. It reminded him what a precious gift life was, and how easily, and how quickly it can be taken away. All the noisy monitoring equipment in the room was now off, the rhythmic beeps and panic-inducing alarms replaced with an eerie silence.

"You have to come closer to see this," said Ms. Moniri.

The two walked slowly closer to the body. She revealed that the man was a cleric who had been shot mercilessly on the street. Hossein cast his inquisitive medical eye down the right side of his body and observed numerous bullet holes all the way from his hip up to his skull. Whoever had inflicted those brutal injuries was clearly devoid of compassion and empathy. Hossein had observed similar sights all too often; he would never understand what could drive a human being to commit such a ruthless act.

"Apparently, this cleric was walking on a sidewalk of the street, not far from the hospital, when two young men on a motorcycle appeared out of the blue. As they drove by, the person sitting in the rear of the motorcycle pulled out a machine gun and fired directly at him, from close range," said Ms. Moniri. "With all those bullet holes in his body, he must have died instantly. The code team could not do anything for him."

Ms. Moniri then covered the body gently and walked to the sink to wash her hands. Once they were dry, she reached into her pocket.

"Take this," she commanded as she passed a piece of paper to Hossein. "It is the contact information for a general surgeon who carries out abortions. He is not a gynecologist, but I know him well; he is a very nice person. Tell him that I advised you and your friend to see him."

"I wonder how he has flown under the radar," Hossein asked warily, "considering how tightly the government has clamped down on doctors. They even carry out surreptitious investigations to stop abortions altogether."

"Because he is a general surgeon, not a gynecologist; that has kept him out of the scrutiny," Nurse Moniri replied.

It made sense. "Thank you so much Ms. Moniri," said Hossein. "I will pass this information on to the person who needs it."

Ms. Moniri simply nodded impassively in response. Hossein left the emergency room, and hurried down the hospital corridors to the ward where he knew Afsaneh was working.

"We need to talk," said Hossein to Afsaneh. He did not have time for polite greetings and small talk. "Seven tonight, your place."

"Yes, sure, that's fine," replied Afsaneh.

Later that day, after a difficult and tiring shift, Hossein headed to Afsaneh's house. Both her parents were home and the dinner table was ready, as beautifully presented as always, and with a place set especially for Hossein. Ordinarily he would have felt honored to be included in such plans, but this was no ordinary situation. The thought of having to sit through dinner without being able to talk freely to Afsaneh was gut-wrenchingly frustrating. They needed to find privacy to discuss the matter that was occupying their minds so intensely.

"Sit down, it won't take long and then we can talk" Afsaneh whispered, as if reading Hossein's thoughts. After what seemed like an excruciatingly long dinnertime, Afsaneh's father went to the backyard to smoke a cigarette while his wife kept herself busy in the kitchen.

Hossein seized the fleeting opportunity.

"Listen, I've got the name of a surgeon who can do it. We need to go and meet with him."

"Shhh, keep your voice down, my parents are not far away, they'll hear!" snapped Afsaneh, before adding, "When?"

"I already called his office and made an appointment for us to go and meet with him. The earliest he could see us was tomorrow at 6pm."

"So you will be skipping the German class?" The situation was far from humorous, but the light-hearted quip momentarily diffused the intensity of the situation in which they had unwillingly found themselves.

"You stopped coming to the class long ago, Afsaneh," said Hossein, with a half-smile.

"Tomorrow after work, we will go there to meet him. Let's hope that he can help us," said Afsaneh.

At that moment, Afsaneh's father reentered the room, but there was no need for further discussion. The plans were already in motion.

The next day, Afsaneh and Hossein drove in a taxi to the surgeon's office. The two barely exchanged a word during the entire trip. When they arrived, they found the waiting area sparsely decorated and impersonal. Neither could find suitable words to express their feelings, so they simply squeezed each other's hand and waited to be summoned. After half an hour, the surgeon appeared and nodded toward Hossein. It was their turn.

"How can I help you today?" asked the surgeon. His friendly and calming tone put the pair at ease.

"Dr. Rezaii, we are here on recommendations from one of our senior nurses from Emam Khomeini Hospital, Nurse Moniri," said Hossein formally.

"I know Ms. Moniri very well. I did my internship and residency at that hospital. She is a wonderful person." Dr. Rezaii seemed completely relaxed, in direct contrast to how Afsaneh was feeling.

"We are both interns there," she said, wondering if this revelation would have any impact on the level of care she might receive from Dr. Rezaii.

"Oh, nice," said the doctor. "So tell me what brings you here today."

"I am pregnant Dr. Rezaii," said Afsaneh. She saw little point in sugarcoating the pill at this stage. "I need an abortion. We wanted to discuss this with you."

"Mrs. Moniri spoke very highly of you," added Hossein. "We really need your help. Can you do this for us?"

Dr. Rezaii remained silent for a while, shifting uncomfortably in his chair. It was as though he were unsure how to react to the turn the conversation had taken.

"Why don't you come over and let me examine you," he eventually said.

They obediently followed the doctor to his examination room. Afsaneh put on a gown, and lay on the table. If she thought she felt uncomfortable before, it paled in comparison to how she felt now.

Dr. Rezaii completed the examination swiftly and with practiced expertise.

"You are about ten weeks pregnant," he said confidently. "We can do this, *but* there are many issues you need to be aware of. Firstly, I will do the procedure right here, in this room, without a nurse and without an assistant, for obvious reasons."

"But perhaps you can help me," said Dr. Rezaii to Hossein. It was more of a statement than a question. The doctor's demeanor had changed entirely, his friendliness now encased in a hard and impenetrable exterior.

"I use a vacuum abortion method," continued the doctor. "This procedure has a two percent risk of infection or bleeding. Afterwards, you will need to go home and rest for 48 hours. Drink lots of fluids, take some antibiotics and then come back and see me one week later."

"Thank you Dr. Rezaii," said Hossein. "What will the procedure cost?"

"My usual fee for this procedure is $5,000 and I accept only U.S. dollars, not rials," said the doctor firmly. He softened slightly when he saw the combined look of shock and dismay plastered across their faces.

"I tell you what, because you are both interns, how about I extend a professional courtesy discount to you? You will need to pay only $4,000."

Hossein sighed. It was a lot of money, but he could not say that he was not expecting such a sum.

"How soon do you think you can do this, Dr. Rezaii?" asked Afsaneh, as she was getting dressed.

"Unfortunately I am going away for a few days, so the soonest that I can do this for you will be next Monday. If that date works for you, you will need to confirm it by tomorrow."

"Can you tell me what the odds of serious complications are? And what do we do if she bleeds excessively after the procedure?" The cautious, medically trained part of Hossein's brain had shifted into gear.

"In my hands, the overall chance of running into a major complication is less than two percent," replied Dr. Rezaii. "Uterine infection and bleeding are the two most common complications. Very rarely the body of uterus is perforated during the procedure."

Afsaneh gasped. In her eagerness to rectify her situation, she had not considered the possibility of such a complication. Dr. Rezaii reacted.

"Afsaneh, believe me, the odds of that happening are extremely low. I have not had one happen to me, but I have to tell you about it because it is a known complication of this procedure. Now, is there anything else I can answer for you?" The doctor glanced at the clock on the wall.

"No, thank you, Dr. Rezaii. You covered all the risks and complications," said Afsaneh. "Oh, there is just one thing you did not answer before. If, for example, the most unlikely thing happens and my uterus is perforated…" the words left a bitter taste in her mouth "… then what do we do?"

"Perhaps I did not make this clear," answered the doctor coldly. "Once we are done with the procedure, you go home. If anything goes wrong, you go to any local hospital and seek help. You must understand that we do this in complete secrecy. You are never to tell anyone what happened. You never mention that you had an abortion, much less tell anyone who did the procedure. And if you do, I will deny it. So, to make it absolutely clear, I will be happy to do the procedure for you, and the odds of anything going wrong are very low. If, however, something does go wrong, taking care of it is your responsibility and your responsibility alone. We all take some risks in our lives. You took a risk and became pregnant; I am taking a huge risk by performing an abortion. It is our choice to take these risks, and so we must deal with the potential consequences. Under the circumstances, if the government learns about my doing abortions, they will execute me the next day. I select my patients carefully, and I need you to understand all this before we proceed. Are there any other questions?"

"No doctor, all is clear," said Afsaneh quietly.

Hossein and Afsaneh left the doctor's office, each going over the events of the last hour in silence.

"We need to get into two taxicabs," said Hossein as they stepped out of the doctor's office, "I will come to your house to talk. I will be there in an hour. I need to do something or I'll go crazy."

"Okay" she replied meekly as she walked down the street to find a taxi, her mind reeling. The things she had just heard dumbfounded her.

Poor Afsaneh, thought Hossein.

Despite her apparent collectedness and self control, he could see straight through to her vulnerability. He chastised himself once more. *How could I have been so stupid? I am a doctor, I knew the risks.* But entertaining such thoughts was pointless. What was done, was done.

Instead of getting into a taxi, Hossein decided to walk for a while. The air was nice and fresh, it was an ideal time of the day, and it provided the perfect opportunity for him to try to compartmentalize the mess of thoughts that twisted and knotted themselves relentlessly in his head. The doctor's office was across from Laleh Park and within walking distance from the medical school. During his first two years there, Hossein used to visit this park on practically all of his lunch breaks. Afsaneh's house was on the opposite side of the park. Hossein desperately desired time alone to think, so he succumbed to the allure of the park's peacefulness and ambled through, slowly.

What if something goes wrong after the abortion? Hossein considered as he strolled down the familiar paths. *Dr. Rezaii is right. Every action we take involves some degree of risk. We do need to take responsibility for our actions and for the risks we take. I know the risk of running into complications following a simple abortion is low, but however low those risks may be, they are unacceptable. I could never forgive myself if something went wrong. Doing the procedure in that medical office as opposed to a sterile operating-room environment carries an additional risk. Not having free access to medical care after the procedure is another major problem.*

Hossein simply could not find a way out of this impossible scenario. He saw a row of benches in front of him and sat down, defeated. For several minutes, he could not think. His mind had given up; he had not slept properly in days. He closed his eyes, and before he knew it, he was asleep. He awoke several minutes later to a warning from an elderly man.

"Wake up young man, it is getting dark, and it is not safe for you to sleep here," said the man.

"Thank you sir," said Hossein startled. He stretched and yawned before offering the man an explanation. "I've had a long day and I'm exhausted, but I still have so much more to do."

The man nodded sympathetically as the two of them stood and walked in the same direction. A thought crossed Hossein's mind: *This old man seems like a sincere and nice person. I am going to ask his advice. He is a complete stranger, he does not know me, and I do not know him. Right now, he seems like the best person to ask. Perhaps he will give me the solution for which I have been searching.*

Hossein surprised even himself by this decision. It was not in his nature to divulge the intricacies of his private life, but liked the idea of talking to the man, of sharing the thoughts that burdened him with a kind and wise old stranger. He slowed. The man did the same.

"Sir, I realize this may sound odd to you, but may I ask you something?" asked Hossein of his elder. 'I'd like to get a fresh perspective."

"Of course you can, I don't know whether I will be able to answer your question though," said the man with a smile on his face. He steadied himself with a cane, and appeared to be in his mid seventies.

"By the way, my name is Hossein."

"I am Manoochehr; it is very nice to meet you Hossein Agha."

"Sir, how much risk should one take in his life?" asked Hossein boldly.

"That is a difficult question, my son," said Manoochehr. "I suppose it all depends on the circumstances and your level of comfort with the situation. At the time of the Shah, I was in the army. I was in charge of several thousand soldiers, and I never took a risk that would needlessly endanger the life of any of my soldiers. A life is precious; it is not something to risk if you can help it."

"What do you do Hossein Agha?" asked the Manoochehr after a short pause.

"I am finishing medical school." answered Hossein, "I will be a qualified doctor in just a few months."

"Well congratulations, that is wonderful," replied Manoochehr. "But why did you ask me this question? Are you facing jeopardy?"

"I have to help a friend make a huge decision, to undergo a medical procedure that carries a very small, yet very serious risk," replied Hossein solemnly.

"I wish I could help you more, but I cannot. You should always help others, give them advice, but never impose your ideas on them. The greatest of friends do not push their ideas or personal opinions onto others. My advice is this: Tell your friend what you think and what you would do, if you were in his shoes."

"Her," corrected Hossein

"Okay then, if you were in her shoes," continued the man. "Let her decide on her own. But with women, be much more careful. If there is one thing I have learned in my life, that is it. Believe me, if something were to go wrong, you would be blamed."

Hossein nodded, thanked the man, and politely made his excuses to leave to go to Afsaneh's house.

"You are late," said Afsaneh with a sigh as she opened the door for Hossein.

"I know. I am sorry. Are your parents' home?"

"My mom is, but she is on the phone with her sister. Their phone calls go on forever. She'll be talking for a long time yet."

They walked to Afsaneh's room and both sat once more on the edge of her bed.

"So what do you think of this doctor?" asked Hossein.

"I am not sure," said Afsaneh. "On one hand, he seems to be a nice person; on the other hand, he will not provide any follow-up. What if something goes wrong? Can you imagine my parents visiting me in the hospital, needing a blood transfusion because of an illegal abortion? My mother could not cope with that."

"I know Afsaneh," replied Hossein. "I am at a loss myself. I do not know what to tell you. I wish there was an easy solution to this."

"Since I learned about my pregnancy, I have been doing rigorous exercises, hoping for a spontaneous abortion," Afsaneh confessed. "I have been reading a great deal on the first trimester of pregnancy. About 20 percent abort spontaneously. I am hoping that mine will end that way."

"Yes that's true my love, but 80 percent of the pregnancies do not," said Hossein softly. He did not want to upset her, but she needed to face the realities of her condition head on. "We need a better plan for this. We need to decide and act soon. If you want to get an abortion, we need to do it sooner than later."

The two held each other's hands and remained silent for a while. Afsaneh did not argue—she knew he was right.

"Can you come here over the weekend and be with me?" asked Afsaneh in a small voice. "My father will be out of town and I don't want to be alone."

"My dear Afsaneh, of course I will," replied Hossein, kissing the top of her head gently. Love and pity gripped his heart.

On Friday afternoon, Hossein paid Afsaneh another visit. He rushed impatiently to her house.

"Afsaneh, since we met last, something else has crossed my mind!" He could not speak fast enough. "You have a valid passport and visa to France. We have signed you up to take your ECFMG in Paris. Correct?"

"Yes, I do have a visa. I traveled to France last summer with my mother," said Afsaneh. "Why?"

"Well, considering all the options, one possibility is for you to get an abortion in Europe, where it is completely legal and follow-up services are available," replied Hossein. "Where is your passport? May I see it?"

Afsaneh's face lit up for the first time in days and she rushed to get her passport from her desk.

"Here it is!" she exclaimed.

Hossein opened her passport and flipped through the pages.

"Okay, your passport is valid for four more years," said Hossein. "You have a multiple-entry visa to France, valid until the 10th of August, 1983."

"Oh Hossein, you are a genius," she gushed, "It had not even crossed my mind to go to France for an abortion. I was thinking only of my ECFMG."

"I am surprised myself that I hadn't thought of it earlier, my dear. Under the circumstances, it may be your best option. Getting an abortion in Tehran right now, even if Dr. Rezaii does it, will not be medically safe. God forbid, if something went wrong, it would be a major catastrophe."

"I know, I know," said Afsaneh, unable to hide her relief. "Also, getting an abortion here will cost me even more than going to Paris for a week and getting it done there. You are right, Hossein."

Afsaneh paused for a second as the potential issues surrounding their new plan suddenly demanded her full attention.

"But wait, how can I drop my studies and go? What do I tell my parents? How do I convince them that I have to go to France now, just two months before my ECFMG?"

"Afsaneh, your parents are pleasant and educated, and fortunately money is not an issue for them. Under the current circumstances, traveling to France is by far our best option. What if we talk to your mother about it? I'm sure we can invent a convincing story between us; I doubt she would ever suspect the truth anyway."

"Such as what?" asked Afsaneh.

"We need to devise a good and convincing reason for you to travel to Paris. Can you think of anything? Could you perhaps say that you are depressed or struggling to cope with the stress of your studies and need to take a break? Maybe we could say that the pressure from the Islamic group at the university is pushing you over the edge? Or what about a fictitious medical meeting you are required to attend?"

"I don't know, Hossein, I just don't know," replied Afsaneh. "All of those ideas are plausible, and so convincing her would not be difficult.

The problem is in persuading her that I should drop everything and go immediately."

"True," said Hossein. "But surely we have to try?"

"Hossein, you always devise the most amazing solutions for everything," said Afsaneh, placing her hand affectionately on the side of his face. She could finally see a light at the end of the tunnel and it was all because of the understanding and brilliant man that sat beside her.

"I would have never thought of going to Paris for an abortion. Never. Moreover, you come here, you listen to my cries, comfort me, and resolve my problems. I can finally see a solution. Okay, let me go to the bathroom, wash, put some makeup on, and then go and talk to my mother. In the meantime, please try to think of some good excuses to convince her that I need to drop everything and go to France now. I know you can do it my love."

"Okay, Afsaneh, I will. For you, for us." replied Hossein.

The two stood, Hossein pulled Afsaneh toward him and the two embraced tightly for a long moment. It was a powerful moment for them both, and although they still had so much to do, having a solid plan felt like the end of the traumatic ordeal that had threatened to turn their futures upside down. In that moment, Hossein felt unable to contain his feelings for Afsaneh any longer.

"Afsaneh, I love you. I want to spend the rest of my life with you. I am sorry about the mess that you have to go through, a mess for which I feel so terribly responsible. But now, I am convinced that everything will work out fine. There is so much more in store for us, life is waiting for us to conquer it. I am sure that together, you and I will have a wonderful future. I can just feel it. We are going to overcome this problem and nothing will hamper our plans to leave Iran."

Their eyes locked in an intensely loving gaze and the two kissed passionately, just as they had before they faced this awful dilemma. After many seconds their lips separated, but her eyes remained fixed on his eyes.

"I love you," said Afsaneh, and with those words, she separated herself from Hossein and walked out of the room to freshen up. She was comforted, and she knew that, despite the inevitable difficulties that lay ahead, there was ultimately a solution to her imminent problem.

In that instant, Hossein knew his love for Afsaneh had grown deeper and become more meaningful. It was unchartered territory for him, but although it was frightening, he was ready to face whatever lay ahead; as long she was by his side, he knew he could achieve anything. It was the only encouraging emotion that had come from the whole tribulation—their newfound familial intimacy. Hossein lost himself in poignant contemplation.

Your love for the person whom you cherish the most grows stronger when you struggle together, and it is in defeating hardships that your relationship strengthens its very foundations. In your greatest need, it is the people who are most important to you who carry you through. This is by far the biggest challenge that our relationship has ever faced, and I know now that my unquestionable love for this woman is indestructible. She is the most wonderful thing in my life, and the most beautiful soul I have ever met. She is intelligent, resilient, and strong. I want to spend the rest of my life with her. I can only hope that I am lucky enough for her to feel the same way about me.

"Hossein, you look so very thoughtful again," said Afsaneh, as she reentered the room. "Are you ready to go talk to my mom?"

Hossein smiled, nodded, and followed Afsaneh to the backyard of the house. They found Afsaneh's mother in her flower garden. She was admiring the most beautiful roses and tulips, which were in full bloom.

"Hello, Mrs. Borhan," said Hossein, as the two entered the patio overlooking the backyard of Afsaneh's house. He tried his hardest to display normalcy as he led Afsaneh down the steps that connected the patio to the garden.

"Oh, Hossein, hello," replied Mrs. Borhan, smiling. "So nice to see you again."

"I love your flower garden, Mrs. Borhan," said Hossein casually, "especially your pink roses. They must be very fragrant." If Hossein had learned one thing from working so closely with people, it was that they were generally more amicable if you started the conversation with a compliment.

"Why?—and thank you, Hossein, I am glad that you appreciate them," said Mrs. Borhan. "Am I safe to assume that you are an expert on roses?" she asked playfully, and without actually waiting for a response, she continued. "I am going to give you a little quiz on them now. Are you ready?"

The mischievous glint that danced in her eyes caused both Hossein and Afsaneh to burst into laughter.

"I am ready, Mrs. Borhan," said Hossein, composing himself.

"Okay. I want you to tell me how you think I acquired these roses—these pink ones, your favorites." said Mrs. Borhan.

"Well, I will make a guess, a very wild guess, that you acquired them from the town that is most famous for your lovely pink *Mohammadi* roses, and that is the city of Ghamsar, near Kashan," replied Hossein.

Afsaneh looked simultaneously surprised and impressed by Hossein's correct response. Was there anything this man did not know?

"Wow. Very good, Hossein," replied Mrs. Borhan. "I have to be honest; I didn't expect you to guess correctly. Have you ever been to Ghamsar?"

"I have never been there," replied Hossein, rendering his answer all the more remarkable, "but we all know that the town is famous for its roses and its rosewater industry."

Mrs. Borhan nodded in silent awe.

"So, Hossein, how are things at the hospital for you now?" she asked, changing the subject.

"Well, quite stressful. The Islamic Association at the university and the hospital is working very hard to exert more power over the rest of us," replied Hossein. "Needless to say, we are all living under the shadow of the war. So many of our friends are suffering from depression. There is a sense of downtrodden helplessness throughout the place. "Oh, and you know what the newest development is?"

"What's that?" asked Mrs. Borhan.

"It was common knowledge that male medical school graduates must do their military service immediately after graduation," replied Hossein, "while female graduates could enter into the residency program at that point. Well, all that has changed recently. Now, all female graduates also must carry out their two- to three-year civil service in remote parts of the country, just like their male counterparts. Only upon completing that service can they enroll in a residency program."

"What?" asked Mrs. Borhan, her face enveloped in a look of shocked horror.

"Afsaneh, haven't you told your mother about this?" asked Hossein, turning to his girl.

"Not really." Afsaneh hung her head down, doing her utmost to conceal the smile that would betray the truth.

"Life is becoming more difficult for us," said Afsaneh to her mother. "The outlook is getting gloomier by the day. We are all feeling dejected and low."

At that point, Hossein looked directly and seriously into Mrs. Borhan's eyes, ensuring she followed his gaze to the beautiful Afsaneh, on whom he settled the most sympathetic look he could muster.

"Afsaneh has become so sad and depressed lately. Haven't you noticed?" He was taking the lead effortlessly, his practiced people skills shone as Afsaneh's mother soaked up every convincing word like a sponge.

Afsaneh, unsure of her lines in this production, continued to stare at her feet.

"Actually I have, especially in the past two or three days. She is nervous and anxious," replied Mrs. Borhan, talking about her daughter as though she were not present.

Then, Afsaneh suddenly found her voice, her improvisation only mildly exaggerated.

"I am having nightmares, Mom, all the time. The country is at war, and Iraqis are sending long-range missiles toward Tehran almost every night. We lose electricity constantly. I cannot sleep, I cannot eat properly, I am permanently on edge, and the air-attack sirens make me feel sick. I don't know how much more I can take."

"Mrs. Borhan, half our classmates are taking Valium, some other sedative, or an antidepressant drug," said Hossein. "And on top of that, we have to take care of the growing number of patients who have suffered some form of physical injury during the war. Our work is difficult and mentally exhausting. And the circumstances do not make it any easier. We cannot go out. I cannot go to a movie or dinner with Afsaneh. We cannot even talk to each other in the hospital."

Hossein relented for a moment to let Afsaneh's mother take in all of this.

"However, I am glad we are finally talking about this. Mrs. Borhan, I wanted to share something with you about Afsaneh." He lowered his voice conspiratorially and slowed the pace of the conversation. This was the climax of the routine, and it was essential they get it right.

"What is it, Afsaneh? Are you okay, my love?" asked Mrs. Borhan, as she turned to look at her daughter, a veil of concern clouding her face.

"Mom…" said Afsaneh quietly. "I do not think I can cope any more. I am under so much stress. I am nervous, frightened, and terrified for my future, for our future."

She paused for maximum effect.

"Mom, I cry every day. I just don't know what to do."

She could not make her tears fall on cue, so she settled on a giveaway quiver in her voice. Everything she was saying was true, but the pressure of deceiving her mother into believing she needed to get away prevented real emotion from surfacing.

Once again, Hossein confidently took charge.

"The way things are going now, I am afraid that your daughter may also need to take antidepressant medications," he said, turning to Afsaneh. "Afsaneh, I am sorry that I am talking about this, but your mother needs to know how much pressure you are under."

"It's okay," said Afsaneh.

"What can we do to help you my dear?" asked Mrs. Borhan who at this point looked like she herself might burst into tears.

"I don't know, Mom," said Afsaneh. All of a sudden, the look of desperation and sadness painted on the face of her loving mother prompted the tears that had so far refused to fall.

"Come here, my love, come and sit here with me," said Mrs. Borhan as she extended her hand to her troubled daughter, and led her to the bench in the corner of the garden, away from Hossein.

"What is going on, Afsaneh?" asked her mother once they were beyond Hossein's hearing range. "I did not know that you are under so much stress, my dear. Why do you not talk to me about these things? Why did you not tell me anything sooner?"

"I don't know, Mom. I am trying to hold myself together. All of us are under plenty of stress. I guess I just thought I had to accept it and get on with things."

Mrs. Borhan motioned discreetly for Hossein, who was waiting patiently, to come and join them.

"May I suggest something?" asked Hossein, seizing the moment. "What if Afsaneh were to take some time off? Not long, maybe just for a week or so? To get away and clear her head."

Hossein's heart thumped in his chest as he awaited her mother's response.

"You know what? Hossein is right. That is a good idea," said Mrs. Borhan, addressing her daughter. "Why don't you take some time off my dear? Would you like to go to the Caspian Sea? The city of Ramsar must be beautiful now. All green and peaceful, with thousands of citrus trees that make the air smell so beautiful. Do you want to go there, my dear?"

"I don't know, Mom, I don't know," replied Afsaneh, she had not prepared for such a suggestion.

Hossein knew he had more work to do yet. "I love Ramsar, Mrs. Borhan. As a child, I used to go there with my parents every summer and I have the most beautiful memories from those trips. I loved Ramsar's main boulevard the most. Do you remember the rows of the tall palm trees that stood on both sides of that boulevard, connecting the shoreline all the way to the Casino Ramsar?"

"Of course I remember that," she replied, smiling at the recalled scenes of her past.

"Well, after several years of not being there, I visited Ramsar a few months ago. I stayed at what used to be the Hotel Casino Ramsar," said Hossein. "You know, although the town of Ramsar is still beautiful, it has become depressing. The city does not even maintain the palm trees anymore, and you can see the evidence of neglect on each and every one of them. But more importantly, the clergy and Islamic police rule the city now. Most people dress in black outfits. I could go on, but ultimately what I am trying to say is that Ramsar is not the city it used to be."

Hossein took a deep breath. It was now or never. "Afsaneh went to France last year, and from what I recall, she had a wonderful time there. She has a valid passport, and may already have a valid visa to go there again."

Mrs. Borhan looked contemplatively at both of them before turning to Afsaneh. "Would you like to go to Paris? Your cousin Niloofar lives there. Perhaps you can go and visit her?"

Hossein could not believe it. They had done it—they were another step closer to their solution.

"I really like Paris, Mom. I think that going there might help me relax a bit," said Afsaneh, careful not to sound too eager. "If I go there, I can also explore the possibility of Hossein and me studying there."

"Let's talk to your dad about this when he gets home," said Mrs. Borhan. "But I am in favor of it, as long as you are sure you can take some time off from your hospital work. You should also look at your passport to see if your visa is still valid."

"Yes, Mom, I will do that," said Afsaneh.

"I need to step out for a little while," said Mrs. Borhan. "Why don't you two look into that? Hossein, you are welcome to stay here for dinner."

"Please stay," said Afsaneh.

"Thank you, Mrs. Borhan. It would be an honor to have dinner with you."

Mrs. Borhan left. Hossein and Afsaneh went back to her room, practically skipping with triumph. They sat on the edge of her bed, holding each other's hands once more. Everything was falling into place. Afsaneh rested her head on Hossein's shoulder. She felt so comforted by him, and completely protected, as if nothing in the world could harm her. Hossein stroked Afsaneh's arm gently. Sparks as of electricity surged through her every time he caressed her skin.

"Your mom is out for an hour or so?" asked Hossein.

"Yes?" said Afsaneh, feeling a rush of adrenaline that caught her off guard. The tone of his voice divulged his intentions.

"Well… we do not need to worry about you getting pregnant twice now, do we?" said Hossein, kissing her face lightly.

"You are very bad, Hossein," said Afsaneh. "You wouldn't be proposing we undertake such a sinful act again, would you?" she teased.

* * *

One week later, Afsaneh flew to Paris.

CHAPTER EIGHTEEN
THE SHOW

On a Friday afternoon, Hossein and his family went to Hamid's house for dinner. Once again, this part of Tehran had lost electricity. The sun was gradually going down, turning the western skies a beautiful deep-orange hue. Hamid opened the door for Hossein and his family.

"Welcome, *khale Parvin,*" said Hamid to his aunt as she kissed him on both cheeks. "Unfortunately, we have lost electricity again so the house is a bit dark,"

She sighed, evidently fed up with this frequent occurrence.

"The power usually comes back at about eight, so I don't think we'll have to wait too long," said Hamid.

Everyone walked in. The house was scattered with several half-melted candles and old-fashioned kerosene-burning lamps in preparation for the darkness that would soon descend. Mahmood came to greet Hossein's family, as did Haj Agha. The three were eager to discuss how their plan was progressing, but they could not do so in present company.

"Guys, let's go out for a walk and catch the last light of the day," said Hossein, loud enough for the others to hear. "The sky is so beautiful."

The three excused themselves and strolled out to the street.

"So what is new Hamid?" asked Hossein when they were well out of the others' hearing range. "Where are we with the application process at the health ministry?"

Only after he had started the question did Hossein realize how impatient he was to hear the answer.

"Everything is fine. They asked to see all my medical records, everything from the base I was on, from the military hospital, and from Emam Khomeini Hospital. It seemed to be a pretty extensive investigation," said Hamid. "But my application has finally been completed and submitted. I heard that the review committee will be meeting next week, and my case is on its agenda. So we may know then."

"That's amazing, Hamid," said Hossein. "Everything is progressing the way we had hoped for; this is the final hurdle. If all works out well, we should be able to leave Iran in six to eight weeks. In the grand scheme of things, that is a very short time. Are you ready for it?"

"Yes, Hossein, I am hundred percent ready and set to go," replied Hamid.

"Please let me know as soon as you hear from the health ministry. Once they approve your application, you should be able to get a passport right away."

"Hossein, I have a surprise for you," said Hamid, reaching into his pocket.

"You organized so many things for me that I decided to take the initiative on something myself." He paused for effect.

"You remember when I got my military-exemption card two or three months ago? Well, as soon as I received it, I went straight to the passport office and applied for a passport. All they needed were four photographs, my military-exemption card, a completed application, and the processing fee."

His hand remained firmly in his pocket.

"Look what I received the other day." At that moment, Hamid removed his hand from his pocket, producing a pristine passport, which he handed to Hossein, grinning proudly.

"Oh my God, Hamid, this is wonderful! I am so happy for you. I cannot believe this; you actually have permission to leave the country. We did it!"

"Hamid is free now," said Mahmood.

"That is great, but we still need the approval from the health ministry, so that we can get our ten thousand dollars," said Hossein.

"We worked so hard to make sure that his application at the ministry was complete. We checked it over and over again. I'm really not worried about the outcome of the review committee next week—I have a good feeling about this."

Mahmood's lips suddenly curled into a smile as a flashback from the previous week traversed his mind.

"Hey, you won't believe what our dad did at the health ministry last week."

"What?" asked Hossein.

"There was some minor document missing from the application, and they were threatening to postpone the hearing on Hamid's application until next month. Well, dad blew a fuse, he started yelling and screaming at them, telling them that it was un-Islamic to hold up the application for such a minor thing, when a lifesaving treatment was waiting for his son. They tried to calm him, but he was relentless. He turned to someone else and started yelling at him too, asking what he would do if *his* son had leukemia. It was a truly remarkable show; I did not know he had it in him! I could not decide whether to join in or laugh aloud! In the end, I just stood there frozen to the spot, mesmerized by the incredible spectacle. They agreed to move the application forward, and we saved our laughing for the car ride home."

Hossein's shoulders shook with amusement, as he pictured the comedic scene.

"That's hilarious," he said. "Your dad has a great sense of humor.

"Seriously though, it goes to show the benefits of being a Haj Agha. In this society, only someone with a respected title can get something like that accomplished so quickly. At the ministry, they wouldn't listen to you or me," said Hossein.

"Hamid, once you get a letter from the health ministry, be sure that you enter my name as your companion on the trip."

"Already done," said Hamid with smug pride. "The application form had a place for the name and contact information of the companion, and Haj Agha, with his beautifully neat handwriting, wrote your name in that box. It is all taken care of. They told us that once they approved the application, they will issue a formal letter for the companion, in order for him, *you*, to get a passport and gain permission to leave the country."

Hossein could not believe it was really happening. Had they really pulled this off? He was desperate to give in to his desire to jump up and down in celebration and chat about the exciting possibilities that lay ahead, but he resisted, outwardly remaining his usual pragmatic and sensible self.

"We will need the letter from the health ministry to exchange money. We can take ten thousand dollars with us, which we will split. I will cover five thousand dollars, and you cover the other half."

"That sounds good, Hossein," said Hamid, his childlike expression displaying his excitement.

At that moment, a light came on in a house across the street, signaling that the electricity had come back on. "Look!" said Mahmood. "We have electricity again; today is full of good-luck signs. Come on, let's go and enjoy the dinner with our families."

CHAPTER NINETEEN
THE ILLNESS

Hossein was soon to discover, however, that even the best-laid plans could go awry. The most unexpected things can happen at a time when you are least ready for them. Just one day later, on Saturday morning, everything changed. Hossein went to work at his hospital as usual. He was on duty that day, and scheduled to spend the night at the pediatric unit. But by midday, fever and exhaustion had rapidly and unexpectedly infiltrated his body. He managed to attend his lectures in the afternoon, despite extreme lethargy and weakness. At five, when his night-call shift was to start, Hossein could not take any more; he went to meet his senior resident. With every step, his legs felt like they grew heavier. The senior resident saw immediately that something was wrong.

"You do not look good, Hossein," he said. "Are you okay?"

"No, I don't know what's wrong with me. I feel lousy," replied Hossein. "And even though I have been drinking plenty of water today I am so very thirsty. I need to rest."

"Yes, yes of course, go to bed. I hope that you feel better soon," said his resident.

As a precaution, Hossein went to the on-call room and lay on his bed, hoping that sleep would go some way toward rectifying his condition. He dozed in and out, but was unsettled and getting worse by the hour.

At eight that night, he got up to go for a walk with the intention of forcing himself to eat a little dinner. But as he approached the hospital cafeteria, the smell of the food knocked him sick. He retched; barely reaching the men's room before his stomach violently ejected its contents. The vomiting seemed to never end; it ravaged his entire body to the point where he struggled even to catch his breath. He prayed for it to stop.

After what seemed like hours, his stomach finally settled. Hossein stood to urinate, unsteady on his feet and with sweat pouring from his forehead. What he saw next confirmed the thought that was already circling the periphery of his consciousness; something was seriously wrong. As he looked in front of him, desperately trying to retain his balance, he noticed that the color of his urine had turned dark brown, almost black.

Oh my God; what is wrong with me?

Hossein slept at the hospital that night running a low-grade fever. By the morning, he felt far, far worse and he knew he had to get home. After what felt to Hossein like the longest and most difficult journey of his life, he arrived at his house, to be greeted by a look of extreme concern on his mother's face.

"What is wrong with you, Hossein? You look terrible. Come in."

Hossein's sister was home, and the first thing she commented on was his skin color.

"Hossein you are so yellow. What has happened to you?"

Hossein walked shakily toward a mirror, and looking at his eyes in the daylight, he realized that he was severely jaundiced. He totted up the symptoms in his head, and it suddenly struck him what was wrong. Alarm bells resonated loudly in his skull.

"Mom, I think I have hepatitis," said Hossein. "I need to be hospitalized. Can you take me to the hospital?"

"Oh my dear, of course I can. Are you going to be okay? Shall I take you to your own hospital? To Emam Khomeini?"

"No. I do not want to go to my own hospital. I cannot have my colleagues and classmates see me like this." Hossein was adamant.

Hossein was admitted to Taleghani Hospital that day, a hospital of the Melli University School of Medicine on the northern outskirts of Tehran. He had several friends there, and Mehrdad, one of best high school classmates, was doing his internship at that hospital. He knew he would be in the best hands. By the time he arrived at the hospital, his entire body had turned a deep shade of yellow. It was a far cry from the lively, strong, and vibrant man he was just days earlier. He was severely fatigued, barely able to transfer himself from the wheelchair to his hospital bed. He grabbed to the side rail of his bed for dear life as the kind young nurses assisted him.

Soon after his arrival, the team of on-call interns and residents showed up to examine him. Mehrdad, Hossein's best friend, rushed into the room and took hold of his hand.

"Hossein, don't worry, you will be fine. We will take care of you," he said. And even though Hossein knew it was a line delivered to all patients regardless of their prognosis, it still gave him some comfort.

Hours turned into days, and Hossein's condition continued to deteriorate. His jaundice deepened, and his liver-function tests worsened by the day. The medical team were doing all they could, but it was down to Hossein's own immune system to step up to the challenge and finish off the virus causing his hepatitis.

Hossein had acquired hepatitis B, a blood-born viral illness often transmitted by blood transfusion, or with needle sticks among health-care providers. He recalled an incident that had occurred several weeks earlier while he was working at the hospital clinic. A needle, used to treat a cancer patient, had scratched his hand. Foolishly, Hossein had ignored the tiny graze, and consequently was paying the price—he was fighting for his life.

The hepatitis B virus can vigorously attack the liver, preventing it from functioning correctly. As liver fails to perform its vital tasks, other organs become involved in the affliction. In its most severe and final stages, when liver failure advances, patients develop a fatal complication known as *hepatic encephalopathy*. If this occurs, normal brain functions are disturbed as a result of the build up of harmful chemicals in the blood, chemicals a healthy liver ordinarily filters and excretes from the body. At that point, patients start displaying emotional fragility, become depressed and then delirious, soon comatose and then die.

Hossein's condition was worsening day after day. Full-blown hepatic encephalopathy was just around the corner. Hossein was emotionally and physically drained. He felt like his whole world was falling apart, and all he could do was lie in his hospital bed and wait for this horrific virus to devour him completely.

One evening, at dinnertime, the nurse placed a tray of food in front of Hossein. But before he could reach out his frail hand to grasp a handful of food, another nurse entered the room and demanded that the tray be taken away.

"What is this? This man cannot have French fries. That is not his tray. That is fatty food, which his liver cannot handle. Please remove it immediately. I will bring him his special diet."

Hossein, who never cared much about food, let alone French fries, started crying uncontrollably. Hospital food is bad in the best of times, but at that moment, all Hossein wanted in the world was to eat those French fries, and even that was denied.

"Please don't take this away," pleaded Hossein through ravaged breaths. "I am tired of the bland, tasteless food you serve me every day. Please call the intern in charge tonight. I want… I want to talk to him."

That is it; early signs of hepatic encephalopathy, thought Hossein. *I have never ever cried for food, why now?*

The nurse looked embarrassed and unsure of how to handle the situation that had unfolded before her eyes. She nodded, and quickly scurried away to call the intern, who happened to be on the floor. Within minutes, he strode into the room, heading for the crumpled and defeated, yellow-skinned man who laid beneath the white hospital sheets. Hossein had become familiar with this intern during his stay and liked him.

"Hello, Hossein. How are you doing tonight?" asked the kind intern, and before Hossein could reply, he said, "Look, I know about the food thing. But I have some good news for you. Your lab works today came back slightly better. It does not seem as though you will be leaping into hepatic encephalopathy anytime soon. Seriously though, you are less jaundiced today than yesterday. We think you are on the road to recovery, so I am going to change your diet so you can start eating more regular foods again, but please put a limit on the deep-fried French fries. Okay?"

At that moment, the nurse walked in with a new tray of chicken cutlets, a portion of French fries, and a heartfelt apology for the confusion earlier. For the first time since he was admitted, Hossein managed a smile.

Soon after dinner, as Hossein was dozing back off to sleep, Afsaneh walked in. Up until now she had been in Paris, completely unaware of the state her lover was in back home. This suited Hossein; he had no desire for his beautiful Afsaneh to see him like this. But the night before, she had returned from Paris to the shocking news of Hossein's terrible sickness that other interns had told her.

Afsaneh ran through the door to his bedside.

"Hossein, Hossein, Hossein, oh my God, what happened to you, my love? My God, you look terrible. Oh Hossein, you are okay though, right? You are getting better? Please tell me you're going to be okay!"

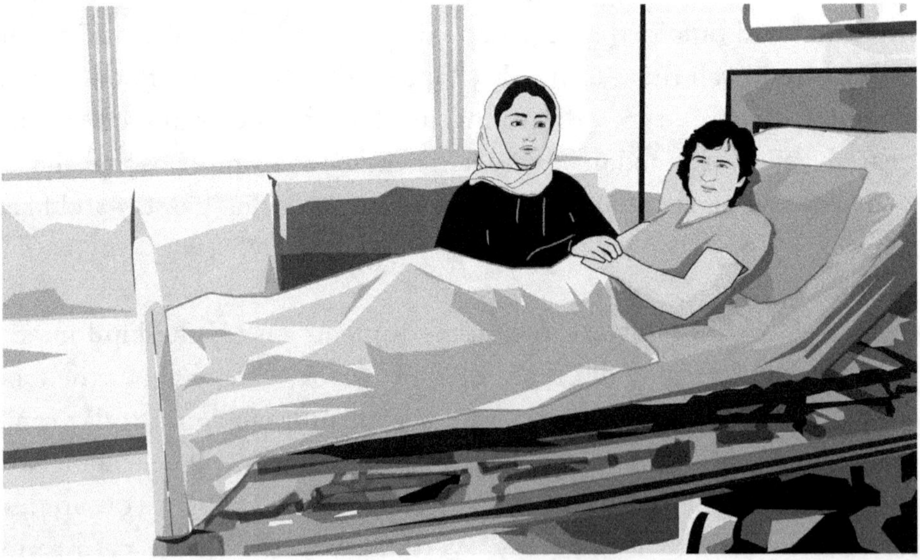

"Afsaneh, I am so glad to see you," Hossein mumbled weakly. He felt a lump rise in his throat. He had been so preoccupied with the state of his health that he had not the time to acknowledge how much he had missed this amazing woman who now stood in front of him. It struck him all at once. "Several weeks ago, a needle barely scratched my right hand, and stupidly I did not think much about it. Well, I got fulminate hepatitis B from it. Can you believe this?"

Hossein spoke slowly; it took all his energy just to talk.

"You will be fine, Hossein. You are a healthy young man otherwise," Afsaneh reassured him. But her moist eyes and the tight grasp of her hands around his betrayed her inner fear for what still could happen. "You are already on your way to recovery. Your liver functions have started to improve. I was out there looking at your chart, and talking to the residents. My love, I know you can fight this. The worst is over."

Hossein suddenly felt very aware of how he must have looked to Afsaneh. He was supposed to be the strong one, the protector, not the weak, frail person he had become. He knew it was illogical, but he could not help feeling that he had failed her.

"I never wanted you to see me like this, Afsaneh, and besides, you were going through enough yourself with the abortion," said Hossein. "You know, you and I have always been on the other side of treatment, on the physician side, caring for sick patients. Now the tables have turned and I am the patient. It feels different, Afsaneh."

Afsaneh was shedding tears as she listened to Hossein's words. It had never occurred to her that she would see him in such a condition, that the tables would turn and she would be the one who had to look after him. It was just so strange.

Hossein was the bulwark of his class, a pillar of strength to all his friends. Others would crowd around him on hospital rounds, desperate for a slice of the seemingly endless knowledge he had on even the most difficult and complicated medical cases. Despite his fragility, he still managed to comfort the lovely woman who stood before him with pity in her eyes.

"Don't cry, my love. I will be fine," said Hossein reaching out slowly to gently wipe tears from Afsaneh's face. "What about you? I have been thinking about you. Tell me how everything went in Paris. Did you have the procedure?"

"Yes, yes, you have nothing to worry about there. Everything went well," said Afsaneh, sniffing. "They did the procedure two days after I arrived, and without complication. I had to rest for only one day. The next day, I was up and about, just as I had been before."

"I am glad to hear that, Afsaneh," said Hossein, genuinely relieved. "But there is one more thing that you need to do now. You need to test yourself for hepatitis B."

Afsaneh froze, fear pooling in the pit of her stomach. In her panic over Hossein, she had completely forgotten that the hepatitis B virus could also be sexually transmitted. She chose to hide her distress. Hossein had been through enough.

"Sure, Hossein, I will get a blood test tomorrow," she said as nonchalantly as she could.

CHAPTER TWENTY
HELPING HANDS

Hossein's condition had terrified his family, and they did little to conceal this in front of him. His mother, Parvin was in tears every day, petrified at the possibility of losing her youngest son to this dreadful illness. But slowly, over the next few days, Hossein's condition took a turn for the better and after two further weeks of bed rest in the hospital, he was finally allowed to return home.

He arrived to good news. The authorities had approved Hamid's application for travel abroad for medical treatment. He had just received the paperwork from the health ministry.

"Hossein, everything worked out just as you thought," said Mahmood, who, accompanied by Hamid, had been one of his first visitors. As he handed a letter to Hossein to read, Mahmood said, "Look at this. This is the confirmation that you can leave Iran with Hamid as his companion. You're free to go too."

"I am so glad to see this," said Hossein. "But now we must plan for the trip to Germany without hesitation. We need to contact several German hospitals, send each one of them a copy of Hamid's medical records, and then hope to receive a letter in return from them, indicating that they are willing to treat him once he is in Germany. It is only with such documentation that they will issue Hamid a visa. Mahmood, can you take the lead on this? I am not only weak from the hepatitis, but I do not have time to do the research. I need you to go to the German Embassy and get a list of the hospitals in Frankfurt and other cities. You also need to translate all his medical records and his high school transcripts into German. Translate them into English as well."

"Sure, Hossein, I will do it," replied Mahmood, impressed by Hossein's rational approach despite his desperate fight for survival during the preceding weeks.

"There is so much to do, Mahmood," said Hossein gravely. "I hope that you two can manage everything. I will have to focus on my own stuff. I have to make plans for my own departure. I have so much to sort out."

"Understood, Hossein," said Mahmood. "Don't worry. We will take care of our end. You focus on the things you need to, and more importantly, on getting better. Hopefully, you and Hamid will depart together soon."

Hossein continued, unable to rest until he was sure that all knew what they had to do.

"Hamid, now that we have both these documents, it is crucial that we file them with the passport office. You need to do this in order to get permission to exchange the ten thousand U.S. dollars at the discounted bank rate. And I will need to file mine to obtain a passport and permission to exit Iran."

"True," said Hamid. "We are going to the passport office tomorrow morning. Are you strong enough to come with us, so you can also make out your application?"

"I think so," said Hossein. "Well, to be honest, I don't have much of a choice. Time is running out. The sooner we do this, the sooner we can get out of here."

The next morning, Hamid and Mahmood arrived at Hossein's house, and together, the three went to the passport office. At the counter, Hamid handed in his new passport and informed the processor about his letter from the health ministry. Once Hamid finished, Hossein stepped forward.

"Good morning, sir. I am here to renew my passport. I am the person accompanying Hamid for his overseas medical treatment."

"Good morning," said the passport officer monotonously, as though he were tired of doing this job day in and day out. "Please complete this application form. Include your old passport, four photographs, and the application fee, which must be paid as a bank check and a copy of the letter from the health ministry. I am assuming you have done your military service?"

"No, sir, I have not. I am still a student at the university," replied Hossein.

The passport officer continued, unfazed by the response.

"Right. Well, in that case you are going to need two more things before you can get a new passport and permission to leave Iran. Write these down," commanded the passport officer. "First, get a letter of good standing from your university's Islamic Association; second, get a certificate from the military, allowing you to leave Iran without having completed your military service. For that, you must go to the Central Military Command Agency. Once you have those, you may get a passport, but then you will need permission to leave Iran, and that has to come from the Ministry of the Interior."

"Oh, okay. Can you think of anything else that I may need to complete this application?" asked Hossein.

"No, that is it," snapped the passport officer. "You can go downstairs to have your pictures taken. There is also a bank where you can get the required check. Bring your completed application, photographs, and the bank check, and we can get the process started. Once you have the other documents, bring them in."

"Thank you, sir," said Hossein.

Hossein did not delay. He put in his application that day. Then the three drove in silence to the Military Command Agency. Luckily, it was not far.

"Fill out this application form. We need a copy of the letter from the Health Ministry," said the military officer. "Because you are still a student, you must also leave a deposit in the amount of one million rials, guaranteeing that you will return to Iran at the end of your travel. You get your money back when you return home. Bring these back, and we will get the paperwork started."

One million rials equaled ten thousand U.S. dollars at the time, an incredibly large sum in 1983. For the past two years, however, Hossein had one goal, one dream—to leave Iran, and in order to achieve that, he had worked tirelessly in a private medical clinic to ensure he could save enough money to cover the initial expenses. Nevertheless, one million rials was a large sum to hand over at one time.

The next morning, Hossein awoke early, and continued with his quest. First, he went to his local bank and transferred the funds into the account of the military, exactly as requested, being careful to leave with a receipt documenting the transaction. Next, he stopped at the military command to complete his application there. He took a deep breath and walked through the door, trying to exude a level of confidence he did not quite feel.

"Would you be so kind and expedite this application?" asked Hossein politely. He trod carefully; it was important to get these people on his side. "My cousin must go overseas for medical treatment, and I am accompanying him."

Hossein need not have worried.

"You are doing a good deed for Islam, my son," was the military officer's response. "Wait here. Let me see if I can get this done for you right away."

To Hossein's surprise, the army officer returned within ten minutes, brandishing a letter of temporary exemption from military service.

Hossein could not believe what he was looking at. This was the most difficult step to achieve, and he had done it. It was working; the pieces of the puzzle were falling into place easier than he had imagined.

The final stop of the day was the office of Islamic Association at the University.

"I need a letter of good standing," said Hossein bluntly, oblivious to the flicker of familiar recognition that danced in the clerk's eyes.

"Hey, I know you. You work at Emam Khomeini Hospital," said the person behind the desk.

"Yes, that's right," said Hossein, cautiously. "But I am afraid I do not remember you."

"You helped my father when he was there few months ago. I remember your face. He liked you very much."

Hossein smiled, relieved. This was unbelievable! Yet another helping hand along the road out of Iran. He was sure that this tenuous connection would work to his advantage.

"Let me get your file."

The person came back moments later with a manila folder, which had Hossein's name on it.

"Do you maintain files on everyone here?" asked Hossein.

"Yes, on everyone," replied the clerk, distractedly scanning the document. "Ah, good, you were not a member of SAVAK. Nor have you ever belonged to any political group."

SAVAK was the old secret service from the time of the Shah, prior to 1979. After the revolution, several students were discovered to have been SAVAK agents, and in 1980 the University expelled all of them.

"You are not a communist," the clerk continued chirpily, "and although you do not belong to the Islamic student group, you have a clean record with us. Therefore, this should be okay. I do not foresee any problems. Come back tomorrow and I will have our manager write the letter you need."

The following day, on his way to the passport office, Hossein stopped by the Islamic Association's office just to see if anything was waiting for him. To his surprise, his letter was ready. He carefully handled the sealed envelope. This was it; he was getting very close to his goal.

Hossein arrived at the passport office just before the end of the working day. As he handed over his documents, he was suddenly very aware of how exhausted he was. The hepatitis virus had certainly left its mark.

"The only thing you now need is the clearance from the Ministry of the Interior," said the clerk at the passport office. "Your passport should be ready one week after we get their approval."

"Thank you, sir," said Hossein, as he left. He was too tired to display the profound elation he felt. All those months of relentless hard work were starting to pay off, and there was only one person with whom he wanted to share the fruits of his labor: Afsaneh. He headed toward her house, fighting off his exhaustion, defiantly refusing to let it slow him down.

It had been several weeks since he had stepped foot in their house, and now, walking down the hallway, the familiar and comforting sights highlighted just how much had happened in such a short time. This house looked exactly the same, yet everything in Hossein's life was different.

"Afsaneh told me about your illness, Hossein," said Mrs. Borhan. "All of us prayed for you every day, and we are all so glad you are feeling better."

"Thank you, Mrs. Borhan," said Hossein. "I am much better now. I had a few rough weeks, but I am determined to put them behind me. My latest blood-test results were good, so I intend to focus fully on my future and put that horrible illness firmly in my past."

Mrs. Borhan hugged Hossein and wished him well. She stepped out to attend to her work, providing some privacy to Hossein and Afsaneh.

"How was Paris, Afsaneh? We never got a chance to talk about it," said Hossein, realizing just how much he had missed.

"Paris was nice," said Afsaneh. "I stayed with my cousin Niloofar. I told her about what had happened. She was so understanding. I did not feel like she was judging me at all. She took me to her own doctor the next morning, who in turn referred me to a private gynecologist in Paris, a specialist in performing abortions. He ran a few blood tests, and I had the procedure first thing on the third day of my stay. Everything went perfectly. They looked after me well, and kept me there for observation until that evening. Niloofar stayed with me all day and took me home that night. And that was it." She paused, realizing she was talking fast.

"What amazed me was the ease of getting an abortion over there. To them, it was no more difficult than extracting a tooth. There was nothing extraordinary about it, no taboos, no shame, and no questions asked. They did it in a clean and safe private setting, and with respect, such a huge contrast to Iran. Did you know, Hossein, that thus far they have executed two physicians here for performing what they call illegal abortions?"

"Yes, Afsaneh, I know that," said Hossein. "I did a lot of research into it when we were looking into having the procedure done here. I also found out that a female practitioner was recently jailed for carrying out abortions in her office. A year or so after the fall of the Shah, some high-ranking cleric at Friday prayers at Tehran University said that all male gynecologists in this country should find a more respectable job for themselves, and give up gynecology. Do you remember that? Crazy."

"Of course I do," said Afsaneh. "You don't forget something like that. I heard it with my own ears. I never listened to that propaganda, but that Friday, for some reason, the TV was on, and the program was broadcast live. It was splashed across all the newspapers, and it was the hottest topic of conversation at the hospital for weeks. What an insult it was to the profession of medicine." If there was one thing she could not stand, it was having her chosen vocation ridiculed. She continued, on a roll now.

"Let me tell you something else that has to do with gynecology," Hossein interjected, in complete agreement with every word she uttered. "This is both funny and sad. Now, I am sure you know that before a high-ranking cleric becomes an *Ayatollah*, he must write a book of dos and don'ts, *Towzih ol-Masael*. I read this in one of those books." Hossein cleared his throat and proceeded to recite the memorized line. "It said the following: 'If a male physician has to examine the genital area of a woman, he must look at her genitalia only through the reflection in a mirror.' Afsaneh, imagine trying to do a PAP smear, or deliver a baby by looking through a mirror! It is a joke! We've come so far in medicine, there have been so many amazing advances, and *this* is what it has come to in our country?!"

"That is why we have lost so many of our good physicians already," said Afsaneh.

"You and I know about the situation in medicine only because we see it firsthand," said Hossein. "Can you imagine how many specialists in other professions have left Iran that we are not aware of?"

Afsaneh sighed. She could continue this conversation for hours, but she made a conscious effort to change the subject to something more upbeat.

"So, Hossein, ECFMG is around the corner. Are you going to make it?"

"I am working on it. Have you bought your ticket to Paris?"

"Yes, I have," she nodded. "As soon as I returned from my trip, I went to the Air France office and bought my ticket. My mother was a little surprised. Somehow, the date of the examination never registered in her mind. She was under the impression that the examination was in September. Perhaps it was better she did not realize until I had returned. Anyway, everything is set. I am leaving right after graduation."

"Be careful about your graduation timelines," warned Hossein. "You know that all male graduates must immediately report to the military and register to serve in the army. For female graduates, the moment you graduate, you will not be able to leave Iran. You automatically become *mamnuol khorouj*, banned from travel outside the country, and you will be stuck here until you do three years of civil service. You must not hand in your thesis yourself, Afsaneh. Have your mother take it to the university after you leave Iran."

"Oh my God, I never thought of that. Thanks, Hossein." Once again, the minefield of Iranian politics became evident. One wrong move and it was game over.

"Hey, do you want to see something interesting?" asked Afsaneh.

"Oh, sure, what is it?"

Afsaneh turned on her heel and returned from her bedroom with small packages.

"This one is for you, an eau de cologne," said Afsaneh. "I hope that you like it. This one, however, I am sure you will appreciate even more now. It is for the both of us."

Afsaneh handed a package of tablets to Hossein.

Hossein gasped. "How did you get these?"

"The abortion clinic, gave them to me," said Afsaneh. "Their policy is to offer birth-control pills to all their patients. I was not going to refuse. This is a six-month supply."

"This is amazing. Once again, the differences between oppressed Iran and the uninhibited Western world are illuminated. Compare the birth-control policy of Iran to that of France," said Hossein. "In one country, they execute physicians for performing abortions; in the other, abortion is a routine and regular medical procedure. Can you imagine the population explosion that we will face in the next few decades? Where on earth is our country heading?"

The poignant question did not require a response.

CHAPTER TWENTY ONE
THE SAVAB

The next day, Hossein went to the Ministry of the Interior. The office that issued clearances for people such as Hossein, and those who were *mamnuol khorouj*, had moved to a separate two-story building, across the street from the main ministry complex in Tehran. It was an unusual place; this office looked like it had been someone's home at some point. Hossein spoke quietly to the two guards at the entrance, explaining in detail why he was there. Once the guards were satisfied with his story, they allowed him inside.

The main building was behind a front courtyard. Hossein entered through a heavy door, which opened into an unimpressive foyer. The foyer had one desk, and several chairs placed against the walls. A middle-aged, heavyset, bearded man was sitting behind the desk. He advised Hossein to take a seat with two others already in the waiting area—a beautiful young woman wearing a scarf and expensive-looking sunglasses, and an older man.

The young woman wore her scarf with a definite air of distain. It was clear to Hossein she would rather not have such a stifling dress code imposed upon her. She went in first and snapped the door shut behind her, yet Hossein was still able to pick up some of the conversation that leaked out from the room. In less than two minutes, the woman returned, visibly upset and trying to prevent tears from spilling past the rim of her sunglasses. Hossein felt for her. He could not begin to imagine the disappointment of not gaining clearance to leave the country.

Next, the older man went in. He too exited the room shortly after a very loud conversation with lots of yelling, most of which came from the office employee to the older man. He too walked out, quite distressed. Obviously, he did not receive the approval he needed from whatever heartless tyrant who was sitting in that room.

Hossein's heart was thumping so fast he thought it might jump right out of his chest. He had not allowed himself to consider the possibility of failing at this, the final hurdle. A voice from inside called, "Next person, come in."

Hossein had never experienced nervousness such as this. His whole body quivered involuntarily, blood pounding through his head. He stood and walked quickly toward the entrance to the room. This was it—judgment day.

Who is this person? What is his position? What qualifications does he have? How powerful is he? How much hatred is in his heart for those who dream only of traveling abroad? These were just a handful of the barrage of questions that pushed through his mind, demanding his attention.

"Have a seat," the man ordered sternly, without even looking at Hossein.

"Thank you, and good morning, sir," said Hossein, determined to remain optimistic as he sat on an old, cheap, folding metal chair across the table from this less-than-pleasant man. The obviously power-hungry bureaucrat kept his eyes down, looking at his desk, writing something on a paper, and placing it inside a manila folder. The room was dark, partly because of the closed window shades. The man eventually raised his head, took off his glasses, and looked at Hossein.

"What can I do for you?"

Hossein knew that winning him over would be no easy feat. But he also knew that doing so was the only way to get his application approved. He eyed the person who stood before him. The man appeared to be in his mid fifties and was short, perhaps no more than about five foot three inches, with cropped gray hair. He wore a dark-gray suit and a gray shirt, typical dress for those who worked in the government. The country had denounced men wearing ties long ago, and now all must dress in gray or muted colors.

And so Hossein began his speech, "Sir, my cousin is sick. He is only nineteen, and he seems to have some sort of bone-marrow disease, like an early form of leukemia. The doctors here cannot treat him and have told us that he may need a bone-marrow transplant. Luckily, his father obtained permission for him to go abroad for treatment. The problem is that his father has five other children, three of whom are much younger than my cousin. He cannot leave his family behind and travel abroad. My cousin does not speak any English; neither does his father, nor anyone else in his immediate family, so they asked me to accompany him. I have hesitantly agreed to go, purely because I know how badly they need my help. My summer vacation from school is coming up in a few weeks, and I thought I could do a good deed for him. Hopefully God will count this act of mine as one that can be rewarded when I die."

At that point, Hossein paused for a response, mentally analyzing everything he had just said. In truth, he was proud of the speech he had just delivered. He could not believe that he could do so well without any preparation, and was eager to see what reaction it elicited. A long pause followed. The man looked suspiciously at Hossein and did not say a thing for a short while. Despite the mysterious silence in the room, Hossein knew he had delivered his speech to the best of his ability. He also knew that the man was waiting for more, but Hossein kept his silence in stubborn mental combat.

Hossein had also considered the psychological impact of his attire for this meeting, and had intentionally dressed in his ugliest gray shirt, teamed with an equally hideous gray pair of un-ironed, loose pants. He had not shaved for a few days, and sported a beard in a mock symbol of commitment to the Islamic regime.

The man did not take his eyes off Hossein for a long time. Eventually, he spoke.

"What paperwork and documents have you brought here with you?"

Hossein hid a victorious smile. The other man felt compelled to break the silence. Now, it was time to make the man believe he was doing the right thing.

"Sir, please allow me to first hand you two letters from the Ministry of Health," said Hossein, and steadying both his hands, he passed the letters to the man. "One is the approval for my cousin to travel abroad, and the other is the letter designating me as the accompanying person. This third letter is a copy of my temporary exemption from military service."

"Do you have something from the university as well?" the man snapped.

"Sure, sir," said Hossein as he handed in the letter of good standing from Tehran University's Islamic Association.

Hossein had nothing else that he could hand in, and there was no more dialogue to deliver. All he could do was wait. Strangely, the man began to quote a verse from the Quran in Arabic, of which Hossein did not understand a word. He hoped this was not a test.

The bureaucrat's tone of voice changed instantaneously. It sported a softer edge as he gently revealed why: "My father died of leukemia several years ago. Back then, there was no treatment. I hope that your cousin can get some help abroad. I am going to approve your application. You are doing *savab* by accompanying him abroad. May God bless you and your cousin."

Hossein noted the man used the word *savab* for "good deed" but he remained silent. This was the time to let the man talk.

Allowing him to talk will make him feel good about approving my application, thought Hossein, his admirable people skills shining through once again.

The man pulled out a blank form from his drawer and started writing something on it. He had addressed the form to the passport office. It affirmed that Hossein had clearance from the Ministry of the Interior. The purpose of the travel was to accompany a sick person.

The form was multilayered, with carbon paper between the layers. The man tore the top sheet, handed it to Hossein, and filed the remaining copies.

"Good luck, son," were his last words.

Hossein stood, thanked him, and walked out. He just wanted to leave that office building as fast as he could. As he exited the room, the young woman whom he had seen earlier approached the door and started begging the bureaucrat again to give her permission to leave Iran.

"Please, sir, please. Please let me go. Half my family is living abroad. I don't have anyone here," cried the woman through her tears.

"I am sorry. According to the laws of Islam, your father committed a crime, which prohibits us from allowing him, or his family, to leave Iran. You and your family are all *mamnuol khorouj.*"

Hossein left that office as quickly as he could, clutching the document he had dreamed of receiving for quite some time. Once on the street, he paused for a minute, in the shade of a tree, to reorganize his thoughts. From distance, he noticed the young woman who was *mamnuol khorouj* exiting the building. He quickly wrote a note to give to the woman who was now getting closer to him.

"This is the phone number for a smuggler, in case you need one," said Hossein to the woman as he handed her the note. "His name is Jahangir. He is highly recommended."

Hossein walked away before she could even thank him. His next stop was the passport office. He dropped off the last needed document that was to secure him a passport. Later that day, Hossein visited Afsaneh.

⋆ ⋆ ⋆

The next Friday, early in the morning, Afsaneh took the Paris-bound Air France flight from Tehran's Mehrabad Airport. Hossein stood next to Afsaneh's tearful parents, waving farewell.

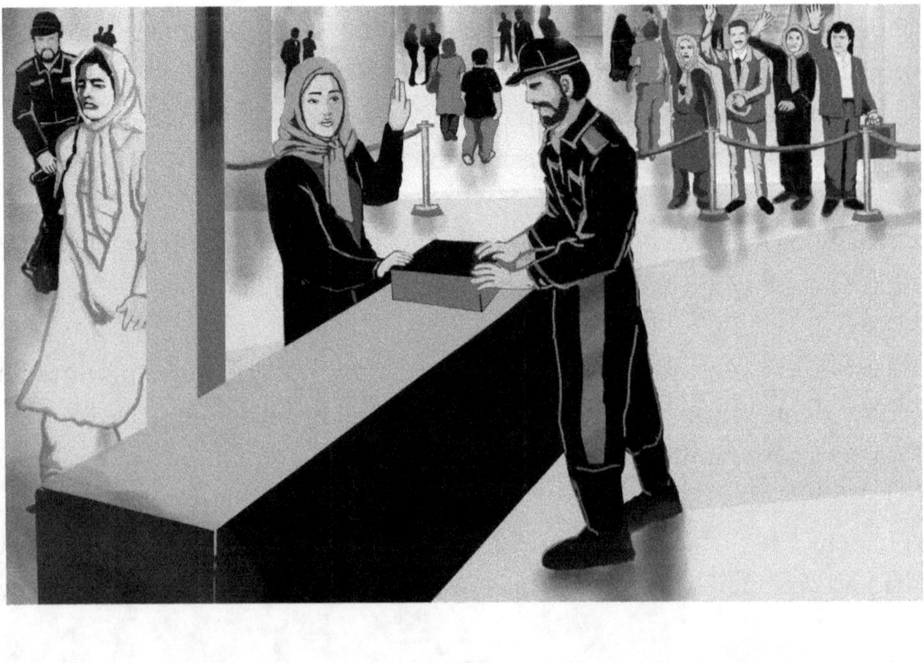

CHAPTER TWENTY TWO
THE CROWD

The next Wednesday, Hossein visited the passport office, still unsure whether his passport would be ready. His heart was pounding. He could barely wait to reach to the counter where he would receive his passport. He walked up the stairs to the second floor. Finally, he was there, standing before the counter, before the man who handed the passports to the travelers.

"I am here to pick up my passport," said Hossein to the clerk.

Minutes later, he was in possession of his very own passport. He stepped aside from the counter and walked to the window overlooking the courtyard of the building. He clutched his passport tightly between his fingers as if he was expecting someone to snatch it from him at any moment. Standing there, with the precious travel authorization in his hand was the most incredible feeling. It was a scene he had been unable to envision fully until this moment. Yet here it was, the moment he had been waiting for.

The events of the past several months passed through his mind like a short but gripping action movie, from Hamid's first blood draw, to his exemption from military duty, and finally to getting permission to leave Iran. Hossein knew that several of his classmates were also planning to leave, but it felt good to know he would be among the first few to depart, a brave trailblazer whom they would all simultaneously admire and envy. He allowed himself to languish in his daydream for a few moments longer.

It is important to remember that for Iranians at the time, obtaining a passport was not enough to gain access to their intended destinations, and although Hossein had legal permission to leave Iran, he now needed to obtain a visa to enter another country. The examination center he had chosen for his ECFMG was Frankfurt. He had verified with the embassy that he was in fact able to get a visa to travel to Germany. This being the case, his next stop that Wednesday afternoon was the Lufthansa office in Tehran. As he walked, he pondered over all the hard work he had done to reach this point, and once again, his decision to maintain secrecy about his plans seemed like the right one. He was not ready to take any risks that would jeopardize his departure from Iran, so he decided to disclose his departure date only to a very intimate group of people, namely, his mother and his siblings. No one else was to know, neither Hamid nor Mahmood.

Of course, Hossein had absolutely no intention of returning to Iran, but in order to remain inconspicuous, secure a visa to Germany, and to prevent his plans from failing, he made the clever decision to purchase a round-trip ticket with a return date two weeks after the departure. To the outside world, it looked completely legitimate.

Once he completed the first task on his list, he headed directly to the central bank so he could exchange his soon-to-be-redundant Iranian currency. The war with Iraq persisted, and in order to discourage travel, the government had severely limited the amount of foreign currency that any regular traveler could take abroad to just five hundred dollars. Thank God, Hamid was able to take ten thousand U.S. dollars with him to pay for the treatments he was presumed to require. Hossein's five-thousand dollar half would be plenty to support him until he got on his feet.

"How do you want your five hundred dollars?" asked the clerk at the bank.

"Does not matter," replied Hossein trying (and succeeding), to look collected and self assured.

Hossein got the five hundred dollars from the bank without question. He crossed Ferdowsi Street with the intention of going to the German Embassy, but when he arrived there, he was disappointed to discover that the visa department was open only from ten in the morning to two in the afternoon; the office had already closed for the day. This minor hitch in Hossein's immediate plan irritated him, but he vowed to return at nine the next morning.

As he walked idly along the streets, Hossein pictured himself at the airport. He knew very well that he and all his belongings would be searched, and that carrying any more than five hundred dollars was illegal. It was a regulation that was strictly enforced, and carrying even one dollar over the limit could jeopardize his chance of traveling. Hossein knew it would be far easier to exchange money in what had become a black market by the dubious *sarrafis,* the private money-exchange businesses, but he chose not to risk it. And although hiding one's money in one's luggage was at the time a norm for most Iranian travelers, for Hossein, the risk of being caught was simply too high. So, with only five hundred dollars in his pocket, staying at any kind of hotel in Frankfurt was out of the question. He had to ensure that the money he took with him would carry him through until Hamid arrived.

Hossein wondered what Hamid had done about his travel plans. After several minutes of inane pondering, Hossein set off to Hamid's house to find out for himself. Chatting to them would help put his mind at ease. Hossein flagged down the nearest taxi, but halfway along the journey he had a sudden change of heart.

"Stop here, please."

"Are you sure? We are not there yet," said the driver, bemused.

"Yes I am sure," replied Hossein obstinately.

Just before Hossein had abruptly asked the driver to stop, he had spotted a huge sporting-goods store out of the corner of his eye. It had triggered the beginnings of a solution to his living concerns in Frankfurt. Hossein scanned the many aisles, displaying various kinds of tools and apparatus. Each aisle was swarming with people. He did not have time to search this maze of a store, so he collared the first employee he could find, the store manager.

"Where do I find the camping equipment?"

"Second floor, to the right of the staircase," replied the store manager. He appeared impatient, as though the question was a great inconvenience.

"You don't happen to sell suitcases as well, do you?" asked Hossein, making the most of this man's knowledge before he scurried away.

"We sell backpacks, not suitcases, but you can go to the shop around the corner and find the best selection of those." Hossein had already started walking away before the man had reached the end of his sentence.

He walked up the stairs and arrived in the camping-equipment section. The vast selection was overwhelming. Hossein had no idea what to choose.

Several wearisome minutes of decision-making later, he walked out carrying a large backpack, sleeping bag, air mattress, and a small tent.

"What are these things Hossein?" asked Parvin as she opened the door for him. It was the tent she identified first. "Are you going camping, my son? With whom?"

"I will tell all of you about it, Mom. Just let me drop the stuff in my room first. These things are deceptively heavy."

Hossein's brother and sister were also home. They all crowded around silently, waiting to hear the story that Hossein had to tell. As he looked around the room, he suddenly felt anxious. He knew that what he was about to disclose would upset them, and he wished he could do something to soften the blow. The love he felt for his wonderful, caring family tugged at his heartstrings as he told them he had received his passport and that he was planning to leave Iran the following week. As expected, they were all shocked by the news that his departure from Iran was imminent.

"But why so soon, Hossein?" asked his mother, unable to conceal the desperation in her voice.

"Mom, please try to understand. Sooner or later, I must leave Iran. I am due to take my ECFMG examination in Frankfurt next Monday, just five days from now."

"How did you manage that?" asked Hossein's brother, incredulous. "It is impossible for someone like you to get a passport. You are expected to go and serve in the military, which you have not done yet."

Hossein felt he owed his family the truth. They at least deserved that much.

"All of you must keep everything that I am about to tell you a complete secret. No one, I repeat, no one should ever know about, or hear, the things I am about to tell you. This includes Hamid, his family, and everyone else. I am telling you this because I love you and trust you. The consequences of this story leaking will be horrendous. Okay?"

They all nodded in silent agreement.

"It is a very long story," said Hossein. "You already know that Hamid is ill and that his father applied for him to go to Europe for treatment. Well, his illness was something I induced and controlled in him so he could get exemption from his military duties. Now, I am leaving Iran to accompany him on his trip. Believe me, pulling this off and getting a passport to leave Iran required months of careful planning."

Several gasps echoed around the room.

"I won't go into all the details now, but I will tell you this much. It was totally worth it. Also, I have spent all my savings. I had to leave a one million rial deposit to get a temporary exemption from the military."

No one spoke for a while, but their stunned expressions said plenty.

"I cannot believe you kept all this to yourself, Hossein," said his brother finally, before adding, "I would have helped you."

Hossein felt a pang of guilt. His brother seemed genuinely hurt that Hossein had not sought his assistance.

"Thank you, I appreciate that, I really do. But I was able to manage everything," said Hossein, turning to his other family members. "My ticket is for this Saturday. I have to get my visa tomorrow, and then drop off my passport at Lufthansa, which they need twenty-four hours before departure to ensure that I am not *mamnuol khorouj*."

Hossein spent the Wednesday night with his family, answering their questions, reassuring them and wrapping up all his last-minute affairs. His examination was on Monday, so the deadline was more than a little tight. He had only one day, Thursday, to get his visa. Fridays are official holidays in Iran, and so the German Embassy was closed. Hossein's flight would leave on Saturday, with or without him.

Thursday morning, Hossein arrived at the German Embassy an hour before the doors were due to open. An unbelievably long line had already formed outside. He had no option but to join the back of the queue.

The main entrance to the embassy was on the busy Ferdowsi Street, across from Iran's Central Bank. And as the time passed, the line grew exponentially. Hossein felt the shift in atmosphere and the increase in anticipation in the moments before the doors opened. As soon at the heavy slabs of wood shifted outwards, the crowd launched itself at the entrance; it was truly every man for himself. In less than a minute, the line had disintegrated into a huge unruly throng in front of the embassy, and with it every scrap of human graciousness and decorum. It was not a scene Hossein had expected, but it emphasized all that was wrong with Iran. He saw that the unruly mob of people forced the brave person who had opened the embassy to reclose it to keep them out. The riled crowd started yelling and screaming in retaliation.

When the embassy doors reopened, they framed a man who stood blocking the entrance with a loudspeaker in his hand.

"The embassy is closed for the rest of the day and will reopen on Monday!" He roared.

Hossein's blood froze. *No. Please, no.* A few months earlier, on the day that he went to the embassy with his initial inquiries, there were no lines at all. Yet today, the only day that he had left to get a visa to travel to Germany, he could not even get close to the entrance to the embassy. He did not leave to go home; he just waited in front of the embassy, praying for a miracle to happen. Several other people appeared to have the same idea. After awhile, it became clear that, miracles were not on the agenda that day. Not for this crowd.

The door remained firmly closed, and as time passed, people slowly dispersed. Just then, Hossein suddenly found his feet. He had never in his life felt desperation like this; his skin was clammy and his heart beat rapidly. Squeezing and pushing through the people in front of him, he realized that he could get himself close to the doors of the embassy. Without hesitation, he rapped loudly on the door, but there was no answer. Someone in the crowd told him that knocking on the doors would upset the embassy staff even more, but he chose to ignore that person, and kept knocking, harder and harder until his knuckles were red and raw. After ten minutes, someone opened the gap of the door, reaffirming that the embassy was closed.

Hossein grasped at the fleeting chance to make himself heard. "Sir, may I have your attention, please?" said Hossein. "This is very important. I have a flight to Germany on Saturday. I have an examination scheduled in Frankfurt for next Monday. I have all my paperwork with me. I need to get a visa today. If I do not get a visa today, I will lose six months of my life. The next time I can take the examination is six months later. Would you kindly let me in? Please?" he begged.

"The embassy is closed today," said the resolute employee in Farsi. "Come back on Monday."

"Sir, please, this is urgent! I cannot come back on Monday. I was here a few months ago. I met with Herr Mueller, who told me I could get a visa, and I have all the necessary paperwork now. Look at my documents. Please listen to me; I have to take an examination in Frankfurt on Monday. Please sir!" said Hossein, unable to comprehend how anyone could show such little empathy for such an anguished man.

"Don't bother showing me your papers. All the people who come here have similar issues and the same kind of papers you have. I cannot differentiate between you and the others. I will not tell you again, the embassy is closed. Come back on Monday. Goodbye." And with that, he slammed the doors tightly shut.

Hossein had lost all hope of getting his visa to Germany. This was a major setback in his plans, a setback to his future, and a setback in his life. He had come so far, and now there was nothing else he could do. His knees refused to carry his weight any longer and he sank to the floor, defeated. There were no words to describe sufficiently the disappointment he felt. He went over and over the situation in his head.

I do not understand. I worked very hard to get Hamid out of the military, and I succeeded. I got him permission to leave Iran, and a passport for myself—an impossible task. Now, this last step, this rather attainable task, became the one that I could not tackle. Whose fault is this? Is it the fault of the Germans behind these walls? Is it the fault of the frantic crowd rushing to the door? Had they stayed in line, had they kept order, I would have been able to get in and get my visa. Why did this happen? Why do all these people want to go to Germany? Perhaps the Germans are the last embassy issuing visas to the Iranian youth?

Thwarted, disillusioned, and resigning himself to the fact that he would never have the answers to these questions, Hossein eventually left to go home. His mind refused to switch off on the journey back.

I cannot fight this one. I will have to find a different country now. The justification to get a visa to travel to Germany was to take the ECFMG examination. No test, no visa. Even if I were to come back here on Monday, there is no way under the sun that they will issue me a visa without an examination to attend. This is going to mess up everything now, even for Hamid and for Afsaneh too. Everything is ruined.

The thought of getting a visa to travel to Austria briefly crossed his mind; he was studying German at the Austrian Cultural Institute after all. The idea lifted his mood momentarily, but he quickly dismissed it. *Why would Austrians give me a visa to go there? I have nothing set up to go there.*

Hossein absent-mindedly walked toward his German-language class on Vila Street. By the time he arrived, it was about one in the afternoon. He was not even sure if the institute would be open. As it happened, the institute was open, but there were no classes there at that time. The hallways, usually filled with students on the nights Hossein took his classes, were vacant and extremely quiet. Hossein knew Herr Schmidt, the director of German Language Studies. Hossein walked toward his office, with no real idea of what he was going to say should he be there. Sure enough, Herr Schmidt was sitting behind his desk, concentrating intensely on a piece of paper in front of him.

"Hello, Herr Schmidt. How are you?" asked Hossein. Herr Schmidt was a tall, blond, blue-eyed, well-mannered man, always impeccably dressed in a smart suit.

"Hello, Hossein, how are you?" replied Herr Schmidt; his tone of voice was friendly as always, despite this interruption from his work. "What brings you in here today?"

"Herr Schmidt, I am in a predicament. I haven't thought too much about the ins and outs of this, but I wanted to talk to you about possibly going to Vienna this summer to improve my German."

"Do you have a passport and permission to leave Iran, Hossein?" asked Herr Schmidt warily.

"Yes, I do." He pulled out his passport and handed it to Herr Schmidt, who regarded it closely.

"Well, through our exchange program, we do help our students to go to Vienna and study German language there. I had no idea you were so serious about improving your German."

"That sounds like a wonderful opportunity, Herr Schmidt," said Hossein, disclosing no more information regarding his circumstances. "How do we do this? What is the process like?"

"It's actually very simple, Hossein," said Herr Schmidt. "If you can bring me a round-trip ticket to Vienna, four photographs, your passport, and the two thousand rials fee for the visa application, I will do the rest for you. I will take your application to our embassy. They process our requests in one to two weeks. If you brought me everything on Monday, I can potentially have your visa in two weeks for you, maybe sooner. How is that?"

"Herr Schmidt, you are very kind," said Hossein, unable to believe the simplicity of it. "I truly appreciate your offer. I will be back on Monday with all that is needed to secure a visa."

Hossein's excitement immediately returned, with a vengeance. He returned his unused Lufthansa ticket back to the airline, and bought a round-trip ticket to Vienna from Iran Air. The ticket scheduled his return exactly one month after his departure date.

Re-motivated at the prospect of going to Vienna, the following Monday he dropped off his visa application package with Herr Schmidt. Several days later, the consular office of the Austrian Embassy in Tehran issued a visa to Hossein. His departure date was now set for Friday, August 5, 1983.

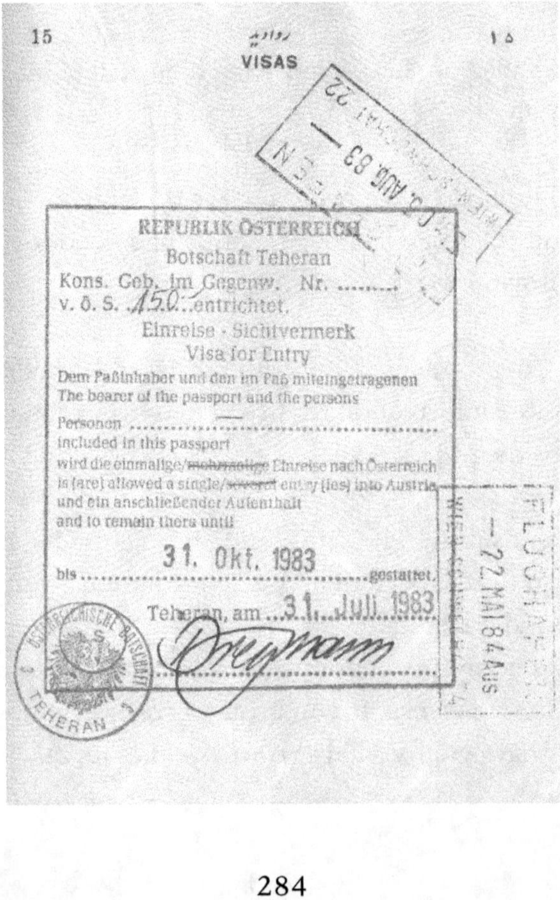
15 روادید ١٥
VISAS
REPUBLIK ÖSTERREICH
Botschaft Teheran
Kons. Geb. im Gegenw. Nr. ....
v. ö. S. 150.– entrichtet.
Einreise - Sichtvermerk
Visa for Entry
Dem Paßinhaber und den im Paß miteingetragenen
The bearer of the passport and the persons
Personen ....
included in this passport
wird die einmalige/mehrmalige Einreise nach Österreich
is (are) allowed a single/several entry (ies) into Austria
und ein anschließender Aufenthalt
and to remain there until
bis 31. Okt. 1983 gestattet.
Teheran, am 31. Juli 1983
ÖSTERREICHISCHE BOTSCHAFT TEHERAN
05. AUG 83
22. MAI 84 Aus

CHAPTER TWENTY THREE
GOODBYE IRAN

For a long time now, Hossein had been determined to go to another country in search of a better life, better opportunities, and a brighter future. By default, Austria had become that country.

Although the United States was his ultimate destination, Hossein knew very well that Austria would be a perfectly adequate temporary home until he could get there. He also was fully cognizant that this trip would spawn a completely new chapter in his life. But to say he was not apprehensive would have been a lie. He was going to live in a foreign country with a very different culture.

While in medical school, Hossein had met several exchange students from Lebanon, who had travelled to Tehran to study medicine at the reputable Tehran University. Over the years, he had several opportunities to socialize with such foreign students. All of them spoke Farsi, but their mouths did not produce the words in the same way that their Iranian peers' did. Instead, they spoke with a thick and distinct accent. This, coupled with their lack of familiarity with the country's culture had greatly distanced them from the Iranian students. Ultimately, they ended up isolated, associating only with other foreign students. Now, Hossein himself was going to become a foreigner, one who would be communicating in German with a distinct foreign accent. He was also realistic enough to acknowledge that during his stay, however long it may be, there would be times when he would encounter local food or customs that he would not understand or appreciate.

As was true in Hossein's case, factors and poignant events in life motivate people to do something outside the ordinary. It is this constellation of motivating factors that drives people and underpins their biggest decisions. The more motivated a person is, the more he will do, and very often the more he will achieve. But intense motivation also exposes individuals to risk, risk that requires the courage to see beyond what others can see in order to reach the goal. Determined to leave Iran, Hossein was ready to face a series of challenges that would deter most people. Given the situation, many would think it was the language barrier that would pose the biggest problem, but for Hossein, learning German was the simplest task, the first step on a staircase stacked with obstacles he would have to overcome to succeed. One such obstacle was living in Vienna on a five-hundred-dollar budget until Hamid, who had been forced to change his travel plans to accommodate Hossein, arrived. Luckily, Hossein had chosen to travel during a season when camping would be a comfortable enough temporary living arrangement.

For Hossein, there was one good thing to come out of his forced change in plans, and that was the opportunity to spend more time with his family before his departure.

With a heavy heart and eyes moist with sadness, Parvin spoke honestly to her son the night before he was due to leave. "Hossein, my wonderful son, I want you to know that I fully support you in your decision to leave this country, and I truly wish you the best."

It was difficult to ignore the lump that had formed in Hossein's throat, but he was so grateful for the words that fell from his mother's mouth, and he wanted to tell her once more what was driving him to take such drastic measures.

"Mom, it is my destiny to take this trip, even with all the foreseeable and unforeseeable challenges that it brings. Only time validates the soundness of our decisions and the appropriateness of our actions. Today, I firmly believe that all the decisions that I have made, and all the actions I have taken, have been correct. After all, you prepared me well to handle the challenges of life. Your own life was full of challenges, as was Dad's until he died. I have learned from you both. As I was growing up, I watched you and Dad withstand so many hardships. Observing you two taught me to do the same, to keep my head up, learn from my mistakes, and move on with life, whatever it may throw at me. There is little point in over-analyzing and critiquing past choices whose consequences have already been realized."

"I know, Hossein, I know," said his mother tearfully. "You are everything a mother could want from a son, and you have in you what it takes to succeed. I wish you a safe trip tomorrow. I will be thinking of you constantly."

Parvin hugged her son tightly as though she never wanted to let go. She was feeling such a mix of emotions. On one hand she was so very happy that her son was finally able to break free from the suppression of Iran and live the life he deserved, but on the other hand, the thought of her precious boy leaving was killing her.

"Go to bed, my love. You have a long day ahead of you tomorrow," she said, wiping the tears from her eyes and fixing a smile on her face.

Everyone chose to sleep on the patio of the house that night. Like many other traditional one-story homes in Iran, in Hossein's house, a raised patio separated the living quarters from the garden. That night was to be the last night that Hossein would spend in Iran—the last night with his family, the last night in his family house, and the last night he would be able to smell the intoxicating scent of his mother's beloved flower garden, blending into the freshness of the crisp night air.

Hossein just could not fall asleep. Tension was high, apprehension reigned over his thoughts, and he was overwhelmed with emotion. In many ways, he had no idea of what life would be like in Vienna. And with no friends or family members waiting there to help ease the transition into his new life, the only thing that gave him hope was his own ability to take on any challenge, the self-confidence that would let him explore this new and exciting land.

He spent much of that night staring blankly at the stars above, waiting impatiently for the sun to rise so he could go to the airport and begin his adventure. He had set two alarm clocks for four in the morning, just to be safe. His flight to Vienna was scheduled for departure at ten, and there was no way he was missing it.

Focusing on the stars, Hossein tried to imagine where he would be the next day, where he would sleep the next night—he faced so many unknowns.

Early on Friday morning, August 5, 1983, Hossein's mother came in to wake him.

"Time to wake," she said gently.

"I am up, Mom, thanks," replied Hossein, his adrenaline levels spiking as he realized that this was it. Today was the day.

The family had a quick breakfast together, although no one had much of an appetite. They were all going to accompany Hossein to the airport. At the door, before they left the house, Hossein's brother brought out his camera and took a photograph of Hossein with his mother and his sister. They all tried to fake a smile for the camera. It was an intensely moving moment.

Hossein's luggage consisted of his briefcase, a box of books, a large suitcase (the largest that he could find in Tehran), and a green backpack that contained all his camping equipment.

"Make sure you take lots of pictures in Vienna. I want to see what Vienna is like," said Parvin, trying to keep the conversation buoyant and upbeat.

Parvin, ever the traditionalist, brought the Quran with her. She held it above Hossein's head and asked him to pass under it three times, praying that her son would remain safe and healthy while he was away from home. Hossein kissed the holy book, took one last look at the house that contained so many happy memories, and followed his beloved family to the car. It was still dark out, and the roads were quiet as they began the journey toward Tehran's Mehrabad Airport.

At the airport, after checking his luggage, it was time for Hossein to say his final goodbyes to his family. Everyone was crying, and Hossein himself was unable to stop his tears from falling. His heart ached; seeing his amazing mother in such distress caused him almost physical pain. Each one in turn squeezed him tightly, mindful of the possibility that this could be the last time they would ever see him. His mother was the last to say goodbye. She clung to him firmly and sobbed onto his shoulder.

"Stay safe my dear son. I am so proud of you."

"I love you, Mom."

And with that, he separated from her and began to walk away. He could still hear their muted cries as he reached the airport's security check.

The airport's staff was mostly depressed-looking young men who sported large beards. He tried not to make eye contact with anyone there, and as he was glancing around the room, he noticed that the security checkpoint had a private space surrounded by dark curtains.

"Follow me," said the officer who was to clear a still-tearful Hossein for his departure. "I will do a manual body search first. Please take off your shoes and belt."

After patting him down, the surly officer searched inside his shoes, the lining of his belt, and even the handle of his briefcase. He emptied all its contents to be certain that he was not hiding money for the trip.

"Okay. You can go now," said the man.

Hossein entered the ground-level gate area, and immediately spotted the gate marked "Iran Air flight to Vienna." He stood dumbfounded as he took his first glimpse of the plane that would whisk him away from the country he despised so much. After a short while, the gate opened, and the passengers quietly entered the open space of the airport to be escorted onto the bus that would transport them to the plane. At the bottom of the staircase to the Iran Air jet, everyone got out of the bus.

Half an hour later, the plane taxied to the runway. As the engine roared into action and the huge jet took flight, Hossein looked melancholically out of the window. The aerial view of Tehran would be his last memory of Iran, and with this in his mind, one phrase repeated itself continually in his head. *Goodbye, Iran, Goodbye, Iran, Goodbye, Iran.*

To be continued!

PERSIAN VOCABULARY

Agha:	Mr.
Ayatollah:	religious leader, highest ranking for an Islamic cleric.
az man:	to become mine
az to:	to you (in this context)
basiji:	Islamic guard
befarmaiid:	please
befrest:	send
Char Shanbe:	Wednesday
Char Shanbe Soori:	festival of fire that is celebrated on the last Tuesday evening of the year.
chelo kabab:	a rice and kebab dish
enshallah:	god willing

Ghormeh Sabzi	a stew made of beef and chopped herbs and vegetables
haft:	seven
Haft Khane Rostam:	the Seven Labors of Rostam, an epic character in Iranian history, similar to the Twelve Labors of Hercules.
Haft Seen:	traditional Iranian New Year Table
Haj Agha:	a Muslim man who has made a pilgrimage to Mecca
Hozeyeh Feizieh	a religious school in Iran's holy city of Qom.
Emam Hossein:	The third of twelve apostles of Islam, famous for his wars to establish Islam
Esfahani:	someone from the Iranian city of Esfahan.
jaan:	a word meaning "life", when it follows a name, it means "dear," as in Hossein Jaan (dearest Hossein)
Karbala:	holy city in Iraq where Emam Hossein fought enemies and died. His burial site is a holy site for Shiite Muslims.
khale:	maternal aunt
khane:	house
Konkoor	Iran's national university entrance examination

mamnuol khorouj:	a person banned from traveling outside Iran
mard:	man
masael:	problems
mehman:	guest
mehman khane:	formal guest-receiving room of an Iranian house
naa:	not
naa-mard:	one who does not adhere to promises he makes (not a man)
na baba:	no way
nooshe jaan:	enjoy, said as an encouragement to someone who is eating something
salam:	hello
salavat:	prayer
salavat befrest:	say prayers
sarraf:	private currency dealer
sarrafi:	private currency exchange agency
soori:	redness
sorkhi:	redness

sorkhi-ye to:	your redness
savab:	a good deed done for the sake of God
taahhod:	commitment to Islam, more so to the ruling clan in charge of the Iran's government
takhassos:	specialized knowledge.
taghooti:	new term that the Islamic government created to refer to those who were rich and connected to the government of the Shah
Tajrish:	northern section of Tehran, which is set at the bottom of the mountain range
towzih:	explanation
Towzih ol-Masael:	a book of dos and don'ts written by an Islamic religious figure in order to be formally recognized as an Ayatollah, a religious leader.
Tork:	individual from northwestern state of Azarbaijan, where the language is Turkish. Iranians make many jokes about Torks,
zardi:	yellowness
zardi-ye man:	my yellowness

AUTHOR'S BIOGRAPHY

Hossein Tirgan was born and raised in Tehran. He lived there throughout the 1979 revolution, and through much of the Iran-Iraq war. Since his relocation to the United States many years ago, New York City has become his home away from home. It is here that Hossein continues to practice medicine, the profession he began studying in Iran and refined in the United States.

* * *

To connect with Hossein, please visit:

www.Goodbye-Iran.com

www.ingramcontent.com/pod-product-compliance
Lightning Source LLC
LaVergne TN
LVHW051514070426
835507LV00023B/3108
* 9 7 8 0 9 8 5 6 5 5 3 0 3 *